INTERNATIONAL LAW

By

Linda A. Malone

Marshall-Wythe Foundation Professor of Law
Marshall-Wythe School of Law
College of William and Mary

SMITH'S REVIEW

Published by

International Law, First Edition (1995)
Emanuel Law Outlines, Inc. • **1865 Palmer Avenue** • **Larchmont, NY 10538**

ISBN 1-56542-159-0

ACKNOWLEDGEMENT

My thanks to Andrew Basham, Marc Bernstein, Ingrid Blanton, Diana Danzberger, Edward Efkeman, Della Harris, Nina Hval, Lee Marsh, Kristin Mueller, Andrew Ollis, Debra Pearson and Chris White for their assistance.

Linda A. Malone
July 1995

TABLE OF CONTENTS

CHAPTER 3

INTERNATIONAL LAW AND MUNICIPAL LAW

CHAPTER 4

STATES

CHAPTER 5

STATE JURISDICTION

CHAPTER 6

INTERNATIONAL ORGANIZATIONS

CHAPTER 7

INTERNATIONAL DISPUTE SETTLEMENT

CHAPTER 8

THE RIGHTS OF INDIVIDUALS — INTERNATIONAL LAW OF HUMAN RIGHTS

CHAPTER 9

THE LAW OF ARMED CONFLICT

CHAPTER 10

THE LAW OF THE SEA

CHAPTER 11

AIR AND SPACE LAW

CHAPTER 12

INTERNATIONAL ENVIRONMENTAL LAW

CAPSULE SUMMARY

This Capsule Summary is intended for review after
studying the main outline. Reading it is not a substitute
for mastering the material in the outline.

CHAPTER 1

THE CONCEPT OF PUBLIC INTERNATIONAL LAW

I. INTRODUCTION

A. Defined: Historically, international law was defined as *"the body of rules and principles of action which are binding upon civilized states in their relations with one another."* The modern approach expands the definition to include relations not only between states but also relations between international organizations and states, among the international organizations themselves, as well as the relationship between states or international organizations and natural or juridical persons, such as the law governing human rights.

B. The importance of public international law: Public international law concerns the conduct of states and international organizations, while private international law focuses on the conduct of individuals, corporations and other private entities. Public international law is important because it 1) defines the very existence of "states", 2) provides the framework for diplomatic relations, 3) governs international agreements, 4) sets forth rules for the operation of international commerce, 5) governs individual human rights, and 6) regulates protection of the global environment, as well as the use of the air, land, sea and other global resources.

C. History of public international law: There have been two main theories in the study of international law: the *natural law approach* of the 16th and 17th centuries and the *positivist movement*, predominant in the 19th and 20th centuries.

   1. Natural law: The theory of natural law is based on the notion that *each state, just as each individual, is endowed with certain natural rights.* These rights are not created but rather are the "dictate of right reason," basic principles of justice with a universal validity.

   2. Positivism: Unlike natural law, which exists without the affirmative consent of nations, positivism teaches that international law is that body of law *to which states have consented to be bound.* A state's consent may be either 1) *express*, as in the form of a treaty, or *implied*, as with acquiescence to customary law.

CHAPTER 2

SOURCES OF INTERNATIONAL LAW

I. THE STATUTE OF THE INTERNATIONAL COURT OF JUSTICE

A. Article 38: The sources of international law, set forth in article 38(1) of the Statute of the International Court of Justice (ICJ), are 1) *international conventions*, whether general or particular, 2) *international custom*, 3) the *general principles of law* recognized by civilized nations, and 4) *judicial decisions* and the *teachings of the most highly qualified publicists* of the various nations, as a subsidiary source.

B. International conventions/treaties: In the broadest sense, an international convention or treaty is *any agreement governed by international law.*

1. **The Vienna Convention:** The Vienna Convention on the Law of Treaties, which entered into force in 1980, is the *primary source for the law of treaties*. Most provisions of the Vienna Convention were declaratory of existing law while others went beyond the existing law to create new law at the time they were adopted. As of 1993, the U.S. had not ratified the Vienna Convention, but the State Department does recognize it as the authoritative guide to current treaty law and practice. The Vienna Convention applies only to those treaties meeting the Convention's requirements for a treaty. Some international instruments that fall outside the Convention's definition of a treaty, however, are nevertheless recognized as treaties.

   a. **Vienna Convention definition of a treaty:** The Vienna Convention sets forth a basic definition for a treaty as "an international agreement concluded between States in written form and governed by international law, whether embodied in a single instrument or in two or more related instruments and whatever its particular designation." In short, to be a treaty within the scope of the Convention, a document must 1) *be between states*; 2) *be in writing*; and 3) be *governed by international law.*

2. **International law governs all treaties:** Governance by international law is required of all treaties, whether or not they are treaties within the scope of the Vienna Convention. Although the presumption is that an agreement between two or more states is a treaty, evidence that domestic law was intended to control the agreement rebuts that presumption.

3. **Non-Vienna Convention treaties:** The concept of a treaty under international law is not limited to that defined in the Vienna Convention. The Vienna Convention states that its definition of a treaty does not affect the legal force or applicability of international law to agreements which do not fall within the definition. Agreements involving international organizations as parties are also generally considered as treaties.

4. **United States distinction between treaties and executive agreements:** U.S. domestic law distinguishes between an executive agreement and a treaty in the procedures necessary for the agreements to be given legal effect and in the legal effect accorded the agreements.

   a. **Treaty:** Treaties are concluded by the President with the advice and consent of the Senate. Senate ratification of a treaty requires a two-thirds majority vote.

   b. **Executive agreement:** An executive agreement is concluded by the President based on authority granted by Congress or based on the inherent authority granted the President by the U.S. Constitution.

5. **Potential conflicts between U.S. domestic law and international law:** It is possible for an agreement to be *denied legal force and effect under U.S. domestic law and yet still be binding under international law.* A state's internal law cannot be invoked as justification for failure to perform a treaty, however.

6. **Name and form of treaty:** "Treaty" is the most common title of an international agreement but the following are also used: convention, act, general act, protocol, agreement, *modi vivendi*, concordance, charter, declaration, and compromise.

   a. **Components of treaty and language:** Although there is no officially correct form, treaties generally comprise four parts: the title, the preamble, the main body, and the final part. There is no universal rule as to what language or what number of languages must be utilized for the text of the treaty. Rather, the language of the treaty is selected by the contracting parties.

   b. **Subject matter of treaty:** The subject matter of the treaty is composed of the rights and obligations of the parties. Two important limitations apply:

      i. ***Jus cogens* restrictions:** The treaty may not set forth rights and obligations which conflict with *jus cogens* (the imperative norms of international law).

     ii. **U.N. Charter restrictions:** The treaty may not set forth rights and obligations which conflict with those obligations a member-state has undertaken under the U.N. Charter.

   c. **Classification of international treaties:** Treaties may be classified by the following criteria: contracting parties, geographic factors, possibility of accession, subject matter, form, or method of conclusion.

7. **Treaty-making power — capacity:** Both the party (the state or international organization) and its representative must have the proper capacity to negotiate and conclude an international agreement.

   a. **Nation-states and international organizations:** It is presumed that nation-states have the necessary capacity to negotiate and conclude treaties. International organizations, however, have the necessary capacity only if the constitution of the organization either expressly or impliedly gives the organization that capacity.

   b. **Component states of a federal union:** An inconsistent area is the capacity of the component states of a federal union. Generally, one constituent state of a federation may enter agreements with other constituent states, but the rules may differ with regards to entering into international agreements. Two determining factors are the constitutional guidelines of the federation and recognition of international legal personality.

   c. **Self-governing territories:** Another troublesome area concerns self-governing territories, as there are conflicting views as to whether they have the capacity to enter international agreements. One view holds that a territory is not a "state" and cannot be regarded as a "distinct juridical person" capable of being "a responsible party to the treaty entirely separate from the parent State." Some conventions, however, specifically include self-governing territories amongst the parties which may sign the convention.

   d. **Authority of persons representing a state or international organization:** Authority is issued in a document entitled a *"full powers"* document, which names those individuals who may negotiate and conclude a treaty on behalf of the state.

     i. **Practice of state:** A state may dispense with full powers if the practice of the state involved demonstrates its intention to consider its representative as being duly authorized.

     ii. **Heads of state:** Full powers are also dispensed with for heads of state, heads of government, ministers of foreign affairs and heads of diplomatic missions. Such officers have inherent capacity to conclude treaties.

   e. **Apparent authority of a state's representative:** A state is bound to a treaty unless it is clearly evident that a representative was acting beyond his authority.

   f. **Subsequent confirmation:** When authority is lacking, the treaty is without legal effect unless the state subsequently confirms the treaty.

8. **The treaty process:** The treaty process includes *negotiation, adoption, authentication,* and *forms of conclusion.*

   a. **Negotiation of treaties:** The negotiation of treaties varies according to whether the treaty is bilateral or multilateral. Bilateral treaty negotiation usually begins in the foreign ministry of one of the parties and is followed up by discussions and exchanges of notes. Restricted multilateral treaty negotiation ordinarily is conducted in the same manner as are bilateral treaties. General multilateral treaty negotiation is generally conducted at diplomatic conferences where diplomatic delegations act on behalf of the states.

   b. **Adoption:** Adoption is generally defined as the *formal act signifying that the form and content of the treaty have been agreed upon.* Adoption signifies that the negotiations have been completed, disputed points have been resolved, and the wording of the final document agreed upon.

   c. **Forms of conclusion:** A party is not bound to a treaty *until it has consented to be bound.* Such consent may be expressed in various ways including signature, the exchange of instruments, acceptance, approval, ratification, and "any other means if so agreed."

   d. **Entry into force:** Entry into force is the *actual implementation of the treaty's terms.* Entry into force often occurs when specific requirements laid out in the treaty have been met. The provisions setting forth the manner of entry into force apply from the moment the text of the treaty is adopted, unlike the remainder of the treaty which is implemented upon entry into force. A provisional application may permit the treaty to be implemented before the formal requirements for entry into force have been met.

9. **Reservations:** A "reservation" is defined as "a unilateral statement, however phrased or named, made by a State, when signing, ratifying, acceding to, accepting or approving a treaty, whereby it purports to *exclude or to vary the legal effect of certain provisions* in their application to that State."

   a. **Permissible reservations:** Article 19 of the Vienna Convention permits reservations to general multilateral treaties, unless the treaty expressly or impliedly prohibits reservations, or the reservations sought are simply incompatible with the object and purpose of the treaty.

   b. **The purpose of reservations:** Many multilateral conventions seek wide participation and reservations encourage participation by allowing a state to be a party without agreeing to every last provision of a treaty.

   c. **Acceptance of and objections to reservations:** A reservation expressly permitted by the treaty does not require acceptance unless the treaty so provides. "When it appears from the limited number of the negotiating States and the object and purpose of a treaty that the application of the treaty in its entirety between all the parties is an essential condition of the consent of each one to be bound by the treaty, a reservation requires acceptance by all the parties." Otherwise unanimous consent to a reservation is not necessary. If the treaty itself does not prohibit a reservation in any way, or expressly permit it, each state is free to decide whether to reject or to accept the reservation.

   d. **Legal effects of acceptances of and objections to reservations:** If a state accepts the reservation, the treaty will enter into force between the accepting and reserving state. The treaty's provisions apply as modified by the reservation. The modification is effective only between the reserving state and the accepting state. If a state objects to a reservation, there are two possible outcomes: 1) the state may object to the reservation, yet still be willing to enter a treaty relation with the reserving state; or 2) the objecting state not only objects, but also expresses its intention that the entire treaty be of no effect between it and the reserving state. In the latter event, the reserving state and objecting state are not parties to the treaty vis-á-vis each other.

   e. **Limitations to reservations:** Reservations are generally narrowly construed and do not apply to other provisions of a treaty by way of implication.

10. **The observance of treaties:** All parties to a treaty must perform their obligations under the treaty in *good faith*.

   a. *Pacta sunt servanda:* Article 26 of the Vienna Convention expresses one of the most fundamental principles of public international law, *pacta sunt servanda:* "Every treaty in force is binding upon the parties to it and must be performed by them in good faith."

   b. **Good faith performance:** Good faith performance is required regardless of any conflicting domestic law. Conflicting domestic law does not excuse a state from its treaty obligations, unless the state's consent to be bound by the treaty was expressed in violation of the state's domestic law. This predominance of treaty obligations over domestic law holds true only in the arena of international law and is not always the rule in domestic courts.

c. **Territorial scope of treaties:** The general rule is that a treaty applies to *all the territory of each party*.

d. **Interpretation of treaties:** There are three basic approaches to treaty interpretation: 1) the *textual approach*, which looks only to the text of the treaty and the "plain and natural meanings of the words;" 2) the *limited contextual approach*, which regards the text as the starting-point for interpretation, ascertaining the intent of the parties from written secondary sources; and 3) the *policy-oriented and configurative approach*, the most liberal and conceptual of the three, which gleans intent from the treaty text and all pre- and post-treaty communications, with no one source predominating over another and intent being considered in the very broad framework of "giving effect to the goals of a public order of human dignity."

e. **Fulfillment of treaties — methods of oversight:** Remedies available for non-fulfillment include submission of the dispute to the International Court of Justice, diplomatic negotiations and arbitration. The treaty itself will often designate the manner in which disputes are to be resolved.

f. **Amendment of treaties:** The general rule is that "a treaty may be amended by agreement between the parties." Amendments take on the character of treaties themselves and are governed accordingly by the general law on treaties.

   i. **"Amendments"** *alter a treaty with respect to all parties*. Article 40 requires notification to all parties of the proposal to amend. All parties have the right to participate in the decision to amend as well as in the subsequent negotiations and conclusions of any amendments.

   ii. **"Modifications"** are *made by a limited number of parties*. Modifications are permitted only if: 1) modifications are permitted by the original treaty; or 2) modifications are not prohibited by the treaty and the modification is one which does not affect object and purpose of the treaty as a whole.

   iii. **Amendment/Modification by tacit consent:** The argument has been made that customary international law recognizes amendment or modification of a treaty by actual practice of the parties which is at variance with the treaty provisions.

g. **Invalidation of treaties:** The grounds for invalidating a treaty are *error, fraudulent conduct, corruption, coercion, conflict with peremptory norms (jus cogens)*, and *conflict with domestic law*. The provisions of the Vienna Convention are controversial and are not necessarily accepted as reflecting customary international law.

   i. **Separability:** Grounds for invalidation generally affect the entire treaty, but article 44 does provide for separability of the treaty provisions if: 1) the treaty itself permits separability; or 2) the objectionable clauses are "separable from the remainder of the treaty with regard to their application", "not an essential basis of the consent" and "continued performance of the remainder of the treaty would not be unjust."

   ii. **Acquiescence:** A party which continues to perform under the terms of a treaty, despite its knowledge that grounds for invalidating it exist, is precluded from later invoking those grounds for invalidation.

   iii. **Termination and suspension of treaties:** Treaties may be terminated or suspended by agreement of the parties, if the treaty so provides, or if the goal of the treaty is realized. Unilateral abrogation of treaties without abrogation or withdrawal clauses is, in principle, not permitted; in practice, however, it is often allowed. Additionally, treaties may be terminated for reasons analogous to contract law defenses.

   iv. **Impossibility of performance:** Impossibility of performance is based on the permanent distinction or disappearance of something indispensable to performance.

CAPSULE SUMMARY

     v. *Rebus sic stantibus*: This doctrine of a fundamental change in circumstances is rarely found applicable. Four criteria must be met: 1) the *change* must be *of a fundamental character*; 2) the change in circumstances must have been *unforeseen by the parties*; 3) the *circumstances* at the time of entering the agreement must have been *an essential basis* of the treaty; and 4) the change in circumstances must radically alter the performance of obligations yet to be performed under the treaty.

     vi. Termination due to breach: The effect of breach varies according to whether the treaty is bilateral or multilateral. In all cases the breach must be material. The breach itself does not automatically terminate the treaty but it may be invoked as a ground for termination.

     vii. Later inconsistent treaty between parties: A treaty is terminated if all parties conclude a later agreement on the same subject-matter and it is implied that the later treaty is to govern; or the later treaty is so incompatible with the earlier treaty that the two treaties cannot be performed at the same time.

     viii. War between contracting parties: The outbreak of an armed conflict does not *ipso facto* terminate or suspend the operation of treaties in force between the parties to the armed conflict. The nature of the treaty dictates the effect of hostilities on its operation.

  h. Effect of state succession on international treaties: Succession of states is the *shift of responsibility over a territory from one state to another state*. Succession affects the legal identity of the state and its treaty obligations, and occurs with secession of states, annexation, merger and consolidation, and decolonization.

     i. Transfer of territory resulting from moving boundaries (Moving Treaty-Frontiers Rule): The international agreements of the state to which the territory once belonged are no longer applicable. The international agreements of the state to which the territory now belongs apply.

     ii. Absorption of an entire state: The international agreements of the absorbed state cease and are replaced by the international agreements of the absorbing state.

     iii. Newly formed states (former colonies or states resulting from separation of a state): The new state does not automatically become a party to the international agreements of the predecessor state. The new state, however, is not precluded from accepting such agreements.

     iv. Territorial and boundary agreements: Such agreements are unaffected by the succession of states.

     v. Newly independent states under the Vienna Convention: The Vienna Convention on the Succession of States in Respect of Treaties distinguishes between newly independent states (*i.e.*, former colonies) and states created by disintegration or secession. The Clean Slate Doctrine states that a newly independent state begins its existence free of the obligations of its predecessor state. The newly independent state does have the Right of Option to be a party to general multilateral treaties by virtue of being a successor state.

     vi. States created by disintegration or secession: A new state created by secession from a former state, or by disintegration of a former state into two or more states, generally succeeds automatically to most of the former state's treaties.

     vii. Effect of governmental succession on international treaties: A change in government has no effect on the legal identity of the state.

C. **International custom:** Along with treaty law, customary international law is *one of the two principal sources of international law.* Customary international law is important for its potentially general application to states not parties to treaties, as well as its ability to supplement areas of international concern not addressed in treaties.

   1. **Two approaches to customary international law:** The two approaches are the *objectivist/sociological approach* and the *participatory/voluntarist approach.*

   2. **Establishment of an international custom:** Customary law follows the basic principle of international law that acts are permitted unless expressly forbidden. Therefore, prohibitions as well as affirmative practices must be proven by the state relying upon them. Quantitative factors in determining an international custom include: 1) *the amount and type of past state practice*; 2) *duration of the state practice*; 3) *consistency of state practice*; and 4) *the number and makeup of states adhering to the practice.* A qualitative factor is the concept of *opinio juris sive necessitates,* the *sense of legal obligation compelling states to follow a certain practice.*

   3. **Use of regional custom:** Customary law may also be limited to a particular region and therefore not be the practice of such a wide variety of states.

   4. **Local customary rights:** Local customary rights may develop from constant and continual practice between two nations, but such customary rights differ from and are independent of general international customary law principles.

   5. **Resolutions and recommendations of international organizations:** General Assembly resolutions are not a form of international legislation and accordingly are *not legally binding.* The resolutions are, however, frequently used as evidence of customary international law. The resolutions are useful as evidence because the votes of the world body may show a consensus (or lack of consensus) on a particular issue.

   6. **Application of international customary law:** The predominant view is that customary international law enjoys universal application, regardless of what nations participated in its formation. Two possible exceptions to application are: 1) a clear and consistent objection, supported by action; and 2) a historic departure from a customary rule and other states' acceptance of that deviation.

   7. **Relationship between treaties and customary international law:** Depending on the situation, treaties may be given equal weight with custom, prevail over custom, be proof of custom, or codify custom.

D. **General principles of law:** A general principle of law "recognized by civilized nations" is one that is *so fundamental that it is a basic tenet in virtually every major legal system.*

   1. **Limited application of general principles:** General principles of law primarily apply to fill in gaps left by treaties and customary law.

   2. **Decreasing importance as a source of international law:** General principles are losing importance in modern international law because many of the norms once recognized as general principles are now incorporated in treaties or are recognized as customary international law. The Restatement now classifies general principles as "a secondary source of international law." General principles continue, however, to be applied in procedural matters and problems of international judicial administration.

E. **Judicial decisions and publicists:** Article 38 includes in its sources of international law judicial decisions, and the teachings of highly qualified publicists as subsidiary means. The judicial decisions may be rendered by either an international tribunal, such as the International Court of Justice, or by a national court adjudicating issues of international law.

   1. **The role of judicial decisions in the development of international law:** Although not required, many courts strive to follow previous rulings (*stare decisis*) and on occasion make new international law. The statute of the International Court of Justice says that judicial decisions have *no binding force* except as between the parties and in respect to that

particular case. Regardless of this prohibition on the doctrine of *stare decisis*, the Court does in fact often look to prior holdings as being ***highly persuasive***. The I.C.J. has made new law when necessary, which subsequently won state acceptance.

2. **Status of the most highly qualified publicists:** The work of scholars is more influential in the international legal system than in municipal legal systems. International groups of publicists serve the development of international law both by codifying existing rules of law and by proposing new rules.

3. **Resolutions of the U.N. and other international law organizations:** The significance of resolutions of the U.N., and other similar international law organizations, as a source of law varies tremendously according to the circumstances. The following factors are to be considered in determining the impact of a General Assembly resolution: 1) internal General Assembly Resolutions; 2) declaratory resolutions; 3) state practice as proof of impact; 4) diverse majority as proof of impact; and 5) the binding effect on dissenting states.

II. *JUS COGENS* — PEREMPTORY NORMS

A. **Generally:** *Jus cogens* or peremptory norms are ***those rules of international law of such fundamental importance that derogation from them is prohibited***. There are few rules which are generally accepted as peremptory norms. Some commonly accepted rules are the basic principles of *pacta sunt servanda*, prohibitions on the use of or threat of force, genocide, slave trade, piracy, and prohibitions on terrorism and the taking of hostages. The controversy surrounding the very existence of *jus cogens*, as well as the difficulty of identifying rules of *jus cogens*, has resulted in sparse application.

III. EQUITY IN INTERNATIONAL LAW

A. **Generally:** Equity in international law can be used if the parties agree to have a case decided *ex aequo et bono*, in which equity overrides all other legal principles in a case. Furthermore, there are substantive concepts of equity common to all modern legal systems which are, therefore, general principles of international law, and may be used to decide international disputes.

CHAPTER 3

INTERNATIONAL LAW AND MUNICIPAL LAW

I. DUALISM AND MONISM

A. **Two theories:** There are two theoretical approaches to the relationship between international law and municipal law: *dualism* and *monism*. Under the dualist theory international law and municipal law are ***entirely separate legal systems***. The monist theory holds that municipal and international law belong to a ***single "universal legal order."*** The diminished role of the state as a legal personality results in a dominant role for international law over municipal law. In actual practice, the dualist approach appears to predominate.

II. TREATIES IN MUNICIPAL LAW

A. **Treaties in U.S. law:** The U.S. Constitution includes provisions on treaties pertaining to the creation of treaties, the judicial power, the relationship of treaties with international law, and limitations on states' power to conclude treaties.

B. **Terminology for treaties:** U.S. domestic law recognizes two types of international agreements: 1) treaties under article II, and 2) executive agreements. Congressional/Executive agreements, also called statutory agreements, are made by the President pursuant to statutes passed by Congress.

C. **Self-executing treaties:** Some treaties may be self-executing under U.S. domestic judge-made law. A treaty cannot be self-executing if the subject matter is one which lies within the exclusive law-making power of Congress, however. A treaty is also non-self-executing if it instructs the legislature to implement enacting legislation.

D. **Treaties and state law — effect of the Supremacy Clause:** Self-executing treaties and legislatively implemented treaties have the status of enforceable federal law and benefit accordingly from the Supremacy Clause.

E. **Treaties and conflicting federal statutes:** Treaty law and federal statutory law are *virtually equivalent* in status. When both address the same issue, courts attempt to interpret the terms of each in such a manner as to avoid outright conflicts. When reconciliation is not possible, the general rule is that *the last in time prevails*. This "last-in-time" rule applies only to article II treaties, and only under U.S. laws — a conflict with domestic law does not excuse the U.S. from international legal obligations.

F. **Treaties and constitutional constraints:** The substantive constraints that the Constitution places on the treaty-making power are not clear, and contrasting views have been opined by the Supreme Court.

G. **Treaties in the laws of other states:** The relationship between international and domestic law varies amongst states. Regarding self-executing treaties, two doctrines dominant: 1) the "English" rule, which only incorporates treaties into municipal law if there is legislative enactment; and 2) the civil law treatment, which generally incorporate treaties into municipal law directly.

III. CUSTOMARY INTERNATIONAL LAW IN MUNICIPAL LAW

A. **Common law countries — international law as common law:** International law derived from sources other than treaties is considered by common law countries to be a special type of common law, one to which the courts resort in the absence of a treaty, executive or legislative act, or judicial decision. The U.S. and other common law jurisdictions consider customary rules to be automatically incorporated into the domestic legal order and thus directly applicable in domestic courts.

  1. **Customary law in the United States:** Customary law, like treaty law, is considered federal law and receives the benefits of the Supremacy Clause. Equal status with federal statutory law, however, is less certain. U.S. courts group customary law together with other non-treaty sources of international law to form what is called international common law, comprising custom, general principles, scholarly works, and judicial opinions.

  2. **Civil law countries — relationship between customary international law and domestic law:** Civil law countries rely on express constitutional provisions to incorporate non-treaty international law into their municipal law.

IV. FOREIGN RELATIONS LAW OF THE UNITED STATES

A. **Generally:** Although U.S. domestic law does not directly impose itself on the international legal order, it does play a major role by allocating power among the three branches of government.

B. **Executive powers:** Article II of the U.S. Constitution expressly grants the President authority for certain international powers. The extent of the President's power to make international agreements is uncertain, although the Supreme Court has upheld various agreements made by the President without Congress' approval. The Executive is also given the authority to receive ambassadors and recognize foreign governments, along with any other powers consistent with article II.

C. **Congressional powers:** Article I of the U.S. Constitution vests the Congress with certain international powers as well. The controversial War Powers Act is one instance of Congressional authority in foreign relations.

D. **Judicial powers:** Article III of the U.S. Constitution allows the Supreme Court to hear cases arising under treaties made by the U.S., cases involving ambassadors and other public ministers and consuls' admiralty and maritime cases, and cases between U.S. states and citizens and foreign states and citizens.

   1. **Act of state doctrine:** The Supreme Court has declined in the past to decide cases on the basis of the act of state doctrine.

   2. **Political question doctrine:** The political question doctrine is also applied by courts to avoid addressing controversies regarding the political functions of the other two branches.

Chapter 4

STATES

I. DEFINITION OF A STATE

A. **Defined:** Under both the Restatement and the Montevideo Convention of 1933 a state is defined as "an entity that has a *defined territory* and a *permanent population*, under the control of its *own government*, and that *engages in, or has the capacity to engage in, formal relations* with other such entities."

   1. **Defined territory:** There is no minimum territory or size requirement. A state need not be established with clearly defined frontiers.

   2. **Permanent population/a "people":** There is no minimum number required. Antarctica, however, has no permanent population and, in part for that reason, is not considered a state.

   3. **Under the control of its own government:** A state's own government must be able to assert itself without the aid of foreign troops and to carry out its duties. Exceptions may be in the cases of: 1) a state temporarily lacking an effective government as a result of civil war, newly gained independence or similar upheavals; 2) a simple change in regime and even conflicting claims of governmental authority; and 3) a state occupied by an enemy in times of war as long as allies are fighting on its behalf against the enemy.

   4. **Capacity to engage in relations with other states:** A state must have the competence, within its own constitutional system, to conduct international relations with other states, as well as the political, technical and financial capabilities to do so.

   5. **Role of recognition in defining a state:** An entity must be treated as a state when it meets the four requirements set forth above. Its existence as a state is independent of any formal recognition.

II. STATE TERRITORY

A. **State boundaries or frontiers:** State boundaries, not only across land but both upwards into the airspace and downwards into the earth, are *most often determined by agreements between the parties*, rather than being dictated by principles of international law. Boundary disputes are common and contests involving relatively small areas of land may be resolved by international litigation or arbitration, or some other settlement, such as a peace treaty.

   1. **Effect of succession:** A succession of states, by itself, is not grounds for affecting boundaries established by treaty, or rights and obligations established by treating and relating to the boundary regime.

B. **Air and outer space:** There are separate sets of treaties and agreements concerning airspace versus outer space.

    1. **Airspace:** The general view is that a state has *complete and exclusive authority* over the airspace above its territory.

    2. **Outer space:** The prevailing theory in the field of outer space is that every state may explore and use outer space, free of national appropriation by another state.

C. **International rivers:** International rivers may flow through a state's territory but not be subject to the absolute authority of the state. An international river has the following characteristics: it is *navigable*; it *flows directly or indirectly into the sea*; it *flows through the territory of two or more states or forms the boundary between them*; and an *international act* proclaims it to be an international river.

D. **State coastal zones:** The sea is divided into several zones: internal waters, the territorial sea, the contiguous zone, the continental shelf, the exclusive economic zone, and the high seas, with the sovereign rights of the coastal state varying with each zone.

E. ***Res nullius* and *res communis*:** *Res nullius*, or unattributed territory, and *res communis*, or common territory, refer to territory which belongs to no state.

F. **Acquisition of territorial sovereignty:** Acquisition of territory may occur in a variety of ways, including: 1) accretion; 2) cession; 3) conquest; 4) contiguity; 5) occupation; and 6) prescription.

    1. **Other considerations:** Other factors are considered in resolving territorial disputes: 1) affiliations of the inhabitants of the disputed territory; 2) geographical, economic and historical considerations; and 3) cultural unity.

III. RECOGNITION OF STATES AND GOVERNMENTS

A. **Recognition generally:** Recognition is best defined as the *willingness to deal with another state or government representing the state as a member of the international community*. Public acts of recognition may take a variety of forms. Maintaining or severing diplomatic relations is not synonymous with recognition or nonrecognition respectively.

B. **Express and implied recognition:** Recognition of a state or government is often done so expressly, but certain conduct may also imply recognition.

C. **Recognition under U.S. law:** Under U.S. law, only the President has the authority to recognize or not recognize an entity as a state.

D. **Whether recognition is discretionary or mandatory:** Generally, *recognition is discretionary*. Two limitations on this discretion exist to prevent premature recognition and premature withdrawal of recognition.

    1. **The Lauterpacht doctrine:** This doctrine, not widely accepted, holds that states have a duty to recognize states or governments which meet the international law requirements for recognition.

    2. **Nonrecognition under the U.N. Charter:** Article 41 authorizes the Security Council to order members of the U.N. to "sever diplomatic relations" with a state or government.

E. ***De jure* and *de facto* recognition:** Under the constitutive theory, treatment of an entity as a state without extending a formal recognition was called *de facto* recognition, as opposed to *de jure* recognition. With regard to governments, *de jure* recognition implies that the government is lawfully in power even though it retains little actual power, while a *de facto* government is impliedly a government which is in control but illegally so.

F. **Conditional recognition:** The prevailing view is that recognition generally cannot be granted subject to conditions, except for assumed conditions such as adherence to international law.

IV. RECOGNITION OF STATES

A. Two theories: There are two theories concerning the legal effects under international law of recognition of states: the ***constitutive theory*** and the ***declaratory theory***. The constitutive theory is that an entity does not exist as a state until it has been recognized by other states; the recognition itself "constitutes" the state. This theory is not widely accepted today. Under the declaratory theory, the facts of statehood (defined territory, permanent population, effective government, and capacity for foreign relations) rather than formal recognition define an entity as a state.

B. Evidentiary value of recognition: Recognition, nevertheless, is useful evidence of the existence of a state if enough other states recognize a state.

V. RECOGNITION OF GOVERNMENTS

A. Recognition generally: Recognition of a government is an ***acknowledgment that it is in effective control of the state***. The traditional approach allows recognition of a government when: 1) it is in effective control of the state without the assistance of foreign intervention; 2) it has the consent, or at least the acquiescence of the people; and 3) it shows its willingness to comply with the state's obligations under international law.

B. Estrada Doctrine: Under the so-called Estrada doctrine, the practice of recognizing governments is eliminated altogether with the focus being on recognition of states.

C. Wilson Doctrine: Under this approach only democratic and constitutional governments were extended recognition. The U.S. itself no longer adheres to this doctrine.

D. Acts of recognition: Recognition of governments is often implied through the continuation or establishment of diplomatic relations.

E. Significance in domestic law of the recognition of states and governments: Under domestic law, recognized governments and states enjoy important benefits. In the United States, these include: 1) access to courts in the United States; 2) entitlement to property belonging to those states located in the United States; and 3) a right to claim sovereign immunity.

VI. RECOGNITION OF INSURGENTS AND BELLIGERENTS

A. Generally: Insurgencies and belligerencies are two types of internal state conflicts, and are discussed *infra* at p. C-26.

VII. THE RIGHTS AND OBLIGATIONS OF STATES

A. Rights: States have the rights that are generally accorded them by the international community. Some rights are protected by the U.N. Charter and other U.N. resolutions.

1. **Right of sovereignty:** The right of sovereignty is ***fundamental*** because it prohibits foreign intervention in internal affairs. A state's authority is supreme within its national territory, although restrictions on territorial jurisdiction may be made in international agreements. There is dispute over how exclusive a state's jurisdiction is within its borders, particularly with respect to human rights. States have a similar qualified right of sovereignty over their natural resources.

2. **Equality of states:** Under international law theory, ***all independent states are equal***. All states are to enjoy equal treatment; thus, no state is permitted to intervene in the affairs of another state.

3. **The right to defense:** A state has the right to take steps necessary to protect a state's security.

    4. **The right of international intercourse:** States are free to establish and regulate their own international relations, as long as they do not violate the accepted rules and principles of international law.

B. **Rights of states under U.S. law:** Under U.S. law, a state has: 1) sovereignty over its territory and general authority over its nationals; 2) status as a legal person; and 3) capacity to join with other states to make international law, as customary law or by international agreement.

C. **General responsibility of states:** A state injuring the rights or property of another state in breach of its international obligations incurs international responsibility. A state may bear political responsibility or civil responsibility.

    1. **Acts attributable to a state:** A state only incurs liability for those individual actions or omissions *which can be attributed to the state.* The acts of its organs or agents generally *are imputed to the state.* A federal state generally cannot deny responsibility for the acts of its member states or provinces.

    2. **Element of fault:** A state is expected to take reasonable care to prevent injury to another state or areas outside its territorial boundaries.

    3. **Defenses to claims against a state:** A state's apparent violation of international law may be justified on the grounds of: consent, *force majeure,* distress, necessity, self-defense, and counter-measures.

    4. **The requirement of injury:** It is generally stated that actual injury is not required to give rise to responsibility to other states for breach of an international obligation, unless the obligation specifically requires injury as an element of its breach.

        a. *Ergo omnes* **obligations:** All states can be held to have a legal interest in the protection of the obligations of a state towards the international community as a whole. These are obligations *ergo omnes.*

        b. **International crimes:** An international crime is an international obligation so essential for the protection of fundamental interests of the international community that its breach is recognized as a crime by that community as a whole.

    5. **Remedies:** Breach of international obligations may give rise to an appropriate remedy, including collective sanctions, restitution, indemnity, and satisfaction.

    6. **Implementing obligations of reparation:** Reparation may be sought through diplomatic channels or through agreed upon procedures of dispute settlement. Regardless of the nature of the procedure, there are several common requirements: 1) standing, 2) laches, 3) prior negotiation of the dispute, 4) exhaustion of local remedies, and 5) consent to third party settlement.

VIII. HEADS OF STATE, GOVERNMENT OFFICIALS, DIPLOMATS, AND OFFICIALS OF INTERNATIONAL ORGANIZATIONS: ROLES AND STATUS IN INTERNATIONAL LAW

A. **Heads of State:** Today most heads of state are considered organs of the state and are limited in their powers by the states' constitutions. A head of state may be held personally responsible for certain international crimes.

B. **Government:** Foreign political acts of a government and statements of a prime minister (or his functional equivalent) made on behalf of the state are binding on the state.

C. **Secretary of State/Minister of Foreign Affairs (or the functional equivalent):** The Secretary of State (or his functional equivalent) is a state's key figure with respect to its foreign affairs; his acts and statements are *binding upon the state*.

D. **Diplomatic agents:** Diplomatic agents are persons empowered to represent a state in a foreign state or in an international organization. The two categories of diplomats (regular and extraordinary) and heads of mission (ambassadors, envoys, and *charges d'affaires*) comprise the diplomatic corps. Permanent diplomatic relations with another state are established by an international agreement followed by the exchange of diplomatic representatives. Diplomatic missions with a particular purpose are terminated with the completion of that job.

1. **Diplomatic immunities and privileges:** The established privileges and immunities of diplomats apply only from the moment the diplomat enters the host country and only for the period in which he is, in fact, a diplomat.

E. **Consuls:** Consuls are authorized to protect the interests of their state in a foreign state with respect to administrative, legal, economic and cultural affairs.

F. **Officials of international organizations:** The status of international officials is regulated by treaties, such as the U.N. Charter and the U.N. Convention on Privileges and Immunities.

CHAPTER 5

STATE JURISDICTION

I. DEFINITION OF JURISDICTION

A. **Generally:** Under international law, jurisdiction is understood to be the ***allocation of power and authority among the states***. Three interdependent types of jurisdiction are recognized: 1) the right to ***prescribe or apply laws*** to persons and activities; 2) the right to ***enforce those laws*** through application of sanctions; and 3) the ***power of courts*** to exercise jurisdiction over a particular person or object.

II. INTERNATIONAL JURISDICTION PRINCIPLES

A. **Five main bases:** There are five recognized bases for such jurisdiction with respect to crimes:

1. **The Territorial Principle:** An essential attribute of a state's sovereignty is to have jurisdiction over all persons and objects within its territory.

   a. **"Pure" territoriality:** The act must be commenced in the state's territory, regardless of where they are concluded or consummated.

   b. **"Objective" territoriality:** The act must either be completed within the state's territory or cause serious and harmful consequences to the social and economic order within the state's territory. U.S. courts have interpreted this principle broadly in the so-called "effects" doctrine.

2. **Active nationality principle based on nationality of the defendant:** The state of a person against whom proceedings are taking place may exercise jurisdiction based on the nationality of the defendant. This is true for corporations, vessels, and aircraft as well.

3. **Protective principle:** A state may exercise jurisdiction over crimes which threaten its security and integrity or its vital economic interests.

4. **Universality principle:** Some offenses, such as piracy on the high seas, slave trading, and war crimes, are considered to be so serious to the general interest of the international community that they are subject to the jurisdiction of all states.

5. **Passive personality principle based on nationality of the victim:** The state of a person suffering injury or damage may assert that person's nationality as a basis for exercising jurisdiction.

B. **Jurisdiction based on agreement:** In addition to the five basic principles of jurisdiction, states may confer jurisdiction through international agreements.

III. EXTRADITION

A. **Extradition generally:** Extradition is the process by which an defendant of a serious crime in one state (the requisitioning state) and found in a second state (the asylum state) is returned to the requisitioning state for trial or punishment. In the absence of a treaty there is *no obligation* to extradite.

B. **Extraditable offenses:** Treaties employ one of two methods for specifying the grounds for extradition: 1) a requirement of double criminality (when the conduct is an offense in both states and punishable by a specified term of imprisonment), or 2) it may list the indictable offenses for which extradition is available.

C. **Nationals of the asylum state:** State treaties sometimes provide that a state may not or cannot extradite its own nationals.

D. **Process of requesting extradition:** Requests for extradition often are initiated along diplomatic channels. The request is then normally subject to a judicial determination followed by consideration in the executive branch, which has some discretion in the final determination.

E. **Standard treaty limitations on extradition:** Some standard treaty provisions may 1) prohibit discrimination against the accused, 2) require probable cause, 3) provide exemptions for political offenses (except terrorism), 4) include a specialty provision (the accused may only be prosecuted for the offenses for which he was indicted), 5) require territorial jurisdiction, or 6) list other non-extraditable crimes.

F. **Methods employed to avoid the safeguards of extradition treaties:** Occasionally, to avoid the terms of extradition treaties, potential asylum states may deport the accused as an undesirable alien. Requisitioning states have been known to abduct the accused from an asylum state, as well.

IV. JURISDICTIONAL PRINCIPLES IN UNITED STATES LAW

A. **U.S. grounds for jurisdiction:** Under the widely accepted "pure" territorial principle, U.S. law may be applied to any conduct taking place in U.S. The controversial effects test of U.S. law is an extension of the objective territoriality principle, in which any minimal effect on the territory of the U.S. is a valid ground for asserting jurisdiction. The protective principle also has been applied in a few cases.

B. **Conflict of laws under U.S. law:** "Comity" is the term used to describe judicial restraint practiced in order to avoid or resolve such conflicts of jurisdictions, and has been used by U.S. courts to refuse jurisdiction in deference to another state. Lack of reciprocity, on the other hand, has been used to justify a refusal to enforce a foreign court's judgment. The doctrine of *forum non conveniens*, an exercise of comity, is an often utilized method for settling problems of concurrent jurisdiction. The sovereign compulsion defense is designed to prevent unfairness to private parties subject to the conflicting commands of several states.

V. IMMUNITIES FROM JURISDICTION

Immunities generally: Both international law and municipal law grant immunities from jurisdiction.

A. **Sovereign immunity:** There are two main theories regarding sovereign immunity. Absolute immunity is based on the notion that all sovereign states are equal and are not subject to each other's authority. The modern view holds that a state may be subject to a foreign jurisdiction when it engages in commercial activity. In addition to the "commercial exception", modern law supports the traditional denial of immunity for claims to property or other immovables acquired by gift of succession, as well as claims in non-commercial torts cases. The Foreign Sovereign Immunities Act of 1976 essentially codified the restrictive theory of immunity.

1. **Foreign Sovereign Immunities Act (FSIA):** Jurisdiction over a foreign state in federal or state courts of the United States may only be obtained through application of the FSIA. A foreign state denied sovereign immunity is liable to the same extent as a private party, except that it will not generally be liable for punitive damages.

2. **Exceptions to immunity:** A state is presumptively immune unless an exception applies. Immunity does not apply under the following statutory exceptions: waivers of immunity, commercial activities, expropriation claims, property claims, non-commercial torts, maritime liens, counterclaims, and international agreements.

B. **Act of State Doctrine:** The act of state doctrine is not a rule of sovereign immunity and, in fact, is not even a rule of international law. It is a domestic court-made doctrine, which protects the sovereignty of states by judicial deference to the public acts of a foreign state done on that state's territory.

1. **Basic doctrine in the U.S.:** There exist today poorly defined parameters for the act of state doctrine based on vague notions of separation of powers in foreign relations between the executive and judicial branches. The Supreme Court now requires the U.S. to deem as valid "the acts of foreign sovereigns taken within their own jurisdictions." There are exceptions, including the treaty exception, the commercial activity exception, and the situs of property exception. Application of the doctrine is especially controversial in anti-trust cases.

2. **Doctrine in other states:** Although international law does not require application of the act of state doctrine as practiced by United States courts, the courts of many other states do, in fact, recognize a similar doctrine.

C. **Immunity of state representatives:** Just as diplomatic and consulate premises enjoy special protection, so also do various state representatives.

1. **Head of State:** The immunity of a head of state relies on both *sovereign immunity* and *diplomatic immunity*.

2. **Diplomatic representatives:** Diplomats (and their family members) enjoy *broad protection* from arrest or detention, as well as immunity from criminal laws, and civil and administrative jurisdiction. The Vienna Convention, also enacted as U.S. federal statutory law, provides that diplomats are, *inter alia*, 1) not required to give evidence; 2) immune from personal service; 3) excused from paying most taxes and social security provisions; 4) excused from customs duties and inspections. The Convention provides that diplomats do not enjoy immunity with respect to: 1) actions involving purely personal property; 2) estate administration in the host state in which the diplomat is involved in a non-official capacity; or 3) any other commercial or professional conduct in which the diplomat is functioning outside his official duties.

   a. **Convention on the Prevention and Punishment of Crimes against Internationally Protected Persons:** This treaty requires states to prosecute or extradite for prosecution anyone who commits a violent crime against any head of state, diplomatic agent, or consular official.

3. **Status of embassies and consulates:** Although such diplomatic premises are within the territory of the receiving state, they do enjoy *special protection*. Diplomatic and consulate premises are "inviolable, and are immune from any exercise of jurisdiction by the receiving state that would interfere with their official use."

4. **Consuls:** Consular immunity has been codified under the Vienna Convention on Consular Relations. Under the Convention, consulars are immune from arrest or detention except for serious crimes or as directed by court decisions, and consular archives are inviolable.

5. **Special missions:** Generally, immunity for special missions is covered by the general provisions of diplomatic immunity.

6. **Representatives to international organizations:** U.N. civil servants are protected under the Convention on the Privileges and Immunities of the United Nations, which generally grants immunities similar to those enjoyed by diplomats and consuls.

D. **Immunity of international organizations, their agents, officials, and invitees:** Immunity of international organizations has been established by treaty rather than by customary law, and not all states have been eager to extend broad protections. The General Convention of the Privileges and Immunities of the United Nations is an example of such a treaty. It provides the following immunities to the U.N.: 1) immunity from all legal process; 2) inviolability of premises, assets, archives and official papers; 3) exemption from direct taxes and customs duties; 4) exemption for staff from income tax on salaries; and 5) diplomatic immunity for the Secretary-General and Assistant Secretaries-General. Other staff members have limited immunities.

CHAPTER 6
INTERNATIONAL ORGANIZATIONS

I. THE UNITED NATIONS

The United Nations generally: International organizations usually refers to public or intergovernmental organizations, in contrast to private or nongovernmental organizations (NGOs). International organizations are established by treaties and governed by international law. The United Nations (U.N.) is a public organization of over 150 states that was established by intergovernmental cooperation on October 24, 1945.

A. **The U.N. Charter:** The U.N. Charter entered into force on October 24, 1945. The four purposes of the United Nations are described in article 1 as to: (1) "maintain *international peace and security*"; (2) "*develop friendly relations* among states"; (3) *achieve international cooperation* in solving economic, social, cultural and humanitarian problems; and (4) *be a center for states* to use to attain these common goals.

1. **Seven guiding principles:** Article 2 lists seven guiding principles for the U.N.: 1) sovereign equality of all member states; 2) fulfillment of states' obligations under the Charter; 3) settlement of disputes by peaceful means; 4) refrainment from the threat or use of force against the territorial integrity of political independence; 5) assistance to the U.N. in any action it takes; 6) adherence by non-member states to these principles insofar as to maintain international peace and security; and 7) non-intervention in matters which are essentially within the domestic jurisdiction of a state.

B. **Nature and function of the U.N.:** The U.N. has organizational personality (legal capacity) and immunity in the international system.

C. **Membership:** There were fifty-one original member states. Since its inception, membership in the U.N. has increased dramatically, doubling by 1965, and tripling by 1985. Membership is open to "all other peace loving states which accept the obligations contained in the present Charter" and are able and willing to carry them out. Although never actually done, a member state may be suspended or expelled.

D. **Charter supremacy:** Under article 103, if a Charter obligation conflicts with any other treaty obligation, the Charter prevails.

E. **The U.N. organs:** There are six principal organs to the U.N. — the *General Assembly*, the *three Councils*, the *Secretariat*, and the *International Court of Justice*.

1. **The General Assembly:** The General Assembly is composed of all member states of the U.N. It is essentially a global forum for the exchange and debate of ideas. Its resolutions are simply recommendations and not legally binding upon members as a matter of Charter law.

2. **The Security Council:** This organ has the primary responsibility for the maintenance of international peace and security. The Security Council consists of five permanent members

and ten rotating members. The permanent members have a veto vote in substantive matters. Decisions of the Security Council are legally binding upon members.

3. **The Economic and Social Council (ECOSOC):** The ECOSOC consists of 54 elected members of the U.N. Its primary responsibilities are to make studies, reports, and cultural matters and to prepare draft conventions for submission to the General Assembly on matters within its competence.

4. **Trusteeship Council:** This organ is responsible for administering trusteeship territories that are not yet self-governing.

5. **International Court of Justice:** The International Court of Justice (ICJ) is the principal judicial organ of the U.N. and the successor to the Permanent Court of International Justice for the League of Nations.

6. **Secretariat:** The Secretariat is composed of a Secretary-General and any required staff of the organization.

F. **Legislative activities of the General Assembly and International Law Commission:** The ILC is composed of leading international lawyers who research international law and draft conventions. When such conventions are adopted by the General Assembly and receive broad support they often become a generally accepted statement of international law in the area.

G. **Specialized agencies:** Specialized agencies are those "established by intergovernmental agreement and having wide international responsibilities, as defined in their basic instruments, in economic, social, cultural, educational, health, and related fields. . . ." Membership in specialized agencies is not limited to members of the U.N. By making recommendations and drafting conventions, specialized agencies have developed international law in many areas.

II. REGIONAL ORGANIZATIONS

A. **Regional organizations generally:** Regional organizations are concerned with problems within a specific region. Some handle only specific concerns such as economic, military or political issues, while others deal with any matter that concerns the nations in that region. The primary function of these regional organizations is to promote cooperation between the member states. Occasionally, the term regional organization has been loosely applied to collective defense arrangements.

B. **Relationship to U.N.:** The United Nations encourages its members in regional organizations to attempt to settle "local disputes" in those organizations before referring them to the Security Council. The issue of regional jurisdiction and the often overlapping authority of the Security Council is unclear.

III. SUPRANATIONAL ORGANIZATIONS

A. **Defined:** Member states of a supranational organization submit themselves and their citizens to the law-making power of the organization through treaties with the other member states. Supranational organizations result in a division of power between the individual member states and the organization. The best example of a supranational organization is the European Community.

C A P S U L E S U M M A R Y

CHAPTER 7
INTERNATIONAL DISPUTE SETTLEMENT

I. DISPUTES GENERALLY

A. Defined: An international dispute is a contest of some specificity, the resolution of which has some practical effect on the relations between the states involved.

II. THE ROLE OF THE U.N.

A. The Charter: The U.N. Charter includes several provisions calling for *peaceful settlement of disputes*, particularly through "negotiation, enquiry, mediation, conciliation, arbitration, judicial settlement, resort to regional agencies or arrangements, or other peaceful means of their own choice."

B. General Assembly: If a state brings a dispute to the General Assembly, the General Assembly may establish fact-finding missions and making recommendations. States are under no legal obligation to cooperate with the fact-finding missions or to follow recommendations.

C. Security Council: The Security Council has discretion to deny a request for dispute settlement or accede to it by placing a dispute on its agenda. The recommendations of the Security Council exert great political influence but create no legal obligations.

III. OTHER TREATY OBLIGATIONS OF PEACEFUL SETTLEMENT

A. Generally: Since the U.N. Charter, the treaties calling for peaceful dispute settlements are primarily regional treaties. In addition, many treaties on various subjects include provisions for peaceful settlement of disputes.

IV. NON-JUDICIAL METHODS

A. Generally: Methods of non-judicial dispute resolution are 1) *negotiation*, a face-to-face discussion between the disputing parties; 2) *inquiry*, an attempt to clarify the facts in the hopes that agreement on factual matters will facilitate a final resolution; 3) *mediation/good offices*, the use of a third party to aid in discussion; and 4) *conciliation*, a non-binding proposal by a fact-finding third party. Each method may be used alone or in any combination with the other methods.

V. QUASI-JUDICIAL METHODS/ARBITRATION

A. Arbitration generally: Arbitration, unlike any of the five methods discussed above, results in *legally binding settlements*. Arbitration has several *advantages*: 1) it is more conclusive than the other forms of non-judicial dispute settlement because the decisions of the arbitral panels are binding upon the parties; 2) the disputing parties retain greater control in the arbitration process because they appoint the arbitrators; 3) the parties may designate the procedures and the laws to be applied; 4) arbitration is less formal and less contentious than adjudication; and 5) both the arbitration proceedings and decisions can be kept confidential, a great advantage in disputes regarding sensitive matters. There are also *disadvantages*, however: 1) if the parties do not specify procedures, arbitration may be a very cumbersome and time-consuming process; 2) arbitration panels do not have the authority of courts to conduct discovery or subpoena witnesses; and 3) the parties themselves pay for the entire cost of the arbitration.

B. Types of international arbitral clauses: Arbitration can be mandated by a treaty clause, may be the main subject of a treaty on dispute settlement, or may be agreed upon after the dispute has risen.

C. **Consent to arbitrate and the *compromis*:**   There is no international law requirement to arbitrate. Parties may consent to arbitrate. The subsequent agreement on the details of the arbitration procedure is called the *compromis d'arbitrage*.

D. **Composition of the arbitral tribunal:**   Normally, a tribunal has a tripartite structure, in which each party selects one member independently and then the third member is selected by a joint decision of the parties.

E. **Choice of location:**   Choice of location can be important because some countries' laws provide that their courts have jurisdiction over arbitration proceedings.

F. **Rules of arbitration/ad hoc versus institutional arbitration:**   Parties may choose between the established sets of rules for arbitration or may develop their own "ad hoc" rules.

G. **Applicable law:**   The *compromis* usually sets forth the governing rules to be applied by the arbitrators and those rules in turn stipulate the choice of law.

H. **Arbitral award:**   As a general rule, arbitral awards are binding on the parties and are not subject to appeal. Certain defenses to enforcement of an award do exist. Some include: 1) the arbitral tribunal exceeded its powers; 2) the enforcement of the award is contrary to the public policy of the forum country; 3) the award resulted from arbitration of matters considered incapable of settlement by arbitration under the laws of the forum country; 4) the defendant proves that he was "not given proper notice ... or was otherwise unable to present his case;" and 5) the award is in "manifest disregard" of the law. Additional bases for challenging an award are: 1) corruption on the part of a member of the arbitral panel; 2) failure to state the reasons for the award; 3) serious departure from a fundamental procedural rule; 4) the agreement to arbitrate or the *compromis* are a nullity; or 5) the tribunal exceeded its powers. Other defenses may be available.

I. **The role of the ICJ:**   A *compromis* may confer jurisdiction of particular legal questions to the ICJ and indicate the rules of law to be applied by the Court.

VI. THE INTERNATIONAL COURTS

A. **The International Court of Justice:**   The International Court of Justice (ICJ) is the ***principal judicial organ*** of the United Nations. Only states may be parties in contentious proceedings before the Court.

1. **Structure and composition:**   The ICJ is composed of fifteen judges elected by both the Security Council and the General Assembly.

2. **Contentious and advisory jurisdiction:**   The Court may only hear cases governed by international law. Contentious jurisdiction is based on either the express or implied consent of the parties Decisions in contentious cases are binding on the parties. The Court also may issue non-binding, advisory opinions.

3. **Compulsory jurisdiction under the optional clause of art. 36(2):**   A state may at any time declare that it recognizes as compulsory *ipso facto* and without special agreement the jurisdiction of the Court in all legal disputes before the Court. A state accepting the jurisdiction of the ICJ under the optional clause does so only with respect to other states which have made a similar declaration. Some declarations state no time limits, while others remain in effect for specific periods (usually five or ten years). Reservations to declarations may be conditioned on other states accepting the Court's compulsory jurisdiction for a certain time, or for a wide variety of reasons. A common reservation is the so-called self-judging reservation, such as the U.S.'s "Connally Amendment," which excludes from the jurisdiction of the ICJ disputes over matters which are essentially within the domestic jurisdiction of a state. Matters related to national security and defense also often are excluded.

4. **Effect and enforcement of judgments:**   Judgments of the ICJ are binding upon the parties. The Security Council makes recommendations or decides upon measures to be taken to give effect to the judgment.

5. **Advisory jurisdiction:** The Court may give advisory opinions on any legal question at the request of a body authorized by the United Nations. Although advisory opinions are legally non-binding, they are, nevertheless, very influential in the development of international law.

B. **Other international courts:** There are also a number of regional and specialized tribunals, particularly in Western Europe. Three regional courts sitting in Europe are the Court of Justice of the European Communities, the Benelux Court of Justice, and the European Court of Human Rights.

CHAPTER 8
THE RIGHTS OF INDIVIDUALS — INTERNATIONAL LAW OF HUMAN RIGHTS

I. STATUS OF INDIVIDUALS

A. **Modern international law:** The human rights of individuals are protected *without regard to their status as nationals or aliens*.

II. BRIEF HISTORY

A. **Generally:** Historically, a state's treatment of individuals in its territory was considered a domestic affair, and not a matter of international law. After World War I, a number of treaties and international organizations began to focus on individual rights. The modern concept of international human rights law is the result of the world's reaction to the Holocaust and other Nazi atrocities during World War II. The body of law concerning international human rights is still growing and evolving.

III. HUMAN RIGHTS AND THE UNITED NATIONS

A. **The United Nations Charter:** The United Nation's Charter was the first attempt to provide comprehensive protection of all individuals. In the decades since its foundation, the U.N. has continued to promote and protect human rights and has drafted treaties for global adoption dealing with many aspects of human rights. The U.N. Charter contains articles concerning human rights, which pledge the members' active support for "human rights and fundamental freedoms." These articles are the foundation of modern human rights law.

B. **The Universal Declaration of Human Rights:** The rights in this General Assembly Resolution fall into two general categories: 1) civil and political rights; and 2) economic, social and cultural rights. Although a simple resolution and not legally binding, some of the rights listed clearly have evolved into customary international law.

C. **The U.N. human rights covenants:** The two groups of rights set forth in the Declaration of Human Rights were the basis for subsequent treaties outlining in greater detail the protected rights of individuals.

D. **The role of specialized agencies of the U.N.:** A number of specialized agencies have been active in the area of developing human rights law.

IV. FUNDAMENTAL HUMAN RIGHTS

A. **The right of peoples to self-determination:** Self-determination is the *right of people in a territory to decide the political and legal status of that territory*. The right of the inhabitants of an *established* state to determine their own government is well established but there is little or no agreement on the right of groups to secede from states of which they form a part, on reunification of peoples in divided states, or the right of minorities to preserve their own separate identities within a state.

B. **Civil and political rights:** These may include prohibition of torture; discrimination on grounds of race, gender, religion, language, political opinion, nationality, ethnicity, birth or other status; and prohibition of arbitrary arrests or interferences with privacy.

C. **Economic, social and cultural rights:** These include the right to social security, full employment, fair work conditions, education, health care, an adequate standard of living, and participation in the community's cultural life.

D. **Prohibition of slavery:** The prohibition against slavery is a fundamental right as a matter of customary international law and the norm is recognized as *jus cogens* from which no derogation is permitted.

E. **Genocide:** Genocide, or acts committed with the intent to destroy a national, ethnic, racial or religious group, is a crime for which individuals are punishable under international law.

F. **Crimes against humanity:** "Crimes against humanity" are defined as "murder, extermination, enslavement, deportation, and other inhumane acts committed against any civilian population, before or during the war, or persecutions on political, racial or religious ground.

G. **Prohibitions of discrimination:** Every individual is protected from discrimination, whether racial, gender-based, religious, or otherwise.

H. **Freedom from torture:** There are no justifications for torture or exceptions to its prohibition. States must adopt measures to prevent torture in their jurisdiction, and ensure that torture, complicity, and attempts to commit torture are criminal offenses.

I. **Rights of refugees:** The 1951 Geneva Convention addresses many civil rights for refugees. At present, customary international law does not appear to recognize a right to asylum, although this rule has been the subject of much criticism.

J. **Newly emerging rights and fundamental rights recognized as customary international law:** Many of the rights recognized in international agreements above are also recognized as customary international law. Customary human rights law may be established through: 1) virtually universal adherence to the U.N. Charter or the Universal Declaration of Human Rights; 2) widespread participation of states in preparation and adoption of international human rights agreements and General Assembly resolutions on human rights; or 3) frequent invocation and application of international human rights principles in both domestic practice and diplomatic practice.

V. ENFORCEMENT OF HUMAN RIGHTS LAW IN THE U.S. COURTS

A. **Current law:** Because the United States has failed to ratify and implement so many human rights treaties, enforcement of human rights law in United States courts is largely dependent on incorporation of custom into United States law and specific legislative provisions, such as the Alien Tort Statute.

VI. DEROGATION FROM PROTECTION OF HUMAN RIGHTS

A. **General concept:** Agreements ensuring protection of fundamental human rights often allow derogation from the rights in times of "public emergencies." The most basic human rights *may not be derogated from*, including torture, slavery, genocide, and like crimes. Examples of the derogation principle may be taken from the International Covenant on Civil and Political Rights and the European Convention for the Protection of Human Rights and Fundamental Freedoms.

1. **The International Covenant on Civil and Political Rights:** Derogation from the Covenant's obligations may be made under the following circumstances: 1) it must be a "time of public emergency which threatens the life of the nation;" 2) the existence of such dire circumstances must be "officially proclaimed;" 3) derogation is permitted "only to the extent strictly

required by the exigencies of the situation;" 4) the measures may not be "inconsistent with their other obligations under international law;" and 5) the measures may not "involve discrimination solely on the ground of race, color, sex, language, religion or social origin."

2. **European Convention for the Protection of Human Rights and Fundamental Freedoms:** The derogation provision of the European Convention is similar to that of the Covenant on Civil and Political Rights. It permits derogation: 1) "[i]n time of war or other public emergency threatening the life of the nation;" 2) "only to the extent strictly required by the exigencies of the situation;" and 3) "provided such measures are not inconsistent with its other obligations under international law."

B. **Clauses of limitation:** A number of the rights enumerated in the European Convention on Human Rights also have their own clauses of limitation, which allow restrictions on the right as necessary to protect national security, safety, and health or morals.

VII. REGIONAL HUMAN RIGHTS LAW AND INSTITUTIONS

A. **Regional human rights generally:** Regional human rights regimes operate mainly in Western Europe, the Americas and Africa.

B. **The European system of human rights law:** European human rights law is contained primarily in the European Convention for the Protection of Human Rights and Freedoms and subsequent protocols for civil and political rights, and the European Social Charter for economic and social rights.

1. **The institutions of the European regime:** The European Convention of Human Rights has established an effective human rights regime, enforcing rights through the European Commission of Human Rights, the European Court of Human Rights, and the Committee of Ministers of the Council of Europe.

2. **The process of implementation and enforcement:** The European Convention and the European Social Charter detail their respective adjudicative procedures.

C. **Inter-American system — human rights law:** Outside of Europe, the most developed regime of human rights law is in the Americas. The primary sources for human rights law in the Americas are the Charter of the Organization of American States (OAS) and the 1969 American Convention on Human Rights.

1. **Institutions of the Inter-American system:** The two organs responsible for supervising implementation and enforcement of human rights are the Inter-American Commission on Human Rights and the Inter-American Court of Human Rights.

2. **Process of implementation and enforcement:** As in the European system, claims of human rights violations are first considered by the Commission, and then referable to the Court.

D. **African regional system— human rights law:** The primary source of law is the African Charter of Human and People's Rights, which differs significantly from the European and American human rights regimes. It guarantees economic, social and cultural rights as well as political and civil rights; it is concerned with the rights of "peoples" as well as individuals; and it proclaims the duties as well as rights of individuals.

1. **Institutions of the African regional system:** The Charter also differs significantly from the European and American human rights regime because it does not provide a human rights court. The Charter does, however, establish an African Commission on Human and People's Rights to consider state and individual petitions.

CHAPTER 9
THE LAW OF ARMED CONFLICT

I. USE OF FORCE UNDER INTERNATIONAL LAW

A. **Generally:** The law of armed conflict is that area of international law which governs the circumstances under which a state may use military force. In addition, once armed hostilities have commenced, the law of armed conflict places limitations upon the means by which force may be exerted and the targets against which such force may be directed. This area of law can be divided into two sections — *jus ad bello*, the law leading up to war, and *jus in bello*, the law during war.

II. WAR AND ARMED CONFLICT

A. **Definition:** The two terms may be used interchangeably to mean any armed conflict of a certain degree between the armed forces of states. The degree of conflict required to constitute a war will vary depending upon the circumstances, the states involved, and other similar factors.

1. **Relevance of a declaration of war:** Traditionally, a state had to declare war before international law would recognize its existence. In recent years, however, many states have engaged in hostilities without a formal declaration of war. The Geneva Conventions are not restricted to declared wars and the U.N. Charter speaks in terms of the use of force, rather than in terms of war.

B. **Legal prohibitions against armed conflict:** During the 19th Century, every sovereign state was considered to have the right to wage war. In the 20th Century, however, many international agreements, most notably article 2(4) of the U.N. Charter, have **renounced force as a policy**, and encouraged first resort to peaceful settlement of disputes.

C. **Use of force consistent with the U.N. Charter:** Even within the U.N. Charter, the prohibition on the use of force is not absolute. The Charter expressly permits member nations to exert force in **self-defense**. The Security Council is also authorized to order force when it finds a threat to peace, breach of peace or act of aggression.

1. **Questions raised by article 51:** Like the prohibition against the use of force, the scope of the right of self-defense has been the subject of considerable debate. There are questions as to whether the conditions in article 51 are the only grounds for self-defense, whether anticipatory self-defense, self-help, or humanitarian intervention are allowed, as well as questions about collective self-defense. Furthermore, it is unclear whether the right of a state to act in self-defense comes to an end as soon as the Security Council has taken action.

2. **Requirements for a valid act of self-defense:** First, there must be a "necessity of self-defence, instant, overwhelming, leaving no choice of means, and no moment of deliberation." Second, the actions justified by the necessity of self-defense "must be limited by that necessity and kept clearly within it." These two requirements are often referred to as the **requirements of necessity and proportionality**. First and foremost, there must be an "armed attack" against a state under article 51.

3. **U.N. Security Council enforcement actions under the U.N. Charter:** The Security Council may act with respect to "threats to the peace, breaches of the peace, or acts of aggression." It may call upon member states to implement measures not involving the use of armed force in order to give effect to its decisions. "Should the Security Council consider that such measures are inadequate, it may use force, including demonstrations, blockade, and other operations by air, sea, or land forces of Members of the United Nations." Action taken under Chapter VII is binding on all members of the U.N., and such decisions are subject to the veto power.

4. **Enforcement action by the General Assembly:** It is questionable whether the General Assembly can take enforcement action under the Uniting for Peace Resolution, in light of the *Certain Expenses* case.

5. **Enforcement actions by regional organizations:** In the past, some regional organizations have tried to justify the use or threat of force under article 53, although such enforcement action is prohibited without the authorization of the Security Council.

D. **Humanitarian intervention as a possible justification for the use of force:** It is generally agreed that the state using force would have to *act from humanitarian motives* (not against "the territorial integrity or political independence" of the target state) and *cease military operations as soon as the humanitarian objective was achieved*, even assuming humanitarian intervention is permissible under international law.

E. **Protection of nationals and property:** Protection of nationals is distinguished from humanitarian intervention based on the nationality of the victims. It is legally distinguishable because advocates of the right have asserted that attacks on a state's nationals triggers a right of self-defense under a broad reading of article 51 or as self-help under customary international law.

F. **Reprisals:** The term "reprisal" means an otherwise illegal act committed by one state against a second state, in order to remedy a prior violation of international law by the second state, to protect its interests, or to achieve some other objective. Often, the illegal act involves the use of force. A state which engages in a reprisal in retaliation for past acts is presumably in violation of international law.

III. THE HUMANITARIAN LAW OF ARMED CONFLICT

A. **Sources of the law of armed conflict:** The International Military Tribunal at Nuremberg found the provisions of the Hague Conventions of 1907 to have entered into customary international law as of 1939. Many international treaties have attempted to regulate the conduct of warfare. Among the more important of these treaties still in force are the Hague Conventions and Declarations of 1907, especially the Convention Respecting the Law and Customs of War on Land and the Protocol for the Prohibition of the Use in War of Asphyxiating, Poisonous or Other Gases, and of Bacteriological Methods of Warfare. The Geneva Conventions of 1949, and the Protocols of 1977 added to them, are also very important in detailing the law of war.

B. **Protections provided by the laws of armed conflict:** Protection in times of war is afforded to certain individuals, including 1) *wounded, sick, or shipwrecked combatants*; 2) *prisoners of war*; and 3) *civilians*. As with individuals, the degree of protection extended to any particular piece of property depends largely upon its nature. As a general rule, the destruction or confiscation of enemy property is forbidden except for situations of military necessity. In no event is looting of enemy property permissible.

1. **The civilian populace:** The 1907 Hague Conventions provided that undefended buildings, towns, and the like were not to be attacked.

2. **Areas with special protection:** The 1949 Geneva Conventions extended special protections to medical facilities (both military and civilian) and provided for the establishment of hospital, neutralized, and safety zones in which attacks are forbidden.

C. **Conflicts encompassed by the Geneva Conventions and protocols:** Which provisions of the Geneva Convention and protocols apply depends upon whether the conflict is an international conflict, civil war or a war of self-determination.

D. **Sanctions and enforcement:** The Hague Conventions of 1907 provided that a state might be required to pay reparations if it, or any member of its armed forces, violated the Convention, although it established no procedural framework for claims. The Geneva Conventions of 1949 provide that once a violation has been established, the parties shall "put an end to it and repress it with the least possible delay." The Geneva Conventions also contain provisions allowing a state to subject any individual, regardless of nationality, to criminal prosecution for violations of the

Conventions. States have an obligation to punish individuals alleged to have committed grave breaches. The Charter of the International Military Tribunal at Nuremberg provides for individual criminal responsibility for "crimes against peace," war crimes, or "crimes against humanity." The fact that an individual acted pursuant to the orders of his government or his superior is not a defense. An official or commander who has, through reports received by him or through other means, information that troops or other persons subject to his control are about to commit or have committed war crimes, and fails to take the necessary and reasonable steps to ensure compliance with the law of war, is responsible for such crimes.

E. **Limitations on the methods of warfare:** There are several limitations imposed on the conduct of warfare by the Hague Conventions of 1907 and the Geneva Conventions of 1949, among other treaties. Restrictions on conduct of warfare cover *types of weaponry* (*e.g.*, prohibitions on poisonous gas and chemical weapons) and *tactics* (*e.g.*, false surrenders). There are also prohibitions on extending warfare to neutral states or demilitarized zones.

IV. CIVIL WARS

A. **Generally:** International law *does not prohibit civil war*. Civil wars may be fought for control of the government of the state, for the creation of a new state, or to gain independence from colonial rule. There are three categories of internal conflicts: (1) *rebellions*; (2) *insurgencies*; and (3) *belligerencies*.

B. **Traditional rule:** Under the traditional rule, states could support the governing authorities *until a belligerency was recognized*, at which point they had to remain neutral. Now, the focus is more upon the general norms of nonintervention and self-determination under the U.N. Charter.

C. **Nonintervention:** Nonintervention is well established as customary law. A state intervenes when it sends armed forces to either side in a civil war, supplies war materials, or allows its territory to be used as a base weapon on forces. It is less clear when aid from a state's nationals is intervention. A state may, however, provide humanitarian aid.

    1. **Possible exception:** It has been argued that outside states may aid insurgents if the war is one of *national liberation*.

    2. **Other justifications:** States have put forth several other justifications for intervention, such as: (1) *consent of governing authorities*; (2) *self-defense*; and (3) *counterintervention*. With the exception of self-defense, recognition of these justifications in post-Charter international law are strongly debated.

CHAPTER 10
THE LAW OF THE SEA

I. NATIONALITY OF VESSELS

A. **Generally:** Three basic principles that govern the freedom of the sea are: 1) *a ship of any state can navigate the oceans freely*; 2) *the state of the ship's nationality has exclusive jurisdiction over the ship on the high seas*; and 3) *no other state can exercise jurisdiction over that ship* absent some affirmative rule authorizing concurrent jurisdiction. The nationality of a ship defines the legal relationship between a state and a ship which is authorized by that state to fly its flag. A ship may only fly the flag of one state. A ship without nationality may be prevented from engaging in international trade or commerce or navigation of any sort on the high seas.

B. **The right of states to confer nationality upon a ship:** Each state may set its own standards for nationality.

1. **Limitations:** A state may not grant its nationality to a ship that is already authorized to fly the flag of another state. Furthermore, a state must have a *genuine link* to a ship in order for a state to confer its nationality upon it. Proof of a genuine link between a flag state and a ship may include: 1) ownership by nationals; 2) national officers; 3) national crew; and 4) national build.

C. **Documentation and registration:** A state that authorizes ships to fly its flag must: 1) *maintain a register* of ships containing the name and description of each ship so authorized; and 2) *issue documents* to the registered ships *evidencing authorization.*

D. **Duties of the flag state:** Under international law, each state has a duty to "effectively exercise its jurisdiction and control in administrative, technical and social matters over ships flying its flag." Each flag state also has the obligation to: 1) maintain a register of ships authorized to fly its flag; 2) govern the internal affairs of the ship; 3) ensure the safety at sea with regard to the seaworthiness of ships, the crews, communications, and the prevention of collisions; 4) ensure the each ship is surveyed by a qualified surveyor of ships and has on board appropriate charts, nautical publications, and navigational equipment; 5) ensure that each ship is manned by a qualified master, officers and crew; and 6) ensure that the master, officers, and the crew are fully conversant with, and are required to observe, applicable international regulations.

II. BASELINE DETERMINATIONS

A. **The baseline generally:** The baseline is the *starting point from which a coastal state's various maritime jurisdictions is measured.* Waters on the landward side of the baseline are considered internal waters of the state.

B. **Delineation of the baseline:** The baseline is the low-water line along the coast.

    1. **Rivers:** If a river flows directly into the sea, the baseline is drawn straight across the mouth of the river between the low-water points of its lands.

    2. **Bays:** Bays are considered to be internal waters of a state when the bay's area is as large or larger than that of the semi-circle for which the diameter is a line drawn across the mouth of the bay, as long as that line is less than 24 nautical miles. If the line between the natural entrance points of the bay exceeds 24 miles, a straight baseline of 24 miles can be drawn so as to enclose the maximum area of water possible with a baseline of that length. Exceptions may be made for "historical bays."

    3. **Islands:** An island is "a naturally-formed area of land, surrounded by water, which is above water at high tide." Every island has the right to claim each and every coastal zone.

    4. **Indented coastlines and island fringes:** A straight baseline method may be used for a fringe of islands or deeply indented coastline by joining appropriate points, if: 1) the baseline does not depart from the general direction of the coast and are sufficiently linked; 2) the low-tide elevation is not used; 3) if the straight baseline does not cut off the territorial sea of another state from the high seas or an exclusive economic zone; and 4) innocent passage is granted through any newly-created internal waters.

C. **Use of baseline with adjacent and opposite states:** Where the coasts of two states are opposite or adjacent to each other, neither state is entitled to extend its territorial sea beyond the median line. The delimitation of the continental shelf and economic zone between states shall be determined by agreement. In the absence of agreement, the boundary shall be the median line, where opposite states are involved; and an equidistant line, where adjacent states are involved.

III. INTERNAL WATERS AND PORTS

A. **General definition:** Internal waters are the *waters of lakes, rivers and bays landward of the baseline of the territorial sea.* A "port" is a place for loading or unloading a ship. A coastal state has *full sovereignty* over its internal waters and ports.

B. Freedom of access to ports: Freedom of access to ports by foreign merchant vessels is governed by the principal of *reciprocity*. Land-locked nations may not be denied freedom of access to ports solely because of their inability to reciprocate. Ports can only be closed to foreign vessels when the vital interests of a state require it. A coastal state may condition a foreign ship's access to port upon compliance with the laws and regulations of the port.

C. Jurisdiction over foreign vessels: A foreign merchant ship which enters any port of a state subjects itself to the administrative, civil and criminal jurisdiction of that state, although a ship's internal matters are left to the flag state. Foreign vessels are not subject to a state's jurisdiction when the vessel is seeking refuge because of distress. The flag state also has jurisdiction, and the LOS Convention grants the port state in certain situations enlarged jurisdiction.

IV. THE TERRITORIAL SEA AND CONTIGUOUS ZONE

A. Coastal state sovereignty over the territorial sea: A state has the *same sovereignty over its territorial sea, air space, seabed, and subsoil thereof as it has with respect to its land.*

B. Breadth of the territorial sea: According to the LOS Convention, every state has the right to establish the breadth of its territorial sea up to 12 nautical miles as measured from the baseline. The United States adheres to a three-mile territorial sea for domestic law purposes. For international relations, however, the United States has extended its territorial sea to 12 miles. Many states have extended their claims of a territorial sea from three miles up to as much as 200 miles.

C. The right of innocent passage: Ships of all states have a *right of innocent passage* through the territorial sea of any coastal state.

    1. General definition: Passage means navigation through the territorial sea for the purpose of either traversing that sea without entering internal waters, or proceeding to or from internal waters.

    2. Prohibited activities for innocent passage: All activities not having a direct bearing on passage violate "innocent passage," including: 1) threat or use of force; 2) exercise or practice with weapons; 3) collecting information that prejudices the defense or security of the coastal state; 4) propaganda affecting the defense or security of the coastal state; 5) aircraft activity; 6) any activity involving a military device; 7) loading or unloading any commodity; 8) pollution in contravention of international law; 9) fishing; 10) research or surveying; or 11) interfering with communications of the coastal state.

    3. Coastal state's rights: Within the territorial sea, the coastal state retains several rights for monitoring activity in the area, including: 1) the unilateral right to verify the innocent character of passage; 2) the ability to suspend the right of innocent passage if essential for protection of the state's security, 3) the adoption of regulations relating to innocent passage; 4) the exercise of fairly broad criminal jurisdiction over foreign ships; and 5) the exercise of more limited civil jurisdiction over foreign ships.

    4. Warships: No prior notification is required for warships in innocent passage under the LOS Convention.

D. Transit passage: The right of transit passage exists "through straits which are used for international navigation between one part of the high seas and another part of the high seas or the territorial sea of a foreign state." The right does not exist where a strait is broad enough to allow navigation through a high seas route in its middle. Unlike innocent passage, transit passage extends to aircraft and submarines, and the *coastal state must place less limitations on it*.

E. Contiguous zone: The coastal state may exercise the control necessary to prevent infringement of its customs, fiscal, immigration or sanitary laws and regulations in a zone contiguous to its territorial sea. The contiguous zone may not extend beyond 24 nautical miles from the baseline from which the breadth of the territorial sea is measured.

V. EXCLUSIVE ECONOMIC ZONE

A. From fishery zones to exclusive economic zone: The Exclusive Economic Zone (EEZ) was created to give coastal states exclusive economic water rights beyond the contiguous zone. The 200-mile zone was adopted at the Third United Nations Conference on the Law of the Sea. The EEZ is generally treated as part of the high seas, although states may exercise exclusive exploitation of its resources. The United States has adopted a 200-mile EEZ.

B. Management and conservation of the living resources within the EEZ: The coastal state has several responsibilities in the management of the resources within the EEZ, including the duty to prevent over-exploitation and to promote optimum utilization of the living resources. In granting access to its EEZ, a coastal state must give special consideration to the rights and needs of geographically disadvantaged and landlocked states in the region.

C. Right of geographically disadvantaged states and land-locked states in the EEZ: Geographically disadvantaged states are coastal states which can claim no EEZ of their own or whose geographic locations make them dependent upon exploitation of the EEZ of other coastal states in the region. These states and land-locked states have the right to participate, on an equitable basis, in the exploitation of any fishery surplus in the EEZs of coastal states in the region.

D. Species subject to special rules: Several species have been singled out for special treatment within EEZs, such as *migratory animals*, *marine mammals*, and *sedentary species*.

E. Enforcement of conservation and management measures: Enforcement of conservation and management measures depends upon whether the violation occurred within the EEZ or beyond it. A coastal state has enforcement rights within the EEZ, but has limited enforcement powers beyond the EEZ.

F. Other uses of the EEZ: A coastal state may exploit non-living resources in its EEZ.

G. Marine scientific research: Coastal states may regulate, authorize and conduct marine scientific research within its EEZ. If the proposed scientific research is for peaceful purposes for the scientific benefit of all mankind, the coastal state must consent to another state's request to do research.

H. Artificial islands and installations: The coastal state has the *exclusive* right to construct and regulate construction, operation and use of any artificial islands, and of installations and structures built for economic purposes in its EEZ if they do not obstruct recognized sea navigation lanes.

VI. CONTINENTAL SHELF

A. Definition and delimitation: The continental shelf is that submarine area which *begins at the shore and ends where the continental slope to the deep seabed begins*. The 1958 Convention and the LOS Convention establish more detailed measurements.

B. Rights and duties of the coastal state over the continental shelf: The coastal state has limited obligations in managing the continental shelf and has extensive rights over the natural resources of the shelf.

C. Sedentary fisheries: The coastal state has sovereign rights over all sedentary fisheries on its continental shelf.

D. Marine scientific research on the continental shelf: The same rules apply to continental shelf research as those which apply to the EEZ.

E. United States practice and legislation relating to the continental shelf: In the United States, control over the continental shelf area is divided between the federal government and coastal states of the U.S. States have full jurisdiction and rights over the inner continental shelf area. However, the U.S. has reserved its powers to regulate commerce, navigation, defense, and international affairs within the inner shelf.

VII. EXPLOITING THE MINERAL RESOURCES OF THE DEEP SEABED

A. **Current status of the legal regime of the deep seabed:** Three views have developed regarding the legal status of the deep seabed: 1) the **common heritage of mankind** view, adopted in the LOS Convention, which is that the mineral resources of the deep seabed may be exploited only through an international authority acting on behalf of all countries and is advocated by the LOS Convention and the developing states; 2) the **freedom of the high seas** view, which is that the right to explore and exploit the mineral resources of the deep seabed is a freedom of the high seas; and 3) the **res nullius** view, which is that the seabed belongs to no one, and that the mineral resources of the deep sea bed may be explored and exploited to the exclusion of all others by the first state which claims it.

B. **Seabed mining under the LOS Convention:** No state may claim, exercise sovereign rights over, or appropriate any part of the deep seabed or its resources because the mineral resources of the seabed are the common heritage of mankind. The seabed is governed by an Authority established by the Convention to oversee exploitation and distribute the benefits of exploitation through the international community.

C. **United States legislation:** The U.S. has promulgated its own regulations on the seabed in the 1980 Deep Seabed Hard Mineral Resources Act. The United States has rejected the deep seabed regime under the LOS Convention because of the way in which it provides for sharing of technology and profits.

VIII. FREEDOM OF THE HIGH SEAS

A. **General Principles:** Freedoms of the high seas include but are not limited to: (1) **freedom of navigation**; (2) **freedom of overflight**; (3) **freedom of fishing**; (4) **freedom to lay submarine cables and pipelines**; (5) **freedom to construct artificial islands**, installations and structures; and (6) **freedom of scientific research**. These freedoms must be exercised with due regard for the interests of other states. States may exercise high seas freedoms in the EEZs of other states if there is due regard for the rights and duties of the coastal state, and there is compliance with internationally legal regulations of the coastal state.

B. **Reservation of the high seas for peaceful purposes:** The high seas must be used for **peaceful purposes**. Naval forces may use the high seas, but use or threat of force violates the law of the sea and article 2(4) of the U.N. Charter absent other justification of international law (*e.g.*, self-defense).

C. **Freedom of navigation:** Every state has the right to sail ships on the high seas bearing its national flag. Warships and state-owned ships have complete immunity from jurisdiction of any other state than the flag state when on the high seas. The flag state of merchant ships has exclusive jurisdiction in terms of arrest or other physical interference, subject to the following exceptions: (1) treaty provisions allowing interference; (2) collision cases; (3) right of visit; (4) hot pursuit; (5) necessity; (6) self-defense; and (7) action authorized by the United Nations.

D. **Freedom of overflight:** All aircraft have the right to fly over the high seas.

E. **Freedom of fishing and conservation measures:** All states have the right to fish the high seas. This is limited by treaties and regard for the rights and duties of other states.

F. **Freedom to lay submarine cables and pipelines:** Cable and pipeline laying is subject to coastal state regulation on the continental shelf.

G. **Freedom to construct artificial islands:** Construction and operation of artificial islands, installations and structures is subject to coastal regulation of such activities on the continental shelf or in the EEZ.

H. **Freedom of scientific research:** All states and competent international organizations have the right to conduct scientific marine research outside of EEZs.

IX. PRESERVATION OF THE MARINE ENVIRONMENT

A. **Generally:** States must ensure, in exercising their sovereign rights to exploit their resources, "that activities within their jurisdiction or control do not cause damage to the environment or other states or of areas beyond the limit of national jurisdiction."

B. **Third United Nations Conference on the Law of the Sea:** States are required to take all measures necessary to prevent pollution of the marine environment from any source.

C. **Vessel source pollution:** States are required to establish international guidelines governing vessel source pollution through international organizations. Flag states are required to adopt laws and regulations for the prevention of pollution of the marine environment from ships flying their flag or of their registry. Coastal states may adopt laws and regulations for the prevention, reduction and control of marine pollution from foreign vessels within their territorial sea but may not hamper innocent passage. States may regulate vessel source pollution in their EEZs through an international organization or diplomatic conference. A state also may make a request to the appropriate international organization for additional coastal state regulation of vessel-source pollution in the EEZ if international rules provide inadequate protection.

D. **Pollution from land-based sources:** All states must adopt laws or regulations to prevent pollution of the marine environment from land-based sources.

E. **Ocean dumping:** States are required to adopt laws and regulations to prevent pollution of the marine environment by the dumping of sewage, sludge, and other waste materials into the ocean. These laws must be comparable to global standards. Dumping in the coastal zones of states requires consent and also is regulated under the Dumping Convention.

F. **Pollution from seabed activities subject to national jurisdiction:** States are required to adopt all laws and regulations necessary to prevent pollution of the marine environment arising from, or in connection with, their exploration and exploitation of the seabed and subsoil.

G. **Pollution from deep seabed mining:** The LOS Convention authorizes the Authority to adopt appropriate rules and regulations to prevent pollution of the marine environment from deep seabed activities.

H. **Pollution from or through the atmosphere:** All states are required to adopt laws and regulations to prevent pollution of the marine environment from or through the atmosphere.

I. **Protection of fragile ecosystems:** States are obligated to take measures necessary to protect and preserve rare or fragile ecosystems as well as the habitat of depleted, threatened or endangered species and other forms of marine life.

J. **Liability:** A state which fails to fulfill its obligations to protect and preserve the marine environment is liable in accordance with international law.

K. **Enforcement:** Flag states, coastal states and port states may all enforce rules and regulations relating to the marine environments depending on the source of pollution, the location of the violation, and the degree of harm to the environment. A state is obligated to compensate the flag state for any injury or loss attributable to unlawful or excessive measures taken against a foreign ship.

L. **Notification and cooperative action:** As soon as a state is aware that injury to the marine environment has occurred or is imminent, it must notify immediately the appropriate global or regional international organizations and all states likely to be affected.

M. **Government noncommercial ships:** Ships that are used by governments for noncommercial purposes are not subject to the international rules, standards, and enforcement procedures discussed above.

CAPSULE SUMMARY

CHAPTER 11
AIR AND SPACE LAW

I. DEFINING STATE SOVEREIGNTY OVER AIRSPACE

A. Generally: Common law doctrine held that a state's control over airspace *extended to the end of the universe*. Early attempts to define states' sovereignty over airspace balanced the inherent nature of airspace as free from sovereign control against the need of the sovereign to provide for self-preservation and the defense of its citizens.

B. Exclusive control: In 1919, the Paris Convention established each state's *exclusive control over the airspace over its territory and its territorial waters*. No state has control over the airspace over the high seas.

C. Developing law after World War II: With the dramatic rise in international air traffic, a need arose to establish some general principles to govern international air travel.

   1. **The Five Freedoms:** At this time, free airspace had been broken down into five components. These so-called *"five freedoms"* became the basis of the international agreements of the World War II era. The five freedoms are: 1) *overflight*; 2) *non-traffic landing*; 3) *putting down traffic*; 4) *picking up traffic*; and 5) *international traffic*.

   2. **The Chicago Convention:** The most important of the World War II-era agreements was the Chicago Convention, which created the International Civil Aviation Organization and the International Air Services Transit Agreement. It also outlined a number of other general principles.

   3. **International Air Services Transit Agreement extends limited freedoms to scheduled air service:** Only the first two freedoms, *i.e.*, overflights and non-traffic landings, are generally available under the International Air Services Transit Agreement for scheduled air service. The remaining three freedoms generally are not agreed upon.

   4. **Definition of "scheduled international air service":** Because the rules governing scheduled and non-scheduled international air service differ, the International Civil Aviation Organization promulgated the following definition. A "scheduled international air service" is a series of flights that: 1) *overflies more than one state*; 2) is *open to the public*; and 3) *has regular service*.

   5. **Prescriptive jurisdiction for international air travel:** When an aircraft engages in international air travel, it will at all times be traveling either in airspace governed by a state's domestic regulations or in airspace above the high seas. Regulations regarding air travel differ by jurisdiction. When the aircraft is in airspace above a state or its territorial water, the regulations of that state apply. When the aircraft is in airspace above the high seas, rules promulgated by the ICAO under article 12 of the Chicago Convention apply. Additional rules may apply for specially designated zones, such as Flight Information Regions (FIRs) or Air Defense Identification Zones (ADIZs).

   6. **Aircraft has nationality of state of registration:** Article 17 of the Chicago Convention defines the nationality of any aircraft as the state in which it is registered.

II. LIABILITY OF AIR CARRIERS

A. Limitations on liability needed to foster airline industry: The original purpose for placing limits on the recovery from airlines for damages was to assist the growth of the fledgling airline industry. Many United States courts construe the limitation of liability provisions very *strictly* against air carriers on the theory that the original purpose behind the provisions is no longer valid.

B. Standard of liability: In exchange for the limitation on liability, the Warsaw Convention provided a stricter standard of liability for the airlines. Under the Convention, carriers shall be liable for death or personal injury unless it can prove that it or its agents have taken all necessary measures to avoid the damage or that it was impossible for the carrier to take such measures.

C. Jurisdiction: The Warsaw Convention of 1929 specifies when a state has jurisdiction for actions brought under its terms. Under article 28, there is jurisdiction in the state of: 1) the carrier's domicile; 2) the carrier's principle place of business; 3) the location at which the ticket was purchased; and 4) the passenger's place of destination.

III. VIOLATIONS OF AIRSPACE

A. Violation of airspace: Under the various international conventions and bilateral agreements governing international aviation, an aircraft normally needs authorization to enter a state's airspace and is required to follow certain procedures while operating in that airspace.

B. Use of force to terminate a trespass: By analogy to the law of the sea, states may use only "necessary and reasonable force" in response to intruding aircraft.

IV. OFFENSES COMMITTED ABOARD AIRCRAFT

A. Jurisdiction generally: Because an aircraft takes on the nationality of the flag state, that state may assert jurisdiction over offenses committed on board the aircraft. In addition, the subjacent state over which the aircraft flies may assert concurrent jurisdiction based on territoriality. Other states may also assert jurisdiction for offenses committed based on other aircraft principles, such as the nationality of the defendant, universality, or the nationality of the victim.

B. Hijacking and sabotage: Hijacking involves the *use or threat of the use of force to exercise control over an aircraft*. Sabotage generally addresses efforts to place the safety of the aircraft in jeopardy. The international community has established conventions to govern both of these offenses. The Convention for the Suppression of Unlawful Seizure of Aircraft ("Hague Convention") governs hijacking and the Convention for the Suppression of Unlawful Acts Against the Safety of Civil Aviation ("Montreal Convention") deals with sabotage. Many of the articles of the two conventions are identical. Both conventions recognize *hijacking and sabotage as universal crimes*, and require that a state either prosecute or extradite the alleged offenders.

V. OUTER SPACE

A. Definition of "outer space": A controversy exists as to whether a definition of outer space is even necessary and, if it is, whether it should be scientifically based or politically based. At least seven possible definitions have been supported over the years: 1) the *limit of the atmosphere*; 2) the *limit of air flight*; 3) the *point at which the atmosphere will no longer sustain human life*; 4) the *lowest point at which a satellite can orbit*; 5) the *point at which centrifugal force replaces aerodynamic forces*; 6) the *limit of a state's effective control over its airspace*; and 7) the *current orbital minimum*.

B. Control of outer space: The widely adopted Treaty of Principles Governing the Activities of States in the Exploration and Use of Outer Space, Including the Moon and Celestial Bodies ("Outer Space Treaty") generally provides for free access to outer space and celestial bodies by all nations.

C. Liability for damage caused by space objects: Under the Outer Space Treaty and the more detailed Convention on International Liability for Damage Caused by Space Objects ("Liability Convention"), a state which launches or authorizes launching of an object, or from whose territory an object is launched, can be held liable for damages caused by the object. The standard of liability varies depending upon where and how the damage occurs. Damages are determined in the Liability Convention by the amount needed to return the injured party, whether that party is a person, state or international organization, "to the condition which would have existed if the damage had not occurred."

1. **Obligation to consider rendering assistance:** In cases in which the damage caused "presents a large scale danger to human life or seriously interferes with the living conditions of the population or the functioning of vital center," the responsible state shall examine the possibility of rendering assistance to the damaged state.

2. **Responsibility for activities in outer space:** States bear international responsibility for national activities in outer space regardless of whether the activity is carried out by governmental or non-governmental entities.

3. **State retains jurisdiction over objects it launches into space:** States retain jurisdiction over objects launched into space which are registered to it.

D. **Military applications in outer space:** The Outer Space Treaty bans military use of outer space and celestial bodies but permits some military use of orbiting space craft. The Treaty does not, however, prohibit the use of military personnel in the conduct of research or for other peaceful purposes.

E. **Geostationary orbits:** A satellite in a geostationary orbit remains over the same position on earth. Such orbits occur only over the equator. Although some states along the equator claim special rights to geostationary orbits, the prevalent view is that such orbits are properly considered "outer space" and therefore are under no state's control.

1. **Regulated use of geostationary orbits:** Because geostationary orbits are so valuable and are limited in number, the international community has sought agreement on their use.

VI. CELESTIAL BODIES

A. **Territory not subject to state control:** Under the Outer Space Treaty *no state may exercise any claim of right to the moon or any other celestial body*. The moon and other celestial bodies may be used only for peaceful purposes.

B. **Control of resources on the moon and other celestial bodies:** Only a few states have signed the Agreement Governing the Activities of States on the Moon and other Celestial Bodies which addresses exploitation of the moon's resources. The Agreement provides, *inter alia*, for the development of a governing regime for the exploitation of the moon's resources. The treaty also provides that the moon and its resources are the common heritage of mankind.

CHAPTER 12
INTERNATIONAL ENVIRONMENTAL LAW

I. EMERGENCE OF INTERNATIONAL ENVIRONMENTAL LAW

The principles of modern international environmental law began to emerge in 1972 during the Stockholm Conference and recently culminated in the 1992 "Earth Summit" in Rio de Janeiro. Many international organizations, including the United Nations (U.N.), have played a fundamental role in its development.

A. **Stockholm Conference:** The Stockholm Conference, sponsored by the United Nations, was the first global environmental conference. It was attended by 113 parties, who adopted two major documents: the Stockholm Declaration on the Human Environment, and the Action Plan for the Human Environment.

1. **Stockholm Declaration:** The Stockholm Declaration established a global approach to environmental problems. Its most important provisions state the principles that humans have a "fundamental right to . . . an environment of a quality that permits a life of dignity and well-being (Principle 1);" states have the right to exploit their own resources, but must ensure that activities within their jurisdiction do not cause damage to areas outside that

jurisdiction (Principle 21); and noted that states should develop international law regarding liability and compensation for pollution victims (Principle 22).

2. **Action Plan:** In the Action Plan, the parties adopted 109 resolutions aimed to assist states in assessing environmental problems and providing solutions.

B. **United Nations Environment Program (UNEP):** UNEP was established in 1973 partly as a result of the Stockholm Conference. It is a subsidiary organ of the U.N. and coordinates its environmental activities. UNEP has a Governing Council, a Secretariat in Kenya, and an Environment Fund. Functions of UNEP include gathering information on environmental problems, recommending possible solutions, and funding programs. It has played a lead role in the formulation of international environmental law and has sponsored major global agreements.

C. **World Charter for Nature:** The World Charter for Nature was drafted in 1982 by the World Conservation Union (IUCN). Its preamble and 24 articles set forth global environmental principles that focus upon the value of nature, the importance of integrating nature with economic planning, and suggest ways that states can implement these goals.

D. **Draft Articles on State Responsibility:** The International Law Commission (ILC) has drafted various articles that focus upon state liability with regard to transboundary pollution and other environmental damage. Article 1 states that "every international wrongful act of a state entails the international responsibility of that state." Article 19(3)(d) lists among international crimes "a serious breach of an international obligation . . . for the safeguarding and preservation of the human environment . . . ." Articles 29 to 31 describe situations that preclude the liability of a state for an otherwise wrongful act: "1. an act made with consent by the affected state, 2. an act legally made in response to a wrongful act by the affected state, and 3. an act due to extraordinary events that made it materially impossible for the state to act in conformity with its obligations."

E. **Restatement on Foreign Relations Law in the United States:** The American Law Institute has drafted a Restatement on Foreign Relations which provides in section 601 that a state is obligated to take measures the ensure that activities under its control conform to general international principles regarding transboundary pollution and are not conducted so as to cause significant injury to another state. It also states that a state is legally responsible for such an injury.

F. **The 1992 Rio Earth Summit:** The United Nations Conference on Environment and Development (UNCED), or Earth Summit, was held in Rio de Janeiro, Brazil, and was the largest global conference on the environment. The Earth Summit produced five major documents: the Convention on Biological Diversity, the Climate Change Convention, the Declaration of Principles on Forest Conservation, the Rio Declaration and Agenda 21.

1. **The Rio Declaration:** The Rio Declaration, the modern equivalent of the Stockholm Declaration, contains 27 non-binding principles, endorsed by the Conference and U.N. General Assembly. It reflects a compromise between developed and developing nations, and specifically includes the "right to development." Principle 2 provides that states have a right to exploit their resources pursuant to environmental and developmental policies, a revision of Principle 21 of the Stockholm Declaration. Other key provisions relate to notification of environmental disasters, environmental impact assessments, and liability for transboundary pollution and compensation to its victims.

2. **Agenda 21:** This 800-page document contains a plan of action for sustainable development and environmental preservation. It includes a set of priority actions and means to accomplish them. A Commission for Sustainable Development is established to monitor and review implementation of Agenda 21.

II. TRANSBOUNDARY POLLUTION

A. **General Rule:** Generally, *no state may use or permit the use of its territory in a manner that is injurious to another state or its persons or property.*

1. *Trail Smelter* Case: This landmark case, brought by the United States against Canada, established two fundamental principles of liability under international law for transboundary pollution: 1) a state must show damage and causation, and 2) a state has a duty to prevent, and may be responsible for pollution by private parties within its jurisdiction. The Tribunal held that Canada was legally responsible for harm caused to U.S. forests in Washington State by a smelter near Trail, Canada.

2. *Corfu Channel* Case: The Corfu Channel Case was brought in the International Court of Justice (ICJ) by the United Kingdom against Albania for damages to British warships by mines in the Straits of Corfu. The court held against Albania and established the principles that every state has an obligation not to knowingly allow its territory to be used contrary to the rights of other states, and a duty to notify other states of imminent danger.

3. *Lake Lanoux Arbitration*: This case was brought by France against Spain, and established the principle that a downstream state does not have the right to veto an upstream state's use of water, but the upstream state must consider counterproposals of the downstream state.

4. *Nuclear Test* Cases: These cases, brought in the ICJ by Australia and New Zealand against France, left the legality of nuclear testing unresolved on the merits. However, the ICJ did preliminary enjoin France from testing while it heard the dispute.

B. **Theories of liability for transboundary pollution under international law:** Such theories include: 1) strict liability for ultrahazardous activities, 2) liability for negligent or intentional acts ("abuse of rights"), and 3) liability for pollution that exceeds an amount a state's neighbors can reasonably endure ("good neighborliness").

1. **Specific treaties focusing on transboundary pollution:** Treaties in this area take a variety of approaches, including agreeing to try to reach agreement ("framework conventions"), establishing substantive standards, "freezing" pollution at current levels, providing for notification and consultation, and authorizing an international organization to establish rules.

2. **Example — the Acid rain treaties:** Various agreements have been drafted that address the problem of acid rain. The Convention on Long-Range Transboundary Air Pollution of 1979 went into effect in 1983 and had 33 parties, including the U.S., by December of 1991. Its purpose is to "limit, and as far as possible, gradually reduce and prevent air pollution including long-range transboundary air pollution." The Convention provides for research, exchange of information, and an Interim Executive body to monitor pollution in Europe. The Convention does not contain specific ceilings and timetables. Two Protocols to the Convention have been adopted by some of the parties, establishing standards for reduction of sulphur and nitrogen oxides.

III. OZONE DEPLETION AND GLOBAL WARMING

A. **Protection of the ozone layer:** The ozone layer protects the earth by filtering out harmful ultraviolet radiation from the sun. It is *currently being depleted* primarily by chlorofluorocarbons (CFCs) from air conditioning, aerosols, styrofoam, and refrigerators. *Two major treaties* address this problem.

1. **The Vienna Convention for the Protection of the Ozone Layer:** The 1985 Vienna Convention is a framework convention that focuses upon information exchange and cooperation among states for research with a goal to protect human health and the environment from the adverse affects of a diminished ozone layer.

2. **Montreal Protocol on Substances that Deplete the Ozone Layer:** This Protocol to the Vienna Convention was adopted in 1987 and amended in 1990. It sets forth timetables for a 50% reduction in use of CFCs by 1999. The 1990 amendments establish an escalated timetable for reduction in use of CFCs, placing a total ban by the year 2000. The amendments also establish a fund to assist developing countries in the transition to technology free of CFCs.

B. **Protection of the Climate:** Another serious global environmental problem is climate change due to the greenhouse effect which results when certain gases in the air trap infrared radiation near the earth's surface, thus elevating global temperatures.

　1. **United Nations resolutions on climate change:** In 1989, the U.N. passed two resolutions that formally recognized climate change as a global concern to be given high priority. They emphasize the need for governmental efforts to prevent climate change, and reviewed possible elements for an international climate change convention.

　2. **United Nations Framework Convention on Climate Change:** This Convention was signed at the 1992 Earth Summit and emphasizes the global concern about climate change caused by greenhouse gases. Its objective is to stabilize gas concentrations in the atmosphere, with an implicit goal of returning to 1990 levels of emissions by 2000. The parties do not agree to specific goals or deadlines. However, they do commit to periodic national inventories of emissions; mitigation programs; development of technology to control emissions; consider climate change in decision-making processes; and cooperate in the exchange of information, education, and public awareness. Developed countries also agree to use the best available scientific technology, and assist developing countries with financing their obligations under the agreement.

IV. WILDLIFE PRESERVATION

A. **Provisions under the Stockholm Declaration and the World Charter of Nature:**

　1. **Stockholm Declaration:** Principle 4 of the Declaration states that *plants and animals are a world heritage*, and that man has a responsibility to safeguard nature and also consider conservation when planning economic development.

　2. **World Charter for Nature:** Principle 2 of the Charter stresses the *need to safeguard habitats to protect global genetic viability, and maintain animal populations to ensure their survival*. In Principle 3, the Charter states that *all areas of the earth are subject to conservation*.

B. **International Convention for the Regulation of Whaling:** This Convention, adopted in 1946, established the International Whaling Commission, and intended to regulate the fishing industry. It is increasingly being directed to conservation of whales. Under the Convention, an annual schedule of whaling regulations is published, which the Commission may modify. In 1990, the Commission set a ten-year moratorium on whaling. Any member may opt-out of its obligations under the Convention by objecting.

C. **Convention on International Trade in Endangered Species of Wild Fauna and Flora (CITES):** This Convention has over 100 parties, and sets up a system of import and export permits and regulations to protect endangered species from overexploitation. The Convention establishes a Secretariat at UNEP to prepare scientific studies and coordinate national record keeping required by the Convention. The state parties are required to meet every two years to modify the Convention if necessary. The permits required under the Convention are nationally administered, and keyed to categories of endangered species as described in Appendices I-III of the Convention. No permit may be issued for a species, or a recognizable part or derivative thereof, that is threatened with extinction.

D. **United Nations Convention on Biological Diversity:** This Convention was signed at the 1992 Earth Summit. Its objectives include conserving biological diversity and the sustainable use of biological resources, and equitable sharing of the benefits of genetic resources. The parties to the Convention are committed to developing and implementing national strategies to protect biological diversity. The Convention establishes a Conference of the Parties to review implementation and adopt protocols or amendments, a Secretariat to arrange meetings and prepare reports, and a technical body to provide scientific advice to the Conference.

V. HAZARDOUS WASTE, RADIOACTIVE POLLUTION, AND ENVIRONMENTAL EMERGENCIES

A. Early Conventions on civil liability for nuclear damage: These conventions include the Paris Convention of Third Party Liability in the Field of Nuclear Energy of 1960, the Brussels Convention Supplementary to the Paris Convention, the Vienna Convention on Civil Liability for Nuclear Damage of 1963, and the Joint Protocol Relating to the Application of the Vienna Convention and the Paris Convention of 1988.

B. The Chernobyl accident and resulting Conventions: In 1986, an explosion occurred at the Chernobyl nuclear power plant in the Soviet Union. The accident raised questions about the adequacy of international law to address this type of emergency. Two conventions were negotiated as a result of the accident: the Convention on Early Notification of a Nuclear Accident, and the Convention on Assistance in the Case of a Nuclear Accident or Radiological Emergency, both signed in 1986. The Convention on Early Notification provides for notification "forthwith" and information regarding a nuclear accident which may have a transboundary affect. The Convention on Assistance provides for cooperation between states in the event of a transboundary radiological release. It focuses upon efforts prior to and after nuclear accidents. The International Atomic Energy Agency (IAEA) has a central role under this Convention to coordinate emergency response.

C. Basel Convention on the Control of Transboundary Movements of Hazardous Wastes and their Disposal: The Basel Convention regulates international trade in hazardous wastes, with an objective to limit such trade. Under the agreement, a party may not export hazardous waste to another party without consent of that party and proof that it has adequate facilities to dispose of the waste. The Convention contains labeling standards, and prohibits trade with non-parties.

VI. ANTARCTICA

Antarctica comprises about ten percent of the earth's land and water mass and is the *only continent that has not been exploited for commercial purposes*. There are five principle mechanisms that protect the Antarctic environment:

A. Antarctica Treaty of 1959: This Treaty was the first to protect the Antarctic environment. It assured continued scientific research and suspended states the right to claim "sectors" of the continent. The Antarctic Treaty Consultative Parties (ATCPs) include 38 states, 12 original signatories and twenty-six other states who have signed the treaty and conducted substantial scientific activity in Antarctica. Key environmental provisions prohibit nuclear explosions and disposal of radioactive waste, and require the ATCPs to meet annually to consult and formulate, if necessary, measures to preserve or conserve living resources in Antarctica.

B. Convention for the Conservation of Antarctic Seals: This 1972 Convention establishes a regulatory system for the hunting of seals, which had almost disappeared from excessive hunting. Some species are completely protected.

C. Convention on the Conservation of Antarctic Marine Living Resources: This Convention, signed in 1980, establishes a system for conservation of marine resources within the entire Antarctic marine ecosystem extending to the boundaries of the Antarctic Ocean, called the Antarctic Convergence. The Convention permits a "rational use" of resources within the context of its conservation goals.

D. Agreed Measures for the Conservation of Antarctic Fauna and Flora: These measures, adopted by the ATCPs in 1964, declares the Antarctic Treaty Area a "Special Conservation Area," and establishes a *regulatory permit system* for harming wildlife in the area. It also requires that states take steps to minimize habitat interference and water pollution. Areas of scientific interest are designated "Specially Protected Areas," and are subject to special regulatory protections.

E. The 1991 Madrid Protocol: The Madrid Protocol provides the most comprehensive protection of the Antarctic environment. Article 3 establishes the basic environmental principle that protection of the Antarctic environment "shall be the fundamental consideration in the planning and conduct of all activities in the Antarctic Treaty Area." The Protocol provides standards by which to assess the environmental impact of all human activities in the Treaty area, requires that adverse impacts on the environment be limited, and provides for "regular and effective monitoring" to assess environmental impacts. Its annexes provide procedures for environmental impact assessment and waste disposal, and also address conservation of wild flora and fauna, prevention of marine pollution and area protection and management. Most significantly, article 7 of the Protocol effectively bans mining on Antarctica for at least 50 years, when the agreement first becomes open for review by the Conference of the Parties.

VII. DEFORESTATION

Deforestation involves the ***unsustainable use of forests and their genetic resources***. Of primary concern today is the destruction of tropical rainforests.

A. Consequences: A fundamental cause of deforestation is thought to be poverty. Local impacts include floods, droughts, siltation of rivers, destruction of breeding areas, and the threat to the survival of millions of forest dwellers worldwide. Globally, deforestation is considered the primary loss of biodiversity and a major contributor to global warming through the greenhouse effect.

B. The 1984 International Tropical Timber Agreement: This Agreement accounts for 95 percent of the international timber trade and is the only global agreement regulating tropical timber. It is administered by the International Tropical Timber Organization, and includes 46 party states. The Agreement is based upon free trade principles, and is unlikely to be modified for environmental reasons alone.

C. The Rio Forest Principles: The Non-Legally Binding Authoritative Statement of Principles for a Global Consensus on the Management, Conservation, and Sustainable Development of All Types of Forests, or Rio Forest Principles, were proposed by the United States at the 1992 Earth Summit after meeting resistance from developing countries to a more binding forestry agreement. In the Rio Principles, the parties agree to promote international cooperation on forestry, but do not commit to any specific actions.

D. Debt-for-nature swaps: First introduced in 1987 by NGOs, debt-for-nature swaps involve the purchase of foreign debt in exchange for domestic forest reserves or other environmental projects. Countries such as Bolivia and Ecuador have participated in swaps, and many others are currently considering them.

    1. Public vs. private debt-for-nature swaps: The first swaps were "private," meaning at least one of the parties was private. A "second generation" of swaps has emerged, called "public swaps." These occur between sovereign states and account for a greater amount of debt reduction than private swaps. There are three types of public swaps: 1. government debt purchases, 2. government grants to environmental groups, and 3. debt forgiveness.

VIII. DESERTIFICATION/LAND DEGRADATION

Desertification is identified in Agenda 21 as a key global environmental problem that is critically linked to the goal of achieving sustainable development in all countries. It affects about one sixth of the population and one quarter of the total land area of the world. Land that is severely degraded may be permanently lost.

A. Definition: The U.N. has defined desertification as land degradation in arid, semi-arid and dry sub-humid areas (including irrigated cropland) resulting mainly from adverse human impact.

B. The Lome IV Convention: This Convention was signed in 1989 between the European Community and the African, Caribbean and Pacific states, and specifically calls for national, regional, and international action to preserve resources and protect ecosystems against desertification and drought.

   C. **Past U.N. efforts to combat desertification:** The U.N. Conference on Desertification (UNCOD), held at UNEP in Nairobi in 1977, was the first world conference to set out a plan for initiating and sustaining a cooperative effort to combat desertification. It focused on technical and economic reforms, and attempted to integrate national, regional, and international efforts within and outside the U.N., with little progress.

   D. **Current U.N. efforts:** Chapter 12 of Agenda 21 includes six program areas addressing desertification that states agree to focus upon, including developing information and monitoring systems and integrating comprehensive anti-desertification programs into national development plans.

   E. **Treaty envisioned:** Agenda 21 requires the U.N. General Assembly to establish a committee to oversee the creation of an international convention addressing land degradation and drought.

IX. MARINE ENVIRONMENT

   A. **Generally:** The protection and preservation of the marine environment is discussed *supra* at page C-31.

X. INTERNATIONAL TRADE AND ENVIRONMENT

There is a growing recognition that *trade and the environment are inextricably linked*. Thus, the effects of environmental policy on trade, and environmental implications of trade are emerging as issues of international concern.

   A. **The GATT:** The General Agreement on Tariffs and Trade (GATT) codifies most of the rules governing international trade. It was established in 1948 and is periodically reviewed by the parties. GATT rules are based primarily on concepts promoting free trade, and environmental regulations are frequently viewed as a type of non-tariff barrier, to be forbidden under GATT. There is no mention in GATT of environmental protection as a justification for limiting trade. However, states may legitimately restrain trade under article XX if "necessary to protect human, animal or plant life or health" and impose measures "relating to the conservation of natural resources." The Uruguay Round of GATT talks, begun in 1985 and concluded in 1994, was the first round to link international trade and the environment, with the participants signing a pledge that they agreed to undertake a dialogue on the "interlinkages between environmental and trade policies." In 1971, GATT established a Group on Environment Measures and Trade, which first became active in 1991 following a GATT debate on environment and trade. The Group will initially examine trade provisions in existing multilateral environmental agreements, national regulations likely to have an international effect, and trade effects of packaging and labeling requirements aimed at protecting the environment.

   B. **Conflicting views of traditional free trade theorists and environmentally oriented economists:** GATT negotiators have difficulty coming to agreement about the role of the environment in international trade because economists' views in this area conflict. Environmentally oriented economists argue that goods in the international market that do not reflect the environmental costs of production distort the trade process, giving an unfair advantage to those who degrade the environment, termed "ecological dumping." However, under the GATT, this kind of advantage is not recognized as unfair, and the practice is not forbidden.

   C. **The Tuna/Dolphin Decision:** This 1991 decision by a GATT panel was the result of a formal complaint by Mexico against the U.S. claiming that a U.S. embargo on Mexican yellowfin tuna was protectionist and a violation of GATT. The U.S. had imposed the trade sanction to compel Mexico to bring down its kill rate of dolphin in the harvesting yellowfin tuna to U.S. standards. The U.S. argued that it was treating the Mexican product no less favorably than products of national origin, and also invoked the exemption for the protection of natural resources and animals. The panel found that the import ban by the U.S. violated GATT, stating that a product may only be regulated according to its properties, and the natural resources exemption can only be used to protect living or natural resources in the jurisdiction of the party invoking the exemption.

D. The Global Environment Facility (GEF): The GEF was established by the World Bank in 1991 as a pilot program to provide financial assistance to developing countries to help them implement programs addressing global environmental problems including: ozone layer protection, limiting greenhouse gas emissions, protection of biodiversity, and protection of international waters. The 1992 Biodiversity Treaty and the Montreal Protocol both contain the GEF as a funding mechanism. Contributions to the fund are currently voluntary. It is administered by the World Bank, UNEP and UNDP.

E. North American Free Trade Agreement (NAFTA): NAFTA is a unique trade agreement for its incorporation of environmental protections. The preamble states that trade must be consistent with environmental protection and conservation. The agreement calls for "harmonization of the parties domestic standards with international environmental standards, while preserving in certain circumstances each country's ability to maintain domestic environmental standards which exceed prevailing international standards. Disputes over environmental standards may be resolved by an arbitral panel, with the burden under NAFTA on the party challenging the environmental measure. Although NAFTA, by its terms, is generally to be given priority over conflicting international agreements, exceptions are made for several major international environmental treaties. A separately negotiated environmental agreement focuses on cleanup of the Mexico/U.S. border area and establishment of a Commission on Environmental Cooperation to ensure enforcement of environmental standards by the parties.

In *Public Citizen v. U.S. Trade Representative*, 5 F.3d 549 (D.C. Cir. 1993), the D.C. Circuit Court of Appeals held that an environmental impact statement did not have to be prepared for NAFTA because it was not "final agency action" under the Administrative Procedure Act and NEPA itself does not create a private right of action.

XI. MILITARY ACTIVITIES AND THE ENVIRONMENT

The international community is increasingly willing to condemn an aggressor and impose liability for environmental crimes committed during military activities. Liability may arise under a number of international agreements or customary law.

A. Protocol I to the 1949 Geneva Conventions Relating to the Protection of the International Armed Conflicts: This Protocol prohibits warfare methods which "are intended, or may be expected, to cause widespread, long-term and severe damage to the natural environment." It also states that "care shall be taken in warfare to protect the natural environment against . . . damage," and that "[a]ttacks against the natural environment by way of reprisals are prohibited." The Protocol's status as customary law is controversial.

B. Environmental Modification Convention of 1977 (ENMOD): ENMOD was drafted during the Vietnam War in response to concern about the military's use in Vietnam of chemicals that change the "dynamics, composition, or structure" of the environment. ENMOD prohibits member states from using environmental modification techniques that have "widespread, long-lasting, or severe" effects as a means to harm another state.

C. General customary laws of war: Customary laws of war require proportionality and necessity of all methods of warfare. It has been argued that the body of law that restricts the use of certain weapons prohibits any method of war that causes unnecessary suffering. It is not clear whether general norms of international environmental law are suspended during armed conflict.

CHAPTER 1
THE CONCEPT OF PUBLIC INTERNATIONAL LAW

I. INTRODUCTION

To understand international law as a body of law requires one to take a broad view of the term "law" and to consider "law" in a context surpassing the set of well-defined rules which are applied to settle disputes brought before a tribunal. International law is applied not only for dispute resolution in a courtroom, but also is very influential in the policy-making and diplomatic relations of nations. The enforcement of international law also differs from the enforcement of most domestic law. Enforcement is less dependent upon judicially imposed civil or criminal sanctions than expectations of reciprocal behavior among nations.

A. Definition of international law: The definition of international law has changed over time.

   1. **Historical approach:** Historically, international law was defined as ***"the body of rules and principles of action which are binding upon civilized states in their relations with one another."*** J. Brierly, The Law of Nations (1963). *See also The Case of the S.S. Lotus (Fr. v. Turk.)* 1927 P.C.I.J. (ser. A) No. 10, at 21 ("International law governs relations between independent States.").

   2. **Modern approach:** The modern approach expands the definition to include relations not only between states ***but also relations between international organizations and states, among the international organizations themselves, as well as the relationship between states or international organizations and natural or juridical persons,*** such as the law governing human rights. This view is reflected both in the Restatement (Third) of the Foreign Relations Law of the United States § 102 and in the Vienna Convention on the Law of Treaties between States and International Organizations or between International Organizations.

   3. **Public international law distinguished from private international law:** One must carefully distinguish "public international law" from "private international law." This distinction is made because the latter focuses on the conduct, not of states or international organizations, but rather on the conduct of individuals, corporations and other private entities.

Note: The distinction between public and private international law is increasingly difficult to define because many treaties entered into by states actually affect the activities of private corporations and individuals, particularly in the area of overseas trade and investment practices. One such example is the U.N. Convention on the Sale of Goods.

B. **Importance of public international law:** International law is pervasive and directly or indirectly impacts upon many fundamental aspects of human existence. International law:

   1. *Defines the very existence of "states";*

   2. *Provides the framework for diplomatic relations;*

   3. *Governs international agreements;*

   4. *Sets forth rules for the operation of international commerce;*

   5. *Governs individual human rights;* and

   6. *Regulates protection of the global environment,* as well as the use of the air, land, sea and other global resources.

C. **History of public international law:** Once called the law of nations, international law emerged as a distinct body of law during the 16th and 17th centuries as a result of the emergence of the nation-state. Early international law was derived in large part from Roman law and canon law, which were in turn derived from natural law. The natural law approach of the 16th and 17th centuries was criticized by theorists of another jurisprudential movement known as positivism.

   1. **Natural law:** Natural law is based on the notion that *each state, just as each individual, is endowed with certain natural rights.* These rights are not created but rather are the "dictate of right reason," basic principles of justice with a universal validity.

      a. **Influence of Hugo Grotius:** Hugo Grotius (1583-1645) transformed the law of nature from one based on divine authority to a law based on universal reason. Grotius is considered the "father of international law" and is best known for *De Jure Bellis Ac Pacis* (The Law of War and Peace). Three important principles of modern international law can be attributed to Grotius:

         i. The requirement of restitution for harm done by one party to another;

         ii. *Pacta sunt servanda* — the obligation of a state to honor its promises; and

         iii. The principle of freedom of the seas.

      b. Influence of Samuel Pufendorf: Samuel Pufendorf (1632-1694) was a German scholar who furthered the natural law approach by stating that natural law was the true source of international law.

2. **Positivism:** The school of natural law may be best understood by contrasting it to positivism. Unlike natural law, which exists without the affirmative consent of nations, positivism teaches that *international law is that body of law to which states have consented to be bound.* Its best known proponent is John Austin (1790-1859) who defined law as the commands of the sovereign, supported by sanctions.

      a. Express consent: Consent may be express, as in the form of a treaty.

      b. Implied consent: Consent may be implied, as with acquiescence to customary law.

3. **In summary:** Positivism became the predominant theory of the 19th and 20th centuries, although there was a resurgence of the natural law approach following World War I. The positivist approach, with its emphasis on sovereign commands and traditional sanctions as fundamental to the distinction between law and morality, is the foundation for much of the controversy over whether international law is really "law."

Chapter 2

SOURCES OF INTERNATIONAL LAW

I. THE STATUTE OF THE INTERNATIONAL COURT OF JUSTICE

The sources of international law, set forth in article 38(1) of the Statute of the International Court of Justice (ICJ), are:

1. *"international conventions*, whether general or particular, establishing rules expressly recognized by the contesting states;" Stat. of the I.C.J., art. 38, ¶ 1(a).

2. *"international custom*, as evidence of a general practice accepted as law;" art. 38, ¶ 1(b).

3. *"the general principles of law* recognized by civilized nations;" art. 38, ¶ 1(c).

4. *"... judicial decisions and the teachings of the most highly qualified publicists* of the various nations, as subsidiary means for the determination of rules of law." art. 38, ¶ 1(d).

II. INTERNATIONAL CONVENTIONS/TREATIES

In the broadest sense, an international convention or treaty is *any agreement governed by international law.* Although treaties have been in use for centuries, many have been concluded since World War II. More than 30,000 treaties have been registered with the United Nations since 1945, and the majority of those treaties are bilateral treaties or treaties between a small number of states.

A. **Introduction:** The *Vienna Convention on the Law of Treaties,* which entered into force in 1980, is the *primary source* for the law of treaties. Most provisions of the Vienna Convention were declaratory of existing law while others went beyond the existing law to create new law at the time they were adopted. The argument has been made, and disputed, that the "progressive development" provisions of the Convention have been so widely accepted that they have been transformed into customary law.

Note: As of 1993, the U.S. had not ratified the Vienna Convention, but the State Department does recognize it as the authoritative guide to current treaty law and practice.

1. **History of the Vienna Convention:** Work commenced on the Convention in 1949 by the International Law Commission and the

Convention was regarded from the beginning as primarily a codification of existing treaty law. From the outset it was assumed that the provisions would form a multilateral treaty rather than an "expository code." Drafts and commentaries were prepared by a group of four preeminent legal scholars called *special rapporteurs*. The four scholars, who are still oft quoted, are James Brierly, Sir Hersh Lauterpacht, Sir Gerald Fitzmaurice and Sir Humphrey Waldock. The *travaux preparatoires* are made up of the reports and records of the International Law Commission and the special rapporteurs and are critical for understanding and interpreting the Vienna Convention.

    2. Alternate forms of treaties: Although the Vienna Convention is the primary source of treaty law, it is not the sole source. The Vienna Convention *applies only to those treaties meeting the Convention's requirements for a treaty.* Some international instruments that fall outside the Convention's definition of a treaty, however, are nevertheless recognized as treaties.

B. The Vienna Convention definition of a treaty — requirements: The Vienna Convention sets forth a basic definition for a treaty as *"an international agreement concluded between States in written form and governed by international law, whether embodied in a single instrument or in two or more related instruments and whatever its particular designation..."* Vienna Convention on the Law of Treaties, *opened for signature* May 23, 1969, U.N. Doc. A/Conf. 39/27, art. 2, ¶ 1(a), 8 I.L.M. 679, 681 [hereinafter *Vienna Convention*]. In short, the Convention requires that an international agreement meet the following criteria in order to be a treaty within its scope:

1. It must be *between states*. The Convention excludes treaties between states and an international organization or between international organizations.

2. The agreement must be *in writing.*

3. The agreement must be *governed by international law.*

C. International law governs all treaties: Governance by international law is required of all treaties, whether or not they are treaties within the scope of the Vienna Convention. Although the presumption is that an agreement between two or more states is a treaty, evidence that domestic law was intended to control the agreement rebuts that presumption. Following are examples of agreements which are not treaties because they are not governed by international law:

Example: A standard contract between two governments for the sale of beef, the contract being one normally used in the meat trade among private parties.

Example: The purchase of land or buildings in a transaction which is made subject to domestic rather than international law.

Note: The transfer of land however from one state to another could, under different circumstances, be governed by international law. For example, the cession of a small parcel of land by France to Switzerland to enlarge the Geneva airport was done by means of a treaty, because the sovereignty of that parcel was transferred and sovereignty is governed by international law.

D. **Non-Vienna Convention treaties:** The concept of a treaty under international law is not limited to that defined in the Vienna Convention. The Vienna Convention states that its definition of a treaty does not affect the legal force or applicability of international law to agreements which do not fall within the definition. Vienna Convention, art. 3. A more recent treaty (Vienna Convention on the Law of Treaties between States and International Organizations or between International Organizations) expands the definition to include agreements not only between states but also includes agreements involving international organizations as parties.

E. **United States distinction between a treaty and an executive agreement:** While international law recognizes as treaties all agreements meeting the above described requirements for a treaty, U.S. domestic law distinguishes *between an executive agreement and a treaty* in the procedures necessary for the agreements to be given legal effect and in the legal effect accorded the agreements.

1. **Treaty:** Treaties are *concluded by the President with the advice and consent of the Senate.* Senate ratification of a treaty requires a two-thirds majority vote. U.S. CONST. art. II, § 2.

2. **Executive agreement:** An executive agreement is *concluded by the President based on authority granted by Congress or based on the inherent authority granted the President by the U.S. Constitution.* It is unclear under U.S. constitutional law as to what matters must be concluded by treaties with Senate ratification and what may be done by executive agreement as part of the inherent authority of the President.

   a. **Limitations upon presidential power and congressional domain:** The President may not conclude executive agreements regulating areas clearly within the congressional domain. The regulation of foreign trade, for instance, is vested in Congress. *See United States v. Guy W. Capps, Inc.,* 204 F.2d 655 (1953), *aff'd*, 348 U.S. 296 (1955).

  b. Presidential power in foreign affairs: The President may, however, conclude executive agreements extinguishing U.S. nationals' claims against foreign countries. *See Dames & Moore v. Regan*, 453 U.S. 654 (1981).

3. Potential conflicts between U.S. domestic law and international law: It is possible for an agreement to be *denied legal force and effect under U.S. domestic law and yet still be binding under international law.*

  Example: The President could sign an executive agreement with another state that goes beyond the constitutional authority of the President to enter into such agreements. Without Senate ratification, the agreement has no legal force and effect as a matter of constitutional law. Nevertheless, the Vienna Convention says that a state's consent to be bound can be expressed in almost any manner (Vienna Convention, art. 11), and that a state's internal law cannot be invoked as justification for failure to perform a treaty. Vienna Convention, art. 27.

  Note: The Vienna Convention does provide, however, that failure to comply with an internal law concerning competence to conclude treaties may invalidate a state's consent if that violation was "manifest and concerned a rule of its internal law of fundamental importance." Art. 46, ¶ 1. A violation is manifest if it would be "objectively evident to any State conducting itself in the matter in accordance with normal practice and in good faith." Art. 46, ¶ 2.

F. Name and form of treaty: As indicated in the Vienna Convention's definition of a treaty, *a treaty may be designated by a wide array of names.* "Treaty" is the most common title but the following are also used: convention, act, general act, protocol, agreement, *modi vivendi*, concordance, charter, declaration, and compromise.

1. Components of treaty and language: Although there is no officially correct form, treaties generally comprise four parts: the title, the preamble, the main body, and the final part.

  a. Title: A description of the type of treaty and the subject matter, the title often also includes the names of the contracting parties. Treaties concluded in simplified form do not usually have titles.

  b. Preamble: Following the title and serving as an introduction, the preamble states the reasons for the treaty, the names of the negotiating representatives, and the authority with which the representative is cloaked.

c. **Main body:** This sets forth the rights and obligations of the parties.

d. **Final part:** The final part comprises the provisions setting forth the guidelines for entry into force, termination of the treaty, revisions, accessions, reservation, publication, and languages in which the text will be written. The treaty finally concludes with the date and place of conclusion and the signatures and seals of the contracting parties.

e. **Language:** There is no universal rule as to what language or what number of languages must be utilized for the text of the treaty. Rather, the language of the treaty is selected by the contracting parties. When a treaty is published in more than one language, the treaty itself should clarify which text is to be the authentic and authoritative one.

2. **Subject matter of treaty:** The subject matter of the treaty is composed of the rights and obligations of the parties. Two important limitations apply:

a. *Jus cogens* **restrictions:** *The treaty may not set forth rights and obligations which conflict with jus cogens* (the imperative norms of international law) (*See* p. 36, *infra*, for discussion of the concept of *jus cogens*.).

b. **U.N. Charter restrictions:** *The treaty may not set forth rights and obligations which conflict with those obligations a member-state has undertaken under the U.N. Charter.* U.N. Charter, art. 103.

   Example: Treaties condoning wars of aggression, slavery or genocide are prohibited.

3. **Classification of international treaties:** Treaties may be classified by the following criteria: *contracting parties*, *geographic factors*, *possibility of accession*, *subject matter*, *form*, or *method of conclusion*.

a. **According to number of contracting parties:** Treaties may be bilateral, multilateral, restricted multilateral, and general multilateral according to the number of contracting parties.

   i. **Bilateral treaties:** Agreements *between two parties* are termed bilateral. They are by far the most common type of treaty and are similar to contracts in that they express a mutual exchange of rights and obligations. Bilateral treaties come in a wide variety of forms, ranging from detailed agreements effective for a fixed period of time to agreements simply stating general norms or intentions to form alliances. Some general treaties in fact state principles so widely accepted as to be considered customary law.

 ii. **Multilateral treaties:** Multilateral treaties are divided into two categories: *restricted multilateral treaties* and *general multilateral treaties*.

  (1) **Restricted multilateral treaties:** Restricted multilateral treaties are agreements *involving close cooperation among a limited number of states for specific purposes;* *e.g.*, construction of a hydroelectric dam and other similar projects and treaties of economic integration, such as the treaties establishing the European Communities. Because restricted multilateral treaties set forth interdependent rights and obligations, the consent of all states is often necessary to adopt the text of the treaty.

  (2) **General multilateral treaties:** General multilateral treaties, on the other hand, are *open to all states or to at least all states within a large geographic region* (*i.e.*, Europe). Unlike bilateral treaties, which are often akin to contracts between parties, general multilateral treaties are more legislative in character. In contrast to restricted multilateral treaties, general multilateral treaties ordinarily do not require unanimity for adoption or entry into force.

 b. **According to geographical factors:** General multilateral treaties are open to all states, no matter what continent or region they belong to. Regional treaties, on the other hand, are restricted to a defined area of the world. Problems arise when a region is not well-defined. For example, there had been considerable debate in the European Community as to whether Turkey was a "European" country for purposes of becoming a party to many treaties of the European Community.

 c. **According to possibility of accession:** A closed treaty contains no provisions allowing for subsequent accession or the joining of a treaty by a new contracting party. An open treaty does provide a right of accession to parties not involved in the original drafting and conclusion of the treaty. A hybrid is the semi-open treaty, which allows accession but only after consultation with the original contracting states. The U.N. Commission adheres to the traditional notion that *accession is only possible if the treaty expressly provides for accession or if the original parties subsequently decide to permit accession.*

    d. According to subject matter: Treaties are loosely categorized as political, commercial, technical, administrative or procedural treaties. The categories are merely a matter of convenience and have little bearing on the treaties themselves or their legal effects.

    e. According to form — written and verbal: Although the Vienna Convention states that treaties must be written, the Restatement and custom demonstrate that *oral agreements are also enforceable as treaties. See* Vienna Convention, art. 3; *Legal Status of Eastern Greenland (Den. v. Nor.)* 1933 P.C.I.J., (ser. A/B) No. 53. Even a unilateral promise by a state may be binding under international law if so intended by the state.

    Example: In the midst of controversy over France's testing of nuclear devices in the South Pacific, France's president declares in various public statements that France intends to stop testing. France is then bound by its declaration. *Nuclear Tests (Aus. v. Fr.)* 1973 I.C.J. 99 and *(N.Z. v. Fr.)* 1973 I.C.J. 135.

    f. According to method of conclusion: Treaties may be concluded by solemn or simplified form.

        i. Treaties concluded in solemn form: Treaties concluded in solemn form are concluded by a "special procedure" and "subject to ratification by the highest competent authority."

        ii. Treaties concluded in simplified form: Treaties concluded in simplified form are concluded on the basis of an exchange of notes or letters. One party sends a note or letter including the draft of an agreement, and the other party returns a note or letter expressing its intentions to adopt the text as an international agreement. Ratification is rarely required for treaties concluded in simplified form. Treaties concluded in simplified form usually extend, amend or amplify pre-existing agreements.

G. Treaty-making power — capacity: *Both the party* (the state or international organization) *and its representative* must have the proper capacity to negotiate and conclude an international agreement.

    1. Nation-states and international organizations: It is presumed that nation-states have the necessary capacity to negotiate and conclude treaties. International organizations, however, have the necessary capacity only if the constitution of the organization either expressly or impliedly gives the organization that capacity.

2. **Component states of a federal union:** An inconsistent area is the capacity of the component states of a federal union. Generally, one constituent state (*e.g.*, Connecticut) of a federation may enter agreements with other constituent states (*e.g.*, Michigan), but the rules may differ with regards to entering into agreements which extend beyond the members of the federation. Two determining factors are the constitutional guidelines of the federation and recognition of international legal personality.

    Example: States of the United States must receive approval from Congress before entering "any Agreement or Compact". By contrast, the states of Germany and Switzerland do have the right, without the interference of their respective central governments, to enter certain treaties with one another.

3. **Self-governing territories:** Self-governing territories also present troublesome issues, as there are conflicting views as to whether they have the capacity to enter international agreements.

    a. **No capacity view:** One view holds that a territory is not a "state" and cannot be regarded as a "distinct juridical person" capable of being "a responsible party to the treaty entirely separate from the parent State." *First Report on the Law of Treaties*, [1962] 2 Y.B. Int'l L. Comm'n 27, 37.

    b. **Capacity view:** Some conventions, however, specifically include self-governing territories among those parties which may sign the convention.

4. **Authority of persons representing a state or international organization:** Authority is issued in a document entitled a *"full powers" document*, which names those individuals who are authorized to negotiate and conclude a treaty on behalf of the State.

    a. **Practice of state:** An exception to the requirement of "full powers" is in art. 7 of the Vienna Convention. It recognizes authorization through the full powers, but it also allows states to dispense with full powers if the practice of the state involved demonstrates their intention to consider their representative as being duly designated and authorized.

    b. **Heads of state — exception to the requirement of "full powers":** Full powers are also dispensed with for Heads of State, Heads of Government, Ministers of Foreign Affairs and Heads of diplomatic missions. Such officers have inherent capacity to conclude treaties. (*See Legal Status of Eastern Greenland,*

(*Den. v. Nor.*) 1933 P.C.I.J. (Ser. A/B) No. 53, concluding that the oral statements of Norway's foreign minister were binding upon Norway because he acted within his capacity under international law.) Also having capacity are representatives accredited by states to international conferences or organizations. The latter's authority applies only for the purposes of the treaty concluded by the particular conference or organization.

> **Example:** A U.S. representative to a conference on human rights may have capacity to negotiate and sign a treaty on human rights but lack capacity to negotiate and sign an unrelated treaty on the sale of goods.

5. **Apparent authority of a state's representative:** A State is bound to a treaty unless it is clearly evident that its representative was acting beyond his authority.

6. **Subsequent confirmation:** When authority is lacking, the treaty is without legal effect unless the state subsequently confirms the treaty. Vienna Convention, art. 8. It is not clear whether such confirmation must be expressly made or whether it is sufficient if implied by subsequent conduct.

H. **The treaty process:** The treaty process includes *negotiation, adoption, authentication,* and *forms of conclusion.*

1. **Negotiation of treaties:** The negotiation of treaties varies according to whether the treaty is bilateral or multilateral.

   a. **Bilateral treaty negotiation:** Bilateral treaty negotiation usually begins in the foreign ministry of one of the parties and is followed up by discussions and exchanges of notes, usually through diplomatic channels. Draft texts are prepared by legal advisors and become the basis of further negotiations. The goal, of course, is to create a draft which is acceptable to both parties.

   b. **Restricted multilateral treaty negotiation:** Restricted multilateral treaty negotiation ordinarily is conducted in the same manner as are bilateral treaties.

   c. **General multilateral treaty negotiation:** Negotiation of general multilateral treaties is generally conducted at diplomatic conferences where diplomatic delegations, including legal advisors, act on behalf of the states. The conference typically begins with draft proposals and other working papers which the participating states or organizations had prepared in advance. The proposals and workings papers are the subject of the subsequent negotiations and form the basis for the final text of the treaty. The conference itself functions much like a legislature, with the designation of drafting committees, presentation of amendments, and recording of the working sessions. As with a legislature, the records become an important part of the final product, the treaty. The formal, final result of the conference is entitled the Final Act, which often serves to authenticate the treaty. Note, however, that the Final Act is not usually intended to bring the treaty into force. Vienna Convention, art. 10.

2. **Adoption:** Although the Vienna Convention itself does not provide a definition, "adoption" is generally defined as the ***formal act signifying that the form and content of the treaty have been agreed upon.*** Adoption signifies that the negotiations have been completed, disputed points have been resolved, and the wording of the final document agreed upon.

3. **Forms of conclusion:** Adoption of the text of the treaty does not conclude the treaty but is rather just one step in a series of steps necessary to eventually bring a treaty into force. A party is ***not bound to a treaty until it has consented to be bound.*** Such consent may be expressed in many ways as suggested by articles 7-11 of the Vienna Convention: through signature, the exchange of instruments, acceptance, approval, ratification, and "any other means if so agreed." Parties most commonly express their consent to be bound by the terms of a treaty by means of either ratification or accession.

   a. **Signature:** The signing of the treaty may, by itself, signify the state's definitive consent to be bound when: the treaty states that the signature is a signal of the state's definitive consent; it is otherwise established by the contracting parties; or intent that the signature establishes definitive consent is indicated from the "full powers" document or otherwise expressed during the negotiations. Vienna Convention, art. 12.

      Note: Ratification is superfluous when the signature itself binds the party to the treaty. On the other hand, a treaty which requires the additional step of ratification before the party is bound to its terms, regards the signature primarily as a method of authenticating the treaty's text and it does not signify a promise to ratify later.

   b. **Signature followed by ratification:** Historically, ratification was the process of verifying the authority given the representatives who had negotiated and signed a treaty, but the modern understanding in many states is that ratification is a check on the treaty-making powers of the executive branch by passing the treaty through the parliamentary/legislative branch of government. Ratification provides an additional opportunity to carefully consider the rights and obligations of a treaty before consenting to be bound by its terms. The law of treaties, as reflected in the Vienna Convention, ***does not require ratification*** for a state to be bound by a treaty, and many informal international agreements bind parties on the basis of a signature alone.

   i.   **United States constitutional requirement of ratification:** Under U.S. law, the President must obtain the advice and consent of the Senate to ratify a treaty. The Senate must approve of the treaty by a two-thirds vote. U.S. CONST. art. II, § 2; *see* p. 6.

c. **Obligations of a party which has signed but not yet ratified:** Although a party has not yet ratified a treaty, it may under the following circumstances still have an ***obligation not to defeat the object and purpose of the treaty.*** Vienna Convention, art. 18.

   i.   **Clear intent to no longer be a party:** When a party has signed a treaty or otherwise exchanged instruments indicating that the treaty is subject to ratification, acceptance, or approval, that party is obliged not to defeat the object of the treaty until it clearly expresses its intentions to no longer be a party.

   ii. **Reasonable waiting period for entry into force treaties:** A party is obliged not to defeat the object of the treaty when its consent to be bound to the treaty has been expressly made subject to the entry into force of the treaty, as long as the entry into force is not unduly delayed.

d. **Accession:** Accession is the ***process by which a state which was not a signatory of the treaty may nevertheless become a party to the treaty and be bound to its terms.*** Parties to a treaty are not given different treatment according to the manner in which they became parties.

   Example: A treaty may provide that "this treaty may be ratified by all states signatories thereto. Any other state wishing to become a party to it, may do so by depositing an instrument of accession."

e. **Acceptance:** Article 14 of the Vienna Convention refers to "acceptance" as ***"an expression of consent to be bound either without a signature or after a non-binding prior signature."*** Acceptance is not so much an actual method of consent as it is a term seen in treaty provisions, the meaning of which varies according to the context.

Example: A signature "subject to acceptance" is the equivalent of a signature subject to ratification, but a treaty which is "open to acceptance" is one which is open to accession.

f. **Approval:** The term "approval" was introduced into international law to correspond to the internal procedures of states which call for the "approval" of treaties.

g. **Entry into force:** Entry into force is the ***actual implementation of the treaty's terms*** and in the Vienna Convention is governed by article 24. Entry into force often occurs when specific requirements laid out in the treaty have been met.

   i. **Bilateral treaties:** The contracting states indicate their intention to be bound to the treaty from a specified date and the treaty takes effect as of that date.

   ii. **Multilateral treaties:** General multilateral treaties usually include a provision stating that a specified number of states must ratify or accept the treaty before it is in force between those states. Alternatively, the treaty may specify that it only goes into force when it is ratified or accepted by all the parties. Note that the provisions setting forth the manner of entry into force apply from the moment the text of the treaty is adopted, unlike the remainder of the treaty which is implemented upon entry into force.

   iii. **Consent of all negotiating states:** If the treaty has not laid out specific requirements for entry into force, the treaty is implemented when all negotiating states have consented to be bound.

   iv. **Provisional application:** Provisional application, recognized by article 25 of the Convention, permits the treaty to be implemented before the formal requirements for entry into force have been met. Either the entire treaty or segments of it may be subject to provisional application. Provisional application may be terminated when the terminating party informs the other states of its intent not to become a party bound to the terms of the treaty. Provisional application is increasingly important in the search for quick solutions. Entry into force of a treaty can take years and the delays are frequently unrelated to the actual substance of the treaties. Hurdles to overcome before actual entry into force often relate to translations, administrative matters, and objections by parliaments to marginal provisions.

I. **Reservations:** A "reservation" is defined as *"a unilateral statement, however phrased or named, made by a State, when signing, ratifying, accepting, approving, or acceding to a treaty, whereby it purports to exclude or to modify the legal effect of certain provisions in their application to that State."* Vienna Convention, art. 2, ¶ d.

  1. **Declarations of understanding:** A reservation must be distinguished from a statement which serves as a clarification of the State's position. Unlike reservations, these declarations of understanding have *no legal effect* in varying the terms of a treaty under international law. Their legal effect within a state as a matter of domestic law will vary from state to state.

  2. **Permissible reservations:** Article 19 of the Vienna Convention permits reservations to general multilateral treaties, *unless the treaty expressly or impliedly prohibits reservations, or the reservations sought are simply incompatible with the object and purpose of the treaty.* *See* Reservations to the Convention on Genocide 1951 I.C.J. 15 (May 28). The treaty may prohibit reservations either as a general matter or it may prohibit specific types of reservations.

  3. **The purpose of reservations:** Many multilateral conventions seek wide participation and reservations encourage participation by allowing a state to be a party without agreeing to every provision of a treaty. Some conventions, however, such as the 1982 Law of the Sea Convention, include a general prohibition on reservations because reciprocity may be vital to treaties functioning as a "package deal."

  4. **Acceptance of and objections to reservations:** Reservations are *not applicable to bilateral treaties* because the terms of the treaty are tailored specifically to the interests of the two contracting parties. Either the parties accept one another's terms or they do not accept them. Reservations may apply in multilateral treaties and often complicate the multilateral treaty, transforming it into a series of related bilateral treaties.

    a. **Reservation expressly permitted:** A reservation expressly permitted by the treaty *does not require acceptance* unless the treaty so provides. Vienna Convention, art. 20, ¶ 2. The other parties essentially have already indicated their acceptance by drafting it into the treaty itself.

b. Object and purpose requires consent: "When it appears from the *limited number of the negotiating States and the object and purpose of a treaty that the application of the treaty in its entirety between all the parties is an essential condition of the consent of each one to be bound by the treaty,* a reservation requires *acceptance by all the parties.*" Vienna Convention, art. 20, ¶ 2. Otherwise, unanimous consent to a reservation is not necessary. *See* Reservations to the Convention on Genocide 1951 I.C.J. 15 (May 28).

c. Reservation neither permitted nor prohibited: If the treaty itself does not prohibit a reservation in any way, or expressly permit it, each state is free to decide whether to reject or to accept the reservation.

5. Legal effects of acceptances of and objections to reservations: *States may either accept or object to reservations.*

a. Acceptance of a reservation: If a state accepts the reservation, the treaty will *enter into force between the accepting and reserving state.* The treaty's provisions apply as modified by the reservation. *See* Reservations to Convention on Genocide 1951 I.C.J. 15 (May 28); Vienna Convention, art. 21, ¶ 1. The modification is effective only between the reserving state and the accepting state, and is of no consequence between other parties to the treaty. Art. 21, ¶ 2.

b. Objection to a reservation: If a state objects to a reservation, there are two possible outcomes:

i. Objecting state still a party: The state may object to the reservation, yet still be willing to enter a treaty relation with the reserving state. In that case, the treaty is *in force between the objecting and accepting state, but "the provisions to which the reservation relates do not apply as between the two States to the extent of the reservation."* Vienna Convention, art. 21, ¶ 3. The willingness to preserve the treaty relationship is presumed in the absence of an express objection to the contrary.

ii. Objecting state refuses to be a party: If the objecting state not only objects, but also expresses its intention that the entire treaty be of no effect between it and the reserving state, *the reserving state and objecting state are not parties to the treaty vis-á-vis each other.*

Example: States A, B, C and D are parties to a general multilateral treaty, but State A ratifies the treaty with a reservation to article 10. State B accepts the reservation; State C objects but still wishes to maintain the treaty relationship; and State D objects both to the reservation and to entry into force of the treaty between itself and State A, the reserving party. The possible outcomes are as follows:

(1) The treaty is in force between State A and State B, but art. 10 is modified by the reservation.

(2) The treaty is in force between State A and State C, but art. 10 does not apply between the two states to the extent of the reservation.

(3) The treaty is not in force between State A and State D.

(4) The treaty is in force and unmodified between States B, C and D.

J. Limitations to reservations: Reservations are generally narrowly construed and do not apply to other provisions of a treaty by way of implication. *See* 1984 Advisory Opinion on Restriction of the Death Penalty, American Convention on Human Rights, Inter-American Court on Human Rights, Advisory Opinion No. OC3 [1983] (ser. A) No. 3, 23 I.L.M. 321 (1984).

K. The observance of treaties: *All parties to a treaty must perform their obligations under the treaty in good faith.*

1. *Pacta sunt servanda*: Article 26 of the Vienna Convention expresses one of the most fundamental principles of public international law, *pacta sunt servanda*: "Every treaty in force is binding upon the parties to it and must be performed by them in good faith." This obligation of parties to observe the provisions of a treaty to which they have consented to be bound is closely related to a second fundamental principle underlying international law: good faith performance.

2. **Good faith performance:** Good faith performance is required regardless of any conflicting domestic law. Conflicting domestic law does not excuse a state from its treaty obligations, unless the state's consent to be bound by the treaty was expressed in violation of the state's domestic law and the violation was manifest and concerned an internal law of fundamental importance. Vienna Convention, art. 46.

Note: The predominance of treaty obligations over domestic law holds true only in the arena of international law and is not always the rule in domestic courts. For example, the general rule under U.S. law is that a later federal statute supersedes an earlier treaty. U.S. courts, however, first attempt to avoid conflicts between the treaties and superseding statutes by interpreting the domestic law in a manner consistent with the treaty. *See* p. 7.

3. **Territorial scope of treaties:**   The general rule is that a treaty applies to *all the territory of each party.* "All the territory" is defined as all land, neighboring territorial waters and air space.

   a. **Exceptions:** Territorial scope may be limited by the treaty itself or by means of a reservation. Note that a reservation limiting territorial scope may be invalid if the limitation is incompatible with the object and purpose of the treaty.

4. **Interpretation of treaties:**   There are three basic approaches to treaty interpretation:

   a. **Textual approach:**   The textual approach, advocated by the Institute of International Law, looks *only to the text of the treaty and the "plain and natural meanings of the words."* Adherents of the textual approach do not attempt to ascertain the intent of the parties, except to the extent that the intent is clearly expressed in the words of the text. The presumption is that the four-corners of the document contain all that the parties wished to express.

   b. **Limited contextual approach:**   The limited contextual approach, followed by the International Law Commission and incorporated into articles 31 and 32 of the Vienna Convention, regards the text as the starting point for interpretation. Interpretation, however, is *not necessarily limited to the four-corners of the document.* Intent of the parties may be ascertained from the *travaux preparatoires*, subsequent agreements regarding interpretation of the treaty, subsequent actions or practices of the parties which reflect the parties' understanding, and other relevant rules of international law.

   c. **Policy-oriented and configurative approach:**   The policy-oriented and configurative approach (from M. McDougal, H. Lasswell, & J. Miller, The Interpretation of Agreements and World Public Order) is the most liberal and conceptual of the three. *Intent is defined as the "genuine shared expectations"* and may be gleaned from the *treaty text and all pre- and post-treaty communications.* No one source predominates over another and intent is considered in the very broad framework of "giving effect to the goals of a public order of human dignity."

5. **Fulfillment of treaties — methods of oversight:**   Many of the traditional methods of securing compliance with a treaty have no application today.

    a. Available remedies: Remedies available for non-fulfillment include submission of the dispute to the International Court of Justice, diplomatic negotiations and arbitration. The treaty itself will often designate the manner in which disputes are to be resolved. (For further discussion, *see* International Dispute Settlement, *infra*, at pp. 101-113.)

    Note: Although the Vienna Convention in articles 65-66 sets out the procedures to be followed for peaceful settlement of treaty disputes, the Convention does not address what happens if peaceful methods of settlement should fail.

6. Amendment of treaties: The general rule, as set forth in the Vienna Convention, is that *"a treaty may be amended by agreement between the parties."* Vienna Convention, art. 39. The method of amendment is often specified in the original treaty. Amendments take on the character of treaties themselves and are governed accordingly by the general law on treaties. The Vienna Convention distinguishes between an "amendment" and a "modification."

    a. Amendments (article 40): Amendments *alter a treaty with respect to all parties.* Article 40 requires notification to all parties of the proposal to amend. All parties have the right to participate in the decision to amend as well as in the subsequent negotiations and conclusions of any amendments. Unless a contrary intention is expressed, a party which does consent to be bound by the amendment nevertheless continues its obligations under the original treaty with respect to those parties not joining the amended version. If not all the original contracting parties become party to the amendment, there results a split in the application of the treaty. The only version which applies between any two states is the one to which both states are parties.

    Example: State A and State B are parties to an amended agreement. State C is a party to the original agreement only, having not joined the amended agreement. The rights and obligations of the amended agreement apply only to the relationship between States A and B. Between States A and C and between States B and C the rights and obligations of the original agreement apply.

    b. Modifications (article 41): In contrast to amendments which are open to all parties, modifications are *made by a limited number of parties.* Modifications are permitted only if:

        i. modifications are permitted by the original treaty; or

ii. modifications are not prohibited by the treaty and the modification is one which "does not affect the enjoyment by the other parties of their rights under the treaty or the performance of their obligations; [and] does not relate to a provision, derogation from which is incompatible with the effective execution of the object and purpose of the treaty as a whole." Vienna Convention, art. 41, ¶ b(i-ii).

c. **Amendment/modification by tacit consent:** Although the Vienna Convention has not included such a provision, the argument has been made that customary international law recognizes amendment or modification of a treaty by actual practice of the parties which is at variance with the treaty provisions.

7. **Invalidation of treaties:** The grounds for invalidating a treaty are *error, fraudulent conduct, corruption, coercion, conflict with peremptory norms (jus cogens),* and *conflict with domestic law.* The provisions of the Vienna Convention are controversial and are not necessarily accepted as reflecting customary international law.

a. **Error (article 48):** In actual practice, error is rarely invoked as a grounds for invalidation because the lengthy process of negotiations decreases the possibility of error.

i. **Right to invalidate the treaty:** *Error does not automatically void the treaty,* but provides the right to invalidate consent to the treaty. Consent may be invalidated only if the error pertained to an essential basis of the consent.

ii. **Invalidation not allowed:** If the party in question either contributed to the error or was on notice of the error, the error is not grounds for invalidating its consent.

iii. **Textual errors:** Errors limited to the wording of the text do not affect its validity.

b. **Fraud (article 49):** Fraud is not defined by the Vienna Convention but it is distinguished from innocent misrepresentation and error because fraud not only affects the consent of a party but the entire basis of mutual confidence between the parties. *Fraud, like error, does not void the treaty* but is a ground for invalidating a party's consent to be bound by the treaty.

c. **Corruption (article 50):** Corruption is the exercise of a substantial and inappropriate influence on the representative concluding a treaty on behalf of the state. The improper influence must come from one of the other negotiating states, not from within the representative's own state.

d. Coercion of a representative (article 51):   Coercion goes beyond influence and consists of acts or threats used against a representative in order to procure a state's consent to be bound by a treaty. Consent so procured is *without any legal effect.*

e. Coercion of a state (article 52):   *A treaty concluded with the threat of or use of force in violation of the principles of the U.N. Charter is void.* Force or threat of force is not well defined and potentially could include everything from economic or political pressure to actual military force.

f. Conflict with a peremptory norm (*jus cogens*) (articles 53 and 64):   The generally accepted rule is that *a treaty is void if it conflicts with a rule of jus cogens.* The application of this rule, however, is complicated by the fact that there is much controversy concerning the rules of *jus cogens.* It is difficult to identify which general rules of international law qualify to be rules of *jus cogens*, and the difficulty is amplified by the evolving nature of *jus cogens.* Nevertheless, there are some generally accepted principles.

Example: Treaties contemplating genocide, slavery or the use of armed or physical force against the territorial integrity or political independence of any state are unenforceable as conflicting with *jus cogens.*

g. Conflict with domestic law (article 46):   *See* p. 7 (discussing potential conflicts between U.S. domestic law and international law).

8. **Separability of treaty provisions (article 44):**   Grounds for invalidation generally affect the entire treaty, but in certain circumstances, only parts may be invalidated. In instances of fraud or corruption only the "victim" state may decide whether the whole treaty or parts of the treaty are to be invalidated. In instances of coercion or conflict with *jus cogens*, the entire treaty is void and there is no separability. Article 44 does provide for separability of the treaty provisions if:

   a. Separability specified in treaty: the treaty itself permits separability; or

   b. Treaty provisions are not essential: the objectionable clauses are "separable from the remainder of the treaty with regard to their application," "not an essential basis of the consent" and "continued performance of the remainder of the treaty would not be unjust."

9. **Acquiescence (article 45):** A party which continues to perform under the terms of a treaty, despite its knowledge that grounds for invalidating it exist, is precluded from later invoking those grounds for invalidation. This provision is included to prevent abuses and it does not apply to treaties which have been procured by coercion or are in conflict with *jus cogens.*

10. **Termination and suspension of treaties:** Treaties may be terminated or suspended for one or more of the following reasons.

   a. **Termination of or withdrawal** from a treaty by agreement of the contracting parties: Treaties may fix their own duration, state a date of termination or an event or condition to trigger termination, or set forth the right of the parties to denounce or withdraw from the treaty. Article 54 of the Vienna Convention provides that a treaty may be terminated in accordance with the terms of the treaty or by consent of all of its parties. In the United States, a treaty's termination provision does not require the Senate's consent to a notice of termination, the President may terminate the treaty on his or her own authority. *Goldwater v. Carter*, 444 U.S. 996 (1979).

   b. **Provisional suspension of multilateral treaties as between some of the contracting parties:** Temporary suspension of a multilateral treaty between some of the parties is permitted:

      i. If provided for in the treaty;

      ii. If the treaty ***does not prohibit*** the suspension and the suspension is ***neither prejudicial*** to the rights of the other parties ***nor incompatible*** with the object and purpose of the treaty. Vienna Convention, art. 58.

   c. **Unilateral abrogation of treaties:** Unilateral abrogation by a party, particularly when a treaty neglects to address the subject, is an area in which many treaty disputes occur.

      i. **Intent of parties and nature of treaty:** *Unilateral abrogation of treaties without abrogation or withdrawal clauses is, in principle, not permitted.* In practice, however, the intent of the parties or the nature of the treaty determines whether unilateral abrogation or withdrawal will be allowed. For example, a treaty establishing a territorial boundary by its nature prohibits unilateral abrogation, while a commercial treaty may imply a right of unilateral abrogation. Article 56 of the Vienna Convention has adopted a middle-of-the-road approach by embracing both the principle and the practice for treaties without provisions regarding termination denunciation, or withdrawal. It requires the abrogating party to give 12 months notice of its intent to withdraw from the treaty. However, a treaty is not subject to denunciation or withdrawal unless the parties so intended or such a right can be implied by the nature of the treaty. Vienna Convention, art. 56, ¶ 1(b).

     ii. **Unilateral abrogation provisions:** Unilateral abrogation of treaties containing abrogation clauses can be revoked in accordance with their own provisions. Treaties may either permit unilateral abrogation under fixed conditions or may stipulate that unilateral abrogation is valid only with the consent of all other contracting parties.

   d. **Termination by reason of duration or realization of purpose:** Termination by reason of duration or realization of purpose is fairly straightforward. If the parties have agreed that the treaty is to last for only a specified period of time, the treaty ceases to be valid at the expiration date. The parties may, however, agree to extend the duration and set a new term for the treaty's validity.

   e. **Grounds for termination or withdrawal:** Treaties may be terminated for reasons analogous to contract law defenses.

     i. **Impossibility of performance:** Although the Vienna Convention, article 61, recognizes impossibility of performance (based on the permanent destruction or disappearance of something indispensable to performance) as a grounds for terminating or suspending application of a treaty, the closely related grounds of *rebus sic stantibus* (fundamental change in circumstances) is of more practical importance as grounds for termination or withdrawal.

     ii. **Fundamental change of circumstances (*rebus sic stantibus*) (article 62):** This doctrine is invoked to terminate obligations under long-term treaties, but international courts and arbitrators rarely find the doctrine applicable. The doctrine may not be invoked when: the treaty establishes a boundary; or the change is the result of a breach by the invoking party of either an obligation under the treaty or of any other international obligation owed by it to any other party to the treaty. *Rebus sic stantibus*, under the Vienna Convention, applies only when all of the following requirements have been met:

      (1) **Fundamental change:** The change must be of a fundamental character;

(2) Unforeseen: The change in circumstances must have been unforeseen by the parties;

(3) Essential basis: The circumstances at the time of entering the agreement must have been an essential basis of the treaty. *But see Bremen v. Prussia*, Germany, Staatsgerichtshof 1925-1926 Ann.Dig. 352, No. 266, stating that restrictive clauses forming an essential basis for the treaty may not be abolished without the party's consent; and

(4) Radical alteration: The change in circumstances must radically alter the performance of obligations yet to be performed under the treaty. *See Fisheries Jurisdiction* (*U.K. v. Ice.*), 1974 I.C.J. 3 (July 25)

iii. Termination due to breach (article 60): The effect of breach varies according to whether the treaty is bilateral or multilateral. ***In all cases the breach must be material.*** A material breach consists of a repudiation of the treaty not sanctioned by the Vienna Convention or a violation of a provision essential to the object and purpose of the treaty. The breach itself does not automatically terminate the treaty but it may be invoked as a ground for termination. *See* Advisory Opinion on the Continued Presence of South Africa in Namibia, 1971 I.C.J. Rep. 16.

(1) Bilateral treaties: A material breach by one party entitles the other party to terminate or suspend operation of the treaty in whole or in part. *Charlton v. Kelly*, 229 U.S. 447 (1913).

(2) Multilateral treaties: The following parties to a multilateral treaty may terminate due to breach.

(a) Parties not in breach: By unanimous agreement the parties not in breach may suspend the treaty in whole or in part or terminate it, either between the aggrieved parties and the breaching party or among all parties.

(b) Party specially affected: A party specially affected by a material breach may act alone to unilaterally suspend the treaty in whole or in part between itself and the breaching party.

(c) Radical change in position: Any party may unilaterally revoke the treaty, if the breach is such as to radically and materially change the position of every party to the treaty.

iv. **Later inconsistent treaty between parties (article 59):** A treaty is terminated if all parties conclude a later agreement on the same subject matter and, it is implied that the later treaty is to govern; or the later treaty is so incompatible with the earlier treaty that the two treaties cannot be performed at the same time. The earlier treaty may be merely suspended if there is an implication drawn either from the treaty or otherwise that suspension was intended.

v. **War between contracting parties:** The Vienna Convention addresses the effect of war between the contracting parties only to state that its provisions "shall not prejudge any question that may arise . . . from the outbreak of hostilities between states." Vienna Convention, art. 73. The Institute of International Law has addressed the topic concluding that ***"[t]he outbreak of an armed conflict does not ipso facto terminate or suspend the operation of treaties in force between the parties to the armed conflict."*** The Effects of Armed Conflict on Treaties: Resolution of the Institut de Droit International, article 2 (1985 Helsinki Session). The nature of the treaty dictates the effect of hostilities on its operation. *Factors to consider are:*

(1) **Express termination:** Whether the treaty has been expressly terminated.

(2) **Incompatibility with war:** Whether the treaty's execution is simply incompatible with the state of war. *See Techt v. Hughs,* 229 N.Y. 222, 128 N.E. 185, *cert. denied,* 254 U.S. 643 (1920), stating that treaties not incompatible with the state of war remain in effect unless expressly terminated. Peace treaties or treaties of alliance, for example, are dissolved during a state of war.

(3) **Intent to govern hostilities:** Whether the treaty is in fact intended to govern the hostilities, such as treaties on the rules of war (Hague Convention), or to prevent hostilities, such as treaties governing boundaries.

(4) **Suspension during war:** Law-making treaties, and certain other general multilateral treaties may be simply suspended by war. Such treaties may remain in force because they serve the interests of the entire international community.

11. **Effect of state succession on international treaties:** Succession of states is the ***shift of responsibility over a territory from one state to another state.*** This is to be distinguished from a change in government or regime within an established state, as takes place for example with a social revolution or an election. Succession affects the legal identity of the state and its treaty obligations. Succession occurs with secession of states, annexation, merger and consolidation, and decolonization. Succession has legal consequences concerning the transfer of rights and obligations from the predecessor state to the newly emerged state.

   a. **The Restatement § 201:** The Restatement generally follows the Vienna Convention but does vary in several respects. The Restatement, unlike the Vienna Convention, does not distinguish between newly independent states (*i.e.,* former colonies) and new states resulting from disintegration of a former state or secession from a former state.

   b. **The Vienna Convention on the Succession of States in Respect of Treaties:** As of 1993, this Convention had not entered into force. As with the Vienna Convention on the Law of Treaties, this Convention is intended primarily as a codification of pre-existing customary law. Not all provisions, however, are considered declaratory of existing law. Most of the principles which follow are reflected in the Vienna Convention.

      i. **Transfer of territory resulting from moving boundaries (Moving Treaty — Frontiers Rule):** The international agreements of the state to which the territory once belonged are no longer applicable. The international agreements of the state to which the territory now belongs apply.

      ii. **Absorption of an entire state:** The international agreements of the absorbed state cease and are replaced by the international agreements of the absorbing state.

      iii. **Newly formed states (former colonies or states resulting from separation of a state):** The new state does not automatically become a party to the international agreements of the predecessor state. The new state, however, is not precluded from accepting such agreements, either expressly or impliedly, and may become a party upon the agreement or acquiescence of the other parties.

      iv. **Territorial and boundary agreements:** Such agreements are unaffected by the succession of states. What qualifies as a territorial treaty is controversial. It is generally defined as a treaty which either grants another state a right to use of its territory or places restrictions on the use of its territory. Examples are treaties on the rights of transit on international waterways, rights to pass through a state's airspace, use of international rivers and demilitarization or neutralization treaties.

c. **Newly independent states under the Vienna Convention:** As stated earlier, the Vienna Convention distinguishes between newly independent states (*i.e.,* former colonies) and states created by disintegration or secession.

   i. **The Clean Slate Doctrine:** The basic concept is that *a newly independent state begins its existence free of the obligations of its predecessor state.* Vienna Convention, art. 17; art. 24. There is an exception for territorial treaties, the obligations of which newly independent states do maintain.

   ii. **The right of option:** Although generally free of obligations, a newly independent state does have the right of option to be a party to general multilateral treaties by virtue of being a successor state. In such cases, the newly independent state may choose to become a party to a treaty independently of the consent of other parties to the treaty. This absolute right of option does not extend to restricted multilateral treaties or bilateral treaties. In practice most new states continue to act pursuant to treaties that applied to their territory before their independence.

d. **States created by disintegration or secession:** A new state created by secession from a former state, or by disintegration of a former state into two or more states, succeeds automatically to most of the former state's treaties. Vienna Convention, art. 34. It has been questioned whether this rule for states created by secession reflects customary international law, because such new states have been viewed as entitled to invoke the "clean slate" doctrine.

12. **Effect of governmental succession on international treaties:** A change in government has no effect on the legal identity of the state, and therefore no effect on the legal obligations arising from treaties.

III. INTERNATIONAL CUSTOM

Along with treaty law, customary international law is one of the two principal sources of international law. Despite numerous treaties, there are many topics and many parties which are not covered by treaty law. Customary international law is important for its potentially general application to states not parties to treaties, as well as its ability to supplement areas of international concern not addressed in treaties. Despite its acknowledged importance, customary law is subject to much controversy for it eludes any definite formulation. First, the lack of sufficient consistency in state practices may make it difficult to establish a practice as customary. Secondly, customary law is ascertained by subjective analysis of whether states engaged in a certain practice are acting out of a sense of legal obligation (the *opinio juris* requirement) or for other reasons.

A. **Two approaches to customary international law:** The two approaches are the objectivist/sociological approach and the participatory/voluntarist approach.

1. **Objectivist/sociological approach:** The objectivist/sociological approach is that customary law is ***universal and therefore binding on every state*** of the world community.

2. **Participatory/voluntarist approach:** The participatory/voluntarist approach is that customary law applies ***only to those states which have participated in the custom,*** and newly independent states have the right not to be bound by a previously established practice as customary international law. *See S.S. "Lotus" (Fr. v. Turk.)*, [1927] P.C.I.J. (ser. A) No. 10, at 21 ("The rules of law binding upon States . . . emanate from their own free will as expressed in conventions or by usages generally accepted as expressing principles of law . . .").

   a. **Objections by developing nations:** The former Soviet Union and many developing countries object to the universal application of customary law on the principle that countries outside the developed nations of the western hemisphere had little to do with the establishment of many customary laws and therefore ought not be bound by them.

   b. **Restatement § 201:** The comments to Restatement § 201 reject this position and view all states as bound by whatever customs are established at the time the state comes into existence.

B. **Establishment of an international custom:** There are quantitative and qualitative elements to customary international law. Customary law follows the basic principle of international law that ***acts are permitted unless expressly forbidden.*** Therefore, prohibitions as well as affirmative practices must be proven by the state relying upon them. *See S.S. Lotus (Fr. v. Turk.)* [1927] P.C.I.J. (ser. A) No. 10.

1. **Quantitative factors:** Quantitative factors include past state practice and duration of the state practice.

   a. **State practice generally:** States in the *practice of their international relations* implicitly consent to the creation and application of legal rules. State practice may be ascertained from a wide variety of sources: treaties, executive agreements, legislation, regulations, court decisions, speeches and testimony before national and international bodies.

   b. **Duration of state practice:** The practice must have been followed for an *appreciable period of time.* The notion is that what began as a limited practice may, over time, ripen and widen in its adoption to become customary law. There is, however, no set standard to determine when practice is transformed into law.

      i. **Long-term:** Long-term practice was an important consideration of the Supreme Court in the case of *The Paquete Habana*, 175 U.S. 677 (1900). The court looked at the practices of England, France, Germany and the Netherlands from 1403 to 1898 to conclude that fishing vessels are recognized as exempt from capture as prizes of war.

      ii. **Short-term:** The ICJ held in the *North Sea Continental Shelf Cases*, 1969 I.C.J. 4 (Feb. 20), that a "passage of only a short period of time is not necessarily, or of itself, a bar to the formation of a new rule of customary international law," [if the practice is] "both extensive and virtually uniform."

   c. **Consistency of state practice:** More important than the duration of state practice is the *consistency with which it is applied.* Minor and infrequent inconsistencies do not necessarily negate a custom.

   d. **Number and makeup of states adhering to the practice:** To establish custom definitively, a practice must be followed by *a significant number of states representing diverse geographic, economic and social characteristics.* It has, however, been suggested that the consistent practice of only a handful of states may be sufficient to establish custom, particularly when those states are the only ones capable of engaging in the practice (*e.g.*, nuclear testing on the high seas in the 1950s). The question then becomes whether custom can be established and imposed over the objection of other states. The answer depends on which approach to customary international law is followed, discussed *supra*, at p. 29.

2. **Use of regional custom:** Note, however, that customary law *may also be limited to a particular region* and therefore not be the practice of such a wide variety of states. A state may rely on regional custom but must show its existence by proving both quantitative and qualitative factors. *Asylum (Colombia v. Peru)*, 1950 I.C.J. 266 (Nov. 20).

3. **Local customary rights:** Local customary rights may develop from *constant and continual practice between two nations,* but such customary rights differ from and are independent of general international customary law principles. *Right of Passage Over Indian Territory (Port. v. India)*, 1960 I.C.J. 6 (Apr. 12).

4. **Qualitative factor — *opinio juris*:** In addition to the quantitative factors, international lawyers often refer to the subjective element of *opinio juris sive necessitatis* (called *opinio juris*). *Opinio juris* is the sense of *legal obligation compelling states to follow a certain practice.* The difficulty in ascertaining *opinio juris* is that states rarely acknowledge that they are acting under a sense of legal obligation rather than an as a matter of choice, comity, or convenience.

Example: A ship was flying a French flag and collided with a Turkish ship. Criminal proceedings were brought in Turkey against the French captain of the French ship. The Permanent Court of International Justice held that there was no rule of international law at the time limiting criminal proceedings in a collision on the high seas to the exclusive jurisdiction of the state whose flag is flown on the offending ship. While the Court found that states in Turkey's position had often abstained from asserting criminal jurisdiction, there was no evidence that the abstentions were based on a sense of legal obligation. *S.S. Lotus (Fr. v. Turk.)*, [1927] P.C.I.J. (ser. A, No. 10).

Example: In the *North Sea Continental Shelf Cases*, 1969 I.C.J. 4 (Feb. 20), the ICJ stated that "[t]he States concerned must therefore feel they are conforming to what amounts to a legal obligation. The frequency, or even habitual character of the acts is not in itself enough. There are many international acts . . . which are motivated only by considerations of courtesy, convenience or tradition, and not by any sense of legal duty."

C. **Resolutions and recommendations of international organizations:** The role of international organizations' resolutions and recommendations in establishing custom, in particular the General Assembly of the United Nations, is controversial. General Assembly resolutions are not a form of international legislation and accordingly are not legally binding. Indeed, the U.N. Charter itself refers to the "recommendations" of the General Assembly, in contrast to decisions of the Security Council which are binding on members of the U.N. Charter. U.N. Charter, art. 25. The resolutions are, however, frequently used as evidence of customary international law. The resolutions are useful as evidence because the votes of the world body may show a consensus (or lack of consensus) on a particular issue. A majority vote is more compelling evidence of custom when the majority represents a wide array of developed and developing countries. On the other hand, states vote in the General Assembly without expecting that they must act or have acted in accordance with their vote.

Example: The U.N. Declaration of Human Rights now has been recognized as expressing customary international law because it "create[d] an expectation of adherence" and that expectation was "gradually justified by State practice." *Filartiga v. Pena-Irala*, 630 F.2d 876, 883 (2d Cir. 1980).

D. **Application of international customary law:**   The predominant view is that customary international law enjoys universal application, regardless of what nations participated in its formation. The issue then arises as to whether there is any way for a state to be exempt from application of a law. Two possible exceptions to application follow:

   1. **Clear and consistent objection:** Dissent from a custom in the form of clear and consistent objections supported by action may prevent application of the custom to the objecting state.

   2. **Historic departure:** Historic departure from a customary rule and other states' acceptance of that deviation also provides an exception to the application of a custom. Note that wholesale departure from a custom by a large number of states may eventually result in the creation of a new custom.

E. **Relationship between treaties and customary international law:** Depending on the situation, treaties may be given equal weight with custom, prevail over custom, be proof of custom, or codify custom.

   1. **Equal weight standard:** Although article 38 of the Statute of the International Court of Justice places treaties first on the list of sources of international law, the order does not necessarily establish a hierarchy of sources. In fact, treaties and custom are generally given *equal weight in international law* (although a treaty which is more specific than a custom will prevail) and some peremptory norms of customs (*jus cogens*) preempt conflicting treaty law. *See* p. 8, *supra*, p. 36, *infra*.

2. **Treaty as evidence of custom:** Treaty provisions may become so widely adopted that they are accepted as custom. Treaties can also serve to codify customary international law.

   a. **Multilateral convention provisions as custom:** Provisions of a multilateral convention which becomes widely adopted may be applicable as customary law, and therefore binding on non-party states, if the practice is uniform and widely recognized as a legal obligation. *See North Sea Continental Shelf Cases*, 1969 I.C.J. 4 (Feb. 20).

   b. **Treaties as codification of custom:** In recent years, treaties have been used to codify customary international law, as, for example, with the law of the sea treaties in 1958 and again in 1982, and with the Vienna Convention on the Law of Treaties. When utilizing such treaty provisions as evidence of custom, however, it is important to differentiate provisions which merely reiterate custom from provisions which expand upon custom or represent progressive development (*i.e.*, new) law.

IV. GENERAL PRINCIPLES OF LAW

A general principle of law "recognized by civilized nations" is one *so fundamental that it is a basic tenet in virtually every major legal system.* Unlike treaties or international customary laws, general principles are derived from domestic law and are not principles originating from international relations or obligations.

Example: General principles of law are rules concerning liability for damages, unjust enrichment, right of passage over territory, the doctrine of *res judicata*, some basic humanitarian rights, the prohibition against being a judge in one's own cause, and application of the principle of good faith.

A. **Limited application of general principles:** General principles of law primarily apply to fill in gaps left by treaties and customary law. As international law expands to encompass new subject areas, general principles of law from domestic legal systems may be utilized until custom is established or treaties are developed.

B. **Decreasing importance as a source of international law:** General principles are losing importance in modern international law because many of the norms once recognized as general principles are now incorporated in treaties or are recognized as customary international law. The Restatement (Third) now classifies general principles as "a secondary source of international law."

C. Application of general principles for procedural matters:
Although generally decreasing in importance, general principles continue to be applied in procedural matters and problems of international judicial administration. General principles often relied on are the doctrines of *res judicata* and laches, as well as the rule that judges are to act with impartiality and independence. *Corfu Channel (U.K. v. Alb.),* 1949 I.C.J. 4 (Apr. 9).

V. JUDICIAL DECISIONS AND PUBLICISTS

Article 38 of the Statute of the International Court of Justice includes in its sources of international law judicial decisions and the teachings of highly qualified publicists as subsidiary means. These sources must be used with some caution. No amount of strong language in a judicial decision or scholarly writing stressing that a given rule is the norm will make it a rule of international law if it is not recognized by states as a binding norm. On the other hand, a decision or scholarly article may be very influential in first recognizing a state practice as custom or in highlighting an emerging norm of customary international law.

A. Status of judicial decisions: Judicial decisions are a "subsidiary means for the determination of rules of law" and the decisions may be rendered by either an international tribunal, such as the International Court of Justice, or by a national court adjudicating issues of international law. Many of the cases cited in international law disputes come from national courts. However, great care must be taken to be sure that the domestic court decision is applying international law and not its own domestic law.

B. The role of judicial decisions in the development of international law: Although the scope and affect of international law judicial decisions are supposed to be limited to the parties and the particular case, most courts strive to follow previous rulings (*stare decisis*) and on occasion make new international law.

   1. International Court of Justice view: Article 38 of the Statute of the International Court of Justice says that judicial decisions are a subsidiary source of international law, "subject to article 59." Article 59 of the Statute of the International Court of Justice states that "[t]he decision of the Court has ***no binding force except between the parties and in respect to that particular case.***" (emphasis added).

   2. *Stare decisis* effect: Although article 59 prohibits the ICJ from following the common law doctrine of binding precedent (*stare deci-*

sis), the Court does in fact often look to prior holdings as being *highly persuasive.* Judges of the ICJ, as well as judges in national courts hearing international law issues, strive to follow previous rulings, thereby lending some certainty and predictability to the development of international law.

3. **Law-making:** When necessary, the ICJ has made new law, which subsequently won state acceptance, as in the *Fisheries Case (U.K. v. Nor.)*, 1951 I.C.J. 116 (Dec. 18). However, the role of judges in the development of international law is somewhat contested, especially by civil lawyers who view law-making as belonging only in legislative bodies.

C. **Status of the most highly qualified publicists:** The work of scholars is more influential in the international legal system than in municipal legal systems. International law scholars play an important role in the development of international law, as evidenced not only by the impact of early scholars such as Grotius and Pufendorf, but also by the inclusion of scholarly works as a source of international law in article 38.

1. **Role in systematization and codification:** International bodies of publicists, such as the International Law Commission (an organ of the U.N. General Assembly), the Institut de Droit International, the International Law Association, the Hague Academy of International Law, and the American Law Institute (publisher of the Restatement of the Foreign Relations Law of the United States), have two functions. They have served the development of international law both by codifying existing rules of law and by proposing new rules.

2. **Role of scholarly works in the courtroom:** Reference to scholarly works varies from court to court. British courts, for example, are reluctant to refer to writers while French courts are highly influenced by the works of jurists. The ICJ often takes into account the opinions of highly qualified legal scholars, but is reluctant to actually identify them in issuing their judgments.

D. **Resolutions of the U.N. and other international law organizations:** The significance of U.N. resolutions and other similar international law organizations, as a source of law, varies tremendously according to the circumstances. The role of resolutions is a subject of much controversy because bodies such as the U.N. General Assembly are not intended to be legislative.

E. **Factors influencing impact of General Assembly resolutions:** The following factors are to be considered in determining the impact of a General Assembly resolution:

1. **Internal General Assembly resolutions:** General Assembly resolutions addressed to a subsidiary organ of the U.N. or to the Secretariat are legally binding as a matter of law under the U.N. Charter.

2. **Declaratory resolutions:** A General Assembly resolution (particularly in the form of a declaration) approved of unanimously and supported by state practice is generally regarded as evidence of customary law. Declaratory resolutions are important evidence of *opinio juris* and, if ratified unanimously or by a larger majority, are significant evidence of customary law.

3. **State practice as proof of impact:** Widespread adoption of a resolution, however, does not necessarily make it "instant custom." A General Assembly resolution, even if approved unanimously or by a majority, is not evidence of customary law if not supported by state practice, unless: the states intended for the resolution to express a rule of law; or the states support the resolution by subsequent practice in accordance with the resolution.

4. **Diverse majority approval as proof of impact:** General Assembly resolutions may be evidence of custom if accepted by a majority of member states (rather than unanimously), the composition of which represents a variety of political, geographic and economic interests. *Texaco Overseas Petroleum et al. v. Libyan Arab Republic*, 53 Int'l L. Rep. 389 (1979).

5. **Effect on dissenting states:** Whether dissenting states are bound by a resolution expressing custom depends upon the general rules as to when custom is binding upon a dissenting state or newly independent state. *See* p. 28, *supra* (discussing newly independent states under the Vienna Convention).

    Example: The *Advisory Opinion on the Western Sahara*, 1975 ICJ 12 (Oct. 16), the ICJ stated that the General Assembly's declarations, in regard to decolonization and self-determination, were interpretations by the member-states of the U.N. Charter customary international law that it had established. The ICJ therefore concluded that the right of self-determination for non-self-governing territories had become a norm of customary international law.

VI. *JUS COGENS* — PEREMPTORY NORMS

Jus cogens or peremptory norms are those rules of international law of **such fundamental importance that derogation from them is prohibited.** *Jus cogens* may only be modified by the emergence of new peremptory norms.

A. **Subject to much controversy:** The controversy surrounding the very concept of *jus cogens* centers on the division between the natural law approach and the positivist approach to international law. Adherents of the natural law approach maintain that there are fundamental rules which exist independently of a state's actions. On the other hand, positivists question the existence of any law to which states have not expressly consented. The Vienna Convention on the Law of Treaties refers to *jus cogens*/peremptory norms, but avoids including specific examples of rules of *jus cogens*. *See* p. 22, *supra* (discussing the difficulty in identifying which general rules of international law qualify to be rules of *jus cogens*).

B. **Identifying rules of *jus cogens*:** There are few rules which are generally accepted as peremptory norms. Those generating the least amount of controversy are the basic principles of *pacta sunt servanda* ("agreements of parties must be observed") and prohibitions on the use of or threat of force. Other commonly accepted rules of *jus cogens* include prohibitions on genocide, slave trade, piracy, and prohibitions on terrorism and the taking of hostages.

C. **Actual application of *jus cogens*:** The controversy surrounding the very existence of *jus cogens*, as well as the difficulty of identifying rules of *jus cogens*, has resulted in sparse application.

VII. EQUITY IN INTERNATIONAL LAW

Equity in international law is best understood by distinguishing the reference to decisions *ex aequo et bono* ("by what is fair and good") from application of equity through general principles of law.

A. ***Ex aequo et bono*:** Article 38 states that it "shall not prejudice the power of the Court to decide a case *ex aequo et bono*, if the parties agree thereto." Stat. of the I.C.J. art. 38. This provision has been interpreted to authorize a decision in which equity is not merely applied but is **allowed to override all other legal principles.** Thus far, parties have never agreed to have a case heard *ex aequo et bono* by the ICJ.

B. **General principles of law:** Article 38 does, however, list general principles of law as a source of international law. There are substantive concepts of equity common to all modern legal systems which are, therefore, general principles of international law. Examples are concepts of estoppel, unjust enrichment, and abuse of rights. Furthermore, many legal scholars argue that the less tangible notion of equity as "reasonableness", "fairness", or "natural justice" is also incorporated in all modern legal systems.

C. **Effect of other principals of equity** — *intra legem, contra legem and praetor legem*: Another method used by international lawyers to distinguish authorized from unauthorized use of equity in international tribunals is to classify the principles of equity as: *intra legem* (within the law), *contra legem* (against the law) and *praetor legem* (outside the law). Decisions *contra legem* are unauthorized unless the parties agreed to confer on the Court the power to hear cases *ex aequo et bono*.

Example: The maritime delimitation cases, such as the *North Sea Continental Shelf Cases*, 1969 I.C.J. 4 (Feb. 20) are examples in which the ICJ has applied equity without the parties conferring on the Court the power of *ex aequo et bono*. Equity was applied as a rule of construction to prevent similarly situated states from unjustifiable differences in treatment. Using equity as an instrument of interpretation is *intra legem* (part of the law) as opposed to *ex aequo et bono* (notwithstanding the law).

CHAPTER 3

INTERNATIONAL LAW AND MUNICIPAL LAW

I. DUALISM AND MONISM

There are two theoretical approaches to the relationship between international law and municipal law: *dualism* and *monism*.

A. Dualism defined: Under the dualist theory international law and municipal law are *entirely separate legal systems.* In actual practice, the dualist approach appears to predominate.

1. **Incorporation of international law in the domestic legal order:** A state's constitution and domestic legal doctrines determine the effect of international laws within the domestic legal order. The constitution also imposes on international laws the same limitations imposed on municipal laws.

2. **Incorporation of municipal law in the international legal order:** Ordinarily, a state may not impose its municipal laws on the international legal system. Conflict with a municipal law *does not excuse a state from its international legal obligations.* Thus a state may be legally bound to an obligation under international law which would have no legal force under its own domestic legal system. Although municipal law cannot generally impose itself on the international legal order, there are instances when an international tribunal encounters and must interpret a municipal law at issue between disputing states. In such cases, the international tribunal attempts to interpret the municipal law in conformity with the interpretations of the municipal courts.

B. Monism defined: The monist theory holds that municipal and international law *belong to a single "universal legal order."* The diminished role of the state as a legal personality results in a dominant role for international law over municipal law.

II. TREATIES IN MUNICIPAL LAW

Treaty law is the form of international law most commonly applied in domestic legal practice.

A. Treaties in U.S. law: The U.S. Constitution includes several provisions on treaties:

   1. **Article II treaties:** The President of the United States has the authority to make treaties with the "Advice and Consent of the Senate." Two-thirds of the Senators present must concur. U.S. CONST. art. II, § 2.

   2. **Judicial power over treaties:** The judicial power of the United States extends to cases arising under treaties. U.S. CONST. art. III, § 2.

   3. **Supremacy of treaties:** Treaties, along with the Constitution and federal laws, are "the supreme Law of the Land" and prevail over conflicting state laws. U.S. CONST. art. VI, § 2.

   4. **Limitations on state powers:** The individual states of the United States may not enter into treaties, alliances or confederations with foreign nations. U.S. CONST. art. I, § 10.

B. **Terminology for treaties:** Although "treaties" are often referred to in a generic sense, U.S. domestic law recognizes two types of international agreements — treaties and executive agreements.

   1. **Article II treaties:** Article II treaties are those international agreements made by the President with the two-thirds majority advice and consent of the Senate.

   2. **Congressional/executive agreements:** Also called statutory agreements, these may be made by the President pursuant to statutes passed by a majority of both the House and the Senate. The President's ability to act without any congressional participation in binding the U.S. to international obligations is controversial. *See* p. 44, *infra*.

C. **Self-executing treaties:** The doctrine of self-executing treaties is not explicit in the U.S. Constitution; it is a judge-made doctrine. Self-executing treaties may be applied directly in U.S. courts without the need for implementing legislation by Congress. Whether or not a treaty is self-executing depends on the intent of the government and is an issue for the courts to decide when the treaty is invoked as law. *Foster & Elam v. Neilson*, 27 U.S. (2 Pet.) 253 (1829).

   1. **Origin of self-executing treaty doctrine:** The doctrine emerged in the 1829 case of *Foster & Elam v. Neilson*, 27 U.S. (2 Pet.) 253 (1829), when the Supreme Court made a distinction between treaties ***directly applicable by the courts as U.S. law*** (*i.e.*, self-executing) and treaties aimed at the legislature and requiring implementation before taking effect under the municipal legal order.

2. **Constitutional restraints on the self-executing character of treaties:** A treaty cannot be self-executing if the subject matter is one which lies within the exclusive law-making power of Congress. For example, treaties pertaining to international crimes (*e.g.*, genocide, hijacking) or the raising of revenue require Congressional action before taking effect as domestic law.

3. **Non-self-executing treaties:** A treaty is also non-self-executing *if it instructs the legislature to implement enacting legislation.* Strictly speaking, it is then the implementing legislation which is given effect as U.S. law, not the treaty itself. Difficulties arise if a treaty does not clearly mandate enactment through implementing legislation and the government takes no actions to implement the treaty. The question then becomes whether the treaty is self-executing and enforceable in domestic courts or non-self-executing and unenforceable without Congressional implementation.

D. **Treaties and conflicting state law — effect of the Supremacy Clause:** Self-executing treaties and legislatively implemented treaties have the status of enforceable federal law and benefit accordingly from the Supremacy Clause. *Thus, such treaty provisions prevail over conflicting state law. Asakura v. Seattle*, 265 U.S. 332 (1924). "Treaties" benefitting from the Supremacy Clause include "congressional/executive" agreements and "executive" agreements.

Note: A treaty lacking required legislative implementation does not prevail over conflicting state laws. For example, a California state law barring certain aliens from owning land was upheld against conflicting provisions of the United Nations Charter. The court held that the cited provisions of the U.N. Charter were not "intended to become rules of law for the courts of this country upon ratification of the charter." *See Fujii v. State of California*, 242 P.2d 617, 621 (1952).

E. **Treaties and conflicting federal statutes:** Self-executing and legislatively executed treaties *prevail over state law but do not necessarily prevail over federal statutory law.* Treaty law and federal statutory law are virtually equivalent in status. When both address the same issue, courts attempt to interpret the terms of each in such a manner as to avoid outright conflicts. *See U.S. v. Palestine Liberation Organization*, 695 F. Supp. 1456 (S.D.N.Y. 1988). When reconciliation is not possible, the general rule is that *the last in time prevails. Whitney v. Robertson*, 124 U.S. 190 (1888). A later treaty may supersede an earlier federal law. Likewise, legislative action may supersede an earlier treaty.

1. **The "last-in-time" rule:** This rule applies only to article II treaties, i.e., made with the advice and consent of the Senate. An execu-

tive agreement does not prevail over previously enacted federal statutes.

2. **Effect on international law obligations:** *The "last-in-time" rule applies only under U.S. law.* Under international law, a conflict between treaty obligations and domestic law does not excuse the U.S. from its international legal obligations. *See* p. 7, *supra* (discussing potential conflicts between U.S. domestic law and international law).

F. **Treaties and other constitutional constraints:** It is far from clear what substantive constraints the Constitution places on the treaty-making power.

1. **Treaty better suited to task:** In *Missouri v. Holland*, 252 U.S. 416, 433 (1920), the Supreme Court stated: "We do not mean to imply that there are no qualifications to the treaty-making power; but they must be ascertained in a different way. It is obvious that there may be matters of the sharpest exigency for the national well-being that an act of Congress could not deal with but that a treaty followed by such an act could. . . ."

2. **Constitutional supremacy:** In contrast, in *Reed v. Covert*, 354 U.S. 1 (1957), the Court struck down an executive agreement authorizing military trials (without the full protections of the Bill of Rights) of dependents of armed forces personnel. "The Court has regularly and uniformly recognized the supremacy of the Constitution over a treaty." 354 U.S. 1, 17 (1957).

G. **Treaties and the laws of other countries:** The   relationship between international and domestic law varies amongst states, but broad generalizations are possible with regard to the doctrine of self-executing treaties.

1. **"English" rule:** Most common-law countries other than the United States do not permit treaties to be incorporated as municipal law without legislative enactment. In the United Kingdom, for example, a treaty may be ratified by the Crown alone but is incorporated into British law only by an act of Parliament. Thus, the United Kingdom may be bound by treaty obligations to other contracting parties, but Parliamentary refusal to perform the treaty puts the United Kingdom in default.

2. **Civil law treatment:** Most civil law countries accept the concept of self-executing treaties and explicit constitutional provisions allow for direct incorporation of treaty law into municipal law. The French Constitution, for example, states that "treaties or international agreements regularly ratified or approved have, from the date of

their publication, an authority superior to municipal law on the basis of reciprocity by the other state."

III. CUSTOMARY INTERNATIONAL LAW IN MUNICIPAL LAW

A. Common law countries — International law as common law:
International law derived from sources other than treaties is considered by common law countries to be a special type of common law. As early as 1784 (*Respublica v. De Longchamps*, 1 U.S. 111), **the law of nations was considered to be part of the law of the United States.** This principle was stated in *The Paquete Habana*: "International law is part of our law, and must be ascertained and administered by the courts of justice of appropriate jurisdiction, as often as questions of right depending upon it are duly presented for determination. For this purpose, where there is no treaty, and no controlling executive or legislative act or judicial decision, resort must be had to the customs and usages of civilized nations. . . ." 175 U.S. 677, 700 (1900) (emphasis added).

1. **Incorporation of customary law into domestic law:** The U.S. joins other common law jurisdictions in considering **customary rules to be automatically incorporated into the domestic legal order** and thus directly applicable in domestic courts. *But see* Harold G. Maier, *The Authoritative Sources of Customary International Law in the United States*, 10 MICH. J. INT'L L. 450 (1989) (courts are free to apply custom or not as with other principles under the common law approach). The U.S., England, Canada and India all treat customary rules of international law as part of domestic law.

2. **Supremacy Clause and customary international law:** Customary law, like treaty law, is considered federal law and **receives the benefits of the Supremacy Clause.** *Banco Nacional de Cuba v. Sabbatino*, 376 U.S. 398 (1964). Customary law, thus, has supremacy over state laws. Its status with respect to federal statutory law, however, is less certain. The drafters of the Restatement, Third, rejected their position in an earlier draft that international common law, like treaties, could supersede preexisting federal law. Note again, however, that U.S. courts will attempt to interpret a federal law to avoid conflict with international law, whether the international law is in the form of a treaty or custom. *See The Charming Betsy*, 6 U.S. (2 Cranch) (1804); *see also Garcia-Mir v. Meese*, 788 F.2d 1446 (11th Cir. 1986), *cert. denied*, 479 U.S. 889

(1986) (acts of Attorney General are controlling executive acts which prevail over international law).

3. **U.S. treatment of customary international law:**   U.S. courts group customary law together with other non-treaty sources of international law to form what is called international common law. Custom, general principles, scholarly works, and judicial opinions are all consulted in order to establish a rule of international law. This practice contrasts with that of international tribunals, which consider each a discrete source of law.

B. **Civil law countries — relationship between customary international law and domestic law:** Civil law countries rely on express constitutional provisions to incorporate non-treaty international law into their municipal law. The provisions are varied. The French Constitution expresses a readiness to adhere to rules of public international law. The Philippine Constitution more directly expresses that it incorporates general international law principles into municipal law and assigns the legislature the task of harmonizing any conflicts. The German Constitution goes so far as to give "general rules" of international law priority over domestic law.

IV. FOREIGN RELATIONS LAW OF THE UNITED STATES

Although U.S. domestic law does not directly impose itself on the international legal order, it does play a major role by allocating power among the three branches of government. The tripartite structure created by the U.S. Constitution influences U.S. conduct of foreign relations.

A. **Executive powers:**   Article II of the U.S. Constitution expressly grants the President authority to be "Commander in Chief of the Army and Navy;" to make treaties; to appoint ambassadors, public ministers and consuls; and to receive ambassadors and public ministers.

1. **International agreements:** One of the most controversial issues regarding the executive powers is the President's ability to *make binding international agreements without Congressional participation* (so-called non-Article II treaties). In *United States v. Curtiss-Wright*, 299 U.S. 304 (1936), the Supreme Court took a very broad view of the inherent powers of the President to enter into international agreements. More recently, the Court upheld executive orders to effectuate the settlement agreement between the U.S. and Iran concerning the U.S. hostages seized from the American Embassy in Tehran in 1979. In upholding the President's authority,

the Court emphasized that Congress had acquiesced in the President's action and that there had been a long standing practice of settling claims of U.S. nationals against foreign countries by executive agreement without the advice and consent of the Senate. *Dames & Moore v. Regan*, 453 U.S. 654 (1981).

2. **Recognition of governments:** Implicit in the express Constitutional authorization to receive ambassadors is the exclusive power to ***recognize foreign governments.*** The executive branch has used recognition of governments as a political tool, but the current practice is to recognize any government in effective control of a state.

3. **Other presidential authority:** Any other Presidential authority in international affairs must be premised on the ***inherent authority generally conferred by Article II.*** *See Dames & Moore v. Regan, supra.*

B. **Congressional powers:** Article I of the U.S. Constitution authorizes the Congress to establish and collect taxes and duties; to pay debts and provide for the common defense and general welfare; to regulate trade with foreign countries; to define and punish piracy and other "offences against the Law of Nations;" to raise and support the armed forces; and to declare war. In 1973, Congress passed the War Powers Act to ensure that the President could not commit American troops to combat without consulting Congress. 50 U.S.C. § 1541 *et seq.* The validity of this attempt to restrict presidential powers in international relations has been questioned following *INS v. Chadha*, 462 U.S. 919 (1983) which declared legislative vetos unconstitutional.

C. **Judicial powers:** Article III of the U.S. Constitution vests the Supreme Court with the judicial power of the United States, which includes cases arising under treaties made by the U.S., cases involving ambassadors and other public ministers and consuls, admiralty and maritime cases, and cases between U.S. states and citizens and foreign states and citizens.

1. **Act of state doctrine:** The act of state doctrine exemplifies the tensions which exist between the three branches with respect to international relations. The Supreme Court stated that the act of state doctrine emerged from "the proper distribution of functions between the judicial and political branches of the Government on matters bearing upon foreign affairs." *Banco Nacional de Cuba v. Sabbatino*, 376 U.S. 398 (1964). Applying the act of state doctrine, the Court declined to rule in favor of the expropriated U.S. property owners and left the matter to the executive branch. Congress reacted quickly with passage of The Foreign Assistance Act of 1961

to prevent courts from declining to address similar issues in the future. For further discussion, *see* p. 80, *infra.*

2. **Political question doctrine:** The political question doctrine is also applied by courts to *avoid addressing controversies regarding the political functions of the other two branches. See Baker v. Carr*, 369 U.S. 186 (1962) (formulating a six-point test for determining when a political question precludes jurisdictions).

CHAPTER 4
STATES

States, particularly under the dualist view of international law, are the primary subjects of international law. States have the capacity to make agreements and treaties and to make claims for breaches of international law. States have rights and obligations under international law. In short, states are the *principal entities having legal personality in the international legal order.*

I.   DEFINITION OF A STATE

Under both the Restatement and the Montevideo Convention of 1933, a state is defined as "an entity that has a *defined territory* and a *permanent population*, under the control of its *own government*, and that *engages in, or has the capacity to engage in, formal relations* with other such entities."

A. **Defined territory:** There is no minimum size for a state. Monaco, for example, takes up only 1.5 square kilometers, yet it is a state. A state need not be established with clearly defined frontiers. The United States, for example, was a state despite indeterminate claims westward into unexplored territories. In addition, many states are in existence despite long-standing border disputes with neighboring states.

B. **Permanent population/a "people":** A permanent population or a "people" is similarly not defined by size. The Vatican, with a population of only about 300, is considered a state. Antarctica, however, has no permanent population and is, in part for that reason, not considered a state.

C. **Under the control of its own government:** A state cannot exist without the control of an effective government. The government must be able to assert itself without the aid of foreign troops and to carry out its duties. Exceptions are granted as follows:

1. A state may temporarily lack an effective government as a result of civil war, newly gained independence or similar upheavals.

2. A simple change in regime and even conflicting claims of governmental authority alone will not disqualify an entity from statehood.

3. A state occupied by an enemy in times of war continues to be a state as long as allies are fighting on its behalf against the enemy.

D. **Capacity to engage in relations with other states:** Under the Restatement (Third) § 201, "[a]n entity is not a state unless it has the competence, within its own constitutional system, to conduct international relations with other states, as well as the political, technical and financial capabilities to do so."

> **Note:** *Only capacity is required, not actual practice.* Voluntary relinquishment of partial or complete control over foreign relations does not disqualify an entity from statehood. Liechtenstein, for example, has relinquished control of its foreign relations to Switzerland, yet is still considered a state.

E. **Role of recognition in defining a state:** Under the declaratory theory of recognition and under the Restatement, an entity must be treated as a state when it meets the four requirements set forth above. Its existence as a state is independent of any formal recognition. *See* p. 51, *infra*, on "recognition" of states.

II. STATE TERRITORY

The very existence of a state relies in large part on the concept of territory, that area of land, air, or water circumscribed by the state's frontiers. An entity can be a state only if it can be defined by its territory. Sovereignty is a state's **right to exercise its authority within that territory**. In addition to the right of sovereignty, a state has certain obligations with respect to its territory. Most of the earth's habitable area is indisputably claimed by the many states. Questions with respect to territory arise with respect to boundary disputes, claims to islands, polar regions, and forceful occupations of land.

A. **State boundaries or frontiers:** State boundaries are the barriers distinguishing one state's territory from another state's territory. These barriers extend not only across land but both upwards and downwards into the airspace and subsurface space. Boundaries are most often determined by agreements between the parties, rather than being dictated by principles of international law.

   1. **Boundary dispute resolution:** Boundary disputes are common and contests involving relatively small areas of land may be resolved by litigation before the International Court of Justice, by arbitration, or in conjunction with the resolution of some other settlement, such as a peace treaty.

   2. **Effect of succession:** A succession of states, by itself, is not grounds for affecting boundaries established by treaty, or rights and obligations established by treating and relating to the boundary regime. The International Law Commission does recognize other grounds for challenging a boundary, such as the invalidity of a

treaty or self-determination. For discussion of the effects of succession on treaties, *see* p. 27, *supra*.

B. Air and outer space: Relatively recent developments in the field of aeronautics have raised many issues of territoriality. There are two important considerations. On the one hand, there is respect for the notion that a state has **the right to use and control its airspace**, particularly for reasons of national security. On the other hand, there exists the notion that outer space, like the high seas, cannot be completely within the jurisdiction of any one state. Accordingly, there are separate sets of treaties and agreements concerning airspace versus outer space. For a detailed discussion on air and space law, *see* pp. 192-204, *infra*.

1. **Airspace:** The Chicago Convention, along with a number of supplemental accords and protocols, establishes the rights of states over their territorial airspace, stating that "[t]he contracting States recognize that every State has **complete and exclusive authority over the airspace above its territory."** (emphasis added).

2. **Outer space:** The legal order of outer space first became an issue with the launching of the Sputnik in 1957 and is an area of great uncertainty. Some guidance is available in the Outer Space Treaty (entered into force in 1967) which provides that the "exploration and use of outer space, including the moon and other celestial bodies . . . shall be the province of all mankind" and that "[o]uter space including the moon and other celestial bodies, is not subject to national appropriation."

C. International rivers: International rivers may flow through a state's territory but not be subject to the absolute authority of the state.

1. **Characteristics:** An international river has the following characteristics:

   a. It is **navigable**;

   b. It flows directly or indirectly **into the sea**;

   c. It flows through the territory of **two or more states** or forms the boundary between them; and

   d. An **international act** proclaims it to be an international river.

   Examples: the Danube, the Rhine, the Amazon, the Congo and the Niger Rivers.

2. **The Vienna Conference of 1815:** The Vienna Conference of 1815 established the general principle of freedom of navigation on international rivers. It also established the rights of states along the length of international rivers and imposed on riparian states the

obligations of maintaining barge towing paths and removing obstacles to navigation.

D. State coastal zones: The sea is divided into several zones: *internal waters, the territorial sea, the contiguous zone, the continental shelf, the exclusive economic zone* and *the high seas*. The sovereign rights of the coastal state vary with each zone. Generally speaking, the internal waters of a state are part of its territory and the state may apply and enforce its laws there. The band of sea extending outward from a state's coast, the territorial sea, is also the state's territory and is subject to the state's exercise of sovereignty. That sovereignty, however, is limited by foreign states' right of innocent passage. Beyond the territorial sea, the rights of the coastal state are much more limited and pertain primarily to economic interests. *See* pp. 170-178, *infra* (discussing state sovereignty over the territorial sea, rights of passage, and economic zones).

E. *Res nullius* and *res communis*: *Res nullius* and *res communis* are terms referring to territory which belongs to no state. *Res nullius*, meaning **unattributed territory**, gave rise to the colonial empires in the 15th to 19th centuries. *Res communis* refers to **common or international territory**, such as the high seas, Antarctica, the moon and outer space.

F. Acquisition of territorial sovereignty: Acquisition of territory may occur in a variety of ways, including the following:

1. **Accretion:** Natural processes, such as shifting rivers and growing deltas, may expand a state's territory.

2. **Cession:** Sovereignty over an area may be transferred by means of an agreement between states. Although some hold that territory may be ceded to another state without the consent of the population living there, the actual practice in recent years has been to condition cession on such consent.

3. **Conquest:** Traditionally, property could be annexed through complete and final subjugation followed by the conquering state's declaration of its intent to annex the property. Title by conquest in this manner was rare because the property more frequently passes as a result of a treaty of cession. More importantly, the U.N. General Assembly's Declaration on Principles of International Law Concerning Friendly Relations and Cooperation Among States suggests that territory may not be acquired by another state from the threat or use of force in an international war.

4. **Contiguity:** There is no rule in international law permitting a state to make claims of acquisition over neighboring islands that

are not part of another independent state. Mere geographic proximity is insufficient to claims of acquisition.

5. **Occupation:** Physical presence coupled with continuous and peaceful display of territorial sovereignty over territory belonging to no state (*terra nullius*).

6. **Prescription:** Acquisition of land belonging to another state through prescription under international law is analogous to the concept of adverse possession under municipal law. Lasting possession of an area, as shown by the exercise or display of a state's authority, may confirm title in that state. Prescription is distinguished from occupation; the former involves acquisition of territory previously claimed by another state and the latter involves the acquisition of territory belonging to no state (*terra nullius*).

7. **Other considerations:** Although the ICJ puts great weight on acquiescence and recognition of territorial claims in determining which state is the sovereign power, (*see Temple of Preah Vihear (Thail. v. Cambodia)*, 1962 I.C.J. 6 (Jun 15)) tribunals do consider other factors in resolving territorial disputes: affiliations of the inhabitants of the disputed territory; geographical, economic and historical considerations; and cultural unity. These considerations are controversial and are sometimes described as political rather than legal. *See India v. Pakistan*, [1968] 50 I.L.R. 2 (1976).

III. RECOGNITION OF STATES AND GOVERNMENTS

Recognition is a confusing mixture of international law, domestic law, and politics. It is important to distinguish political considerations from legal considerations, and to separate the legal issues which arise under international law from those arising under the domestic law of the recognizing state. Recognition is best defined as the ***willingness to deal with another state or government representing the state as a member of the international community***. Public acts of recognition include formal notes, letters and telegrams sent through diplomatic envoys; formal oral public announcements; and the conclusion of bilateral agreements. Maintaining or severing diplomatic relations is not synonymous with recognition or non-recognition respectively.

A. **Express and implied recognition:** Recognition of a state or government is often done so expressly, but certain conduct may also imply recognition:

1. *Entry into diplomatic relations implies recognition*, but an exchange of trade missions does not imply recognition. Conversely, the lack of diplomatic relations does not imply a lack of recognition.

2. *Signing a bilateral treaty subject to ratification implies recognition.*

3. *Common membership in international organizations does not imply recognition of one another.* For example, several Arab states which do not recognize the state of Israel are members of the U.N. along with Israel.

B. **Recognition under U.S. law:** Under U.S. law, *only the President has the authority to recognize or not recognize* an entity as a state. This exclusive authority is implied from the powers granted under article II of the U.S. Constitution to appoint and to receive ambassadors. The President may also recognize a state by concluding an international agreement. The U.S. often uses recognition as a sign of approval. The current practice of the executive branch is to recognize any government in effective control of a state. *See* p. 45, *supra*.

C. **Whether recognition is discretionary or mandatory:** Generally, recognition is discretionary, although one influential scholar has taken the view that it should not be. There are two limitations on this discretion to prevent premature recognition and premature withdrawal of recognition.

1. **Recognition is optional:** According to prominent scholar Ian Brownlie, "[r]ecognition, as a public act of state, is an optional and political act and there is no legal duty in this regard. However, in a deeper sense, if an entity bears the marks of statehood, other states put themselves at risk legally if they ignore the basic obligations of state relations."

   a. The Restatement (Third) adds that an entity need not be treated as a state if it has attained the qualifications for statehood by violating international law, for example, by use of or threat of use of force. As early as the 1930s, former U.S. Secretary of State Henry L. Stimson articulated the Stimson Doctrine by proclaiming a refusal to recognize "any situation, treaty, or agreement which may be brought about contrary to the covenants and obligations of the Pact of Paris [Treaty of Paris]."

   b. Note that the obligation to treat an entity as a state when it has met the requirements of statehood considerably diminishes the significance of the constitutive theory of recognition.

2. **The Lauterpacht Doctrine:** A prominent scholar, Sir Hersch Lauterpacht, contended that states had a duty to recognize states or

governments which met the international law requirements for recognition. In practice, states have been reluctant to relinquish their control of recognition to this extent.

3. **Premature recognition:** If a state, or more commonly a purported government, is recognized *before effective control over the territory at issue*, such *premature recognition is illegal.*

4. **Premature withdrawal of recognition:** On the other hand, *if recognition is withdrawn before loss of control, such premature withdrawal of recognition is also illegal.* Again note that severance of diplomatic relations is not the same as withdrawal of recognition. Because premature recognition and withdrawal of recognition are so rare, it is not clear what the remedies are or to whom they are owed.

5. **Nonrecognition under the U.N. Charter:** Article 41 authorizes the Security Council to order members of the U.N. to "sever diplomatic relations" with a state or government, as was done in 1970 with the Smith regime in Southern Rhodesia.

D. *De jure* **and** *de facto* **recognition:** The terms *de facto* and *de jure* result in much confusion because they are used with varying and uncertain meanings. The Restatement avoids the terms altogether. In any case, the terms do not qualify the legal effects of recognition under international law.

1. **States:** Under the constitutive theory, treatment of an entity as a state without extending a formal recognition was called *de facto* recognition, as opposed to *de jure* recognition. Under the more modern declaratory theory, there is little use for the distinction between *de facto* and *de jure* recognition, except that *de jure* recognition may be regarded as having greater evidentiary value than does *de facto* recognition. The terms are more often used with recognition of governments.

2. **Governments:** *De jure* recognition implies that *the government is lawfully in power even though it retains little actual power.* A government-in-exile, for example, may be accorded *de jure* recognition. Conversely, a *de facto* government is impliedly a government which is in control but illegally so. The term *de facto* recognition is most commonly utilized when there exist unstable circumstances and a political reluctance to fully recognize the government. Notice that international law does not specify how a government must be established nor does it prohibit a group from seizing power in a civil war. Any government with effective control is subject to unqualified recognition. Therefore, the terms *de jure* and *de facto* are more often an expression of the recognizing state's

political approval or disapproval of a government or of how the government came to power in its own domestic system than a reflection of legitimacy under international law. One exception is that a government which seized control through gross violations of human rights, a violation of international law, might be referred to as the *de facto* government.

E. **Conditional recognition:** The prevailing view is that recognition generally cannot be granted subject to conditions. Conditional recognition is prohibited for fear that more powerful nations would utilize it as a form of blackmail. Reasonable conditions, however, are assumed under the international legal principles. For example, a state or government must abide by the general principles of international law.

IV. RECOGNITION OF STATES

A. **Two theories of recognition:** There are two theories concerning the legal effects under international law of recognition of states: the constitutive theory and the declaratory theory.

   1. **Constitutive Theory:** The constitutive theory is that ***an entity does not exist as a state until it has been recognized by other states;*** the recognition itself "constitutes" the state. Acts of recognition determine statehood. This theory is not widely accepted today, as is borne out by actual practice. The People's Republic of China, for example, was considered a state long before it was recognized by many states. Furthermore, fewer states today go through the process of formally recognizing another state.

   2. **Declaratory Theory:** Under the declaratory theory, ***the facts of statehood (defined territory, permanent population, effective government, and capacity for foreign relations) rather than formal recognition define an entity as a state.*** Any formal recognition is simply declaratory of the political and legal reality of statehood.

B. **Evidentiary value of recognition:** Recognition, nevertheless, is useful evidence of the existence of a state if enough other states recognize a state and recognition (or non-recognition) is based on principles of international law rather than political considerations. The limitation of the evidentiary value of recognition is that states may grant or withhold recognition for many reasons unrelated to principles of international law.

Example: In an arbitration decision between Great Britain and Costa Rica (the *Tinoco Case*), [1923] 1 R.I.A.A. 369 (1948), Chief Justice Taft as arbitrator found that the Tinoco regime was the government of

Costa Rica because it had been in effective control of the state, despite the fact that it had not been recognized by a number of states including Great Britain. He concluded that the Tinoco regime was clearly the government in control. If control had been less clear, recognition or non-recognition based on the legal requirement of control would have had evidentiary weight in determining whether the Tinoco regime was the government, and thus authorized to act on behalf of Costa Rica.

V. RECOGNITION OF GOVERNMENTS

Recognition of a government is an acknowledgment that it is *in effective control of the state*. Recognition under international law is not dependent upon the constitutionality of a government or its legitimacy under its own domestic laws, but solely on its effectiveness.

A. Traditional approach to recognition: The traditional approach allows recognition of a government when:

1. It is in effective control of the state *without the assistance of foreign intervention.* Revolutionary governments are not recognized until it has clearly established control over most of the state, having reduced the prior government to control of only negligible areas;

2. It has *the consent, or at least the acquiescence, of the people*; and

3. It shows its *willingness to comply with the state's obligations under international law.*

B. Estrada Doctrine: Under the so-called Estrada Doctrine, the practice of recognizing governments is eliminated altogether with the focus being on recognition of states. A number of states claim to apply the Estrada Doctrine, but states often depart from it to use recognition or non-recognition as a political tool.

C. Wilson Doctrine: In the early 1900s, the Tobar Doctrine was adopted by the U.S. and called the Wilson Doctrine. Under this approach only democratic and constitutional governments were extended recognition. The U.S. itself no longer adheres to this doctrine.

D. Acts of recognition: Unlike recognition of states which is more likely to be express, recognition of governments is often implied through the continuation or establishment of diplomatic relations.

E. Significance in domestic law of the recognition of states and governments: Under domestic law, recognized governments and states enjoy important benefits, as exemplified in the Restatement (Third) § 205:

1. *Access to courts* in the United States.

2. *Entitlement to property* belonging to states located in the United States.

3. *A right to claim sovereign immunity*.

VI. RECOGNITION OF INSURGENTS AND BELLIGERENTS

A. **Generally:** Insurgencies and belligerencies are two types of internal state conflicts, and are discussed at p.158, *infra*.

VII. THE RIGHTS AND OBLIGATIONS OF STATES

A. **Rights:**   There is much controversy regarding the basic rights of states, and as yet there exists no finalized written statement of the rights and duties of states. The U.N. Charter as a whole does impose obligations on its members to respect certain rights of states. Such rights and obligations, however, are binding on the international community as a whole only if accepted as customary law with universal application. The rights generally protected by the U.N. Charter and other U.N. resolutions are as follows.

1. **Right of sovereignty:**   The right of sovereignty is fundamental because it *prohibits foreign intervention in internal affairs.* The state is the supreme authority within its national territory. It is said to have territorial sovereignty or territorial jurisdiction. Customary international law also recognizes immunity for warships and limited immunity for merchant ships.

   a. **Restrictions on territorial jurisdiction:**   Restrictions on territorial jurisdiction may be made in international agreements, such as the preamble to the Statute of the International Labour Organization which gives the organization the right to influence labor conditions within the member-states' territories.

   b. **Exclusive, domestic jurisdiction:**   The notion of exclusive, domestic jurisdiction is subject to much controversy, particularly with respect to matters affecting individual rights. The issue is whether protection of the individual is a matter of domestic jurisdiction or a matter falling under international law governing human rights.

   c. **Sovereignty over use of natural resources:**   Under a number of U.N. resolutions, including the Charter of Economic Rights and Duties of States and the Stockholm Declaration on the Human Environment, states are declared to have absolute sovereignty over use of natural resources within their territories. This right has been qualified in recent years by growing recognition that a state has an obligation to ensure activities occurring within its jurisdiction or control do not cause harm in areas beyond its territory, and the International Law Commission has been studying articles of state responsibility to extend state liability to injuries caused by acts lawful *per se*.

2. **Equality of states:** Under international law theory, ***all independent states are equal.*** Neither the size of territories or populations nor the level of development have any bearing on states. The concept of legal equality is set forth in the Statute to the International Court of Justice. "[N]o circumstances may place parties to a dispute in an unequal position before the court." Likewise, states receive equal treatment when disputes arise in international organizations. The concept of sovereignty and equality are closely joined. All states are to enjoy equal treatment. Thus, no state is permitted to intervene in the affairs of another state. The U.N. Declaration on Principles of International Law Concerning Friendly Relations and Cooperation Among States provides that "armed intervention, and all other forms of interference or attempted threats against the personality of the State or against its political, economic and cultural elements are in violation of international law."

3. **The right to defense:** A state has the ***right to take steps necessary to protect a state's security.*** Before the U.N. Charter was adopted, the right to defense included the right to initiate hostilities in anticipation of an attack. A state may no longer engage in anticipatory self-defense without running the risk of being held responsible for an act of aggression in violation of international law. *See* p. 142, *infra* (discussing the right of self-defense under the U.N. Charter).

4. **The right of international intercourse:** States are ***free to establish and regulate their own international relations,*** as long as they do not violate the accepted rules and principles of international law. The U.N. Declaration on Principles of International Law Concerning Friendly Relations and Cooperation Among States in fact imposes a duty on states to cooperate with one another in maintaining international peace and stability and promoting the general welfare of nations.

B. **Rights of states under U.S. law:**   The Restatement (Third) § 206 incorporates some of these rights. A state has:

"(a) *sovereignty* over its territory and general authority over its nationals;

"(b) *status as a legal person*, with capacity to own, acquire and transfer property, to make contracts and enter international agreements, to become a member of international organizations, and to pursue, and be subject to legal remedies;

"(c) *capacity* to join with other states to make international law, as customary law or by international agreement."

C. **General responsibility of states:**   *A state injuring the rights or property of another state in breach of its international obligations incurs international responsibility.* *Chorzow Factory* [1927] P.C.I.J., (ser. A) No. 9 at 21. A state may bear political responsibility (resulting, for example, in disarmament of an aggressor state) or civil responsibility (resulting, for example, in payment of reparations for damages caused by war). State responsibility for "international crimes" is a developing area of liability.

1. **Acts attributable to a state:**   A state can act only through the actions and omissions of human beings, and the state only incurs liability for *those individual actions or omissions which can be attributed to the state.* Questions then arise as to who or what can act on behalf of the state, and what type of conduct is imputed to the state. Articles of state responsibility adopted by the International Law Commission and draft articles currently being considered have been very influential in formulating this area of the law.

   a. **Acts of state organs:**   The basic principle is that the *acts of state organs or agents are imputed to the state.* An organ may be part of the formal structure of the state government or it may be an entity empowered to exercise elements of governmental authority. The position of the organ in the organization of the state is irrelevant. It does not matter whether its function is legislative, executive, or judicial or whether it has any responsibility for foreign affairs.

   b. **Acts of state agents:**   Agents may be official authorities in government or other persons actually and justifiably exercising elements of governmental authority. Conversely, the conduct of persons not acting on behalf of the state is not considered an act of state.

   c. **Acts of officials:**   The state maintains responsibility for the conduct of its officials and organs with little regard to whether or not the official or organ acted within the limits of its competency. A state may not be held responsible for insurrectional movements which do not succeed in becoming the new government of a state.

    d. Acts of member states or provinces: A federal state cannot generally deny responsibility for the acts of its member states or provinces, for a federal state is expected to uphold its international obligations regardless of internal divisions in government.

2. Element of fault: The issue of whether a state can incur liability without fault arises most commonly in connection with transboundary pollution. On the one hand, a state is obliged not to use its territory in a manner injurious to other states. *See, e.g., Trail Smelter Arbitration (U.S. v. Canada),* [1941] 3 R.I.A.A. 1911 (1949). On the other hand, many lawful uses of a state may have an adverse effect on neighboring states. *See generally* G. Handl, *Territorial Sovereignty and the Problem of Transnational Pollution,* 69 A.J.I.L. 50 (1975). Section 601 of the Restatement (Third) provides:

> ". . . A state is obligated to take such measures as may be necessary, to the extent practicable under the circumstances to ensure that activities within its jurisdiction or control
>
> (a) conform to generally accepted international rules and standards for the prevention, reduction, and control of injury to the environment of another state or of areas beyond the limits of national jurisdiction; and
>
> (b) are conducted so as not to cause significant injury to the environment of another state or of areas beyond the limits of national jurisdiction."

3. Defenses to claims against a state: A state's apparent violation of international law may be justified on the grounds of: consent, *force majeure,* distress, necessity, and self-defense.

    a. Consent: The International Law Commission has stated that "[t]he consent validly given by a State to the commission by another State of a specified act not in conformity with an obligation of the latter State towards the former State precludes the wrongfulness of the act . . . to the extent that the act remains within the limits of that consent." In no case, however, may there be any derogation from a peremptory norm.

    Example: The entry of foreign troops into the territory of another is normally unlawful, but is legitimate if done with the consent of that state.

b. *Force majeure*: An act, normally in violation of international law obligations, may be excused if the act was:

  i. "due to an irresistible force or to an unseen external event"

  ii. "beyond its control"

  iii. "which made it materially impossible for the State to act in conformity with that obligation or to know that its conduct was not in conformity with that obligation." (I.L.C.)

This defense is not available to states contributing to the occurrence of the event. Claims of *force majeure* most often arise in connection with vessels or aircraft which have entered the territory of another state without that state's consent. Claims of *force majeure* are generally not successfully invoked in seeking excuse from payment of a debt.

c. **Distress:** Wrongful conduct of a state may be excused if the state is acting to save the lives of persons entrusted to its care. This defense is closely related with *force majeure*, except that conformity to its obligations is actually possible for the state although it would result in a loss of lives. Incursions into foreign territory in order to save lives may be excused by the defense of distress.

d. **Necessity:** A state may act in violation of its international obligations in order to protect an essential state interest threatened by grave and imminent peril, but may not do so if its conduct imperils the comparable or superior state interests of the other state. The defense of necessity does not apply if:

  i. the state acting in violation of its international obligations caused the situation of "necessity";

  ii. the international obligation which the state is in breach of a peremptory norm of international law (in particular, prohibitions on acts of aggression); or

  iii. the defense of necessity is precluded by the terms of an applicable instrument. (Human rights treaties, for example, often preclude necessity as a defense.)

The International Law Commission suggests that the pertinent essential state interests are the existence of the state, maintenance of essential services, keeping the domestic peace, the survival of part of its population, and ecological preservation of its territory.

e. **Self-defense:** To assert this defense, the state must be acting in self-defense in accordance with the U.N. Charter. *See* p. 142, *infra* (discussing the right of self-defense under the U.N. Charter).

4. **The requirement of injury:** It is generally stated that **actual injury is not required** to give rise to responsibility to other states for breach of an international obligation, unless the obligation specifically requires injury as an element of its breach. The relative unimportance of the injury raises difficulties in determining which states are entitled to seek reparations from the offending state.

   a. ***Erga omnes* obligations:** In *Barcelona Traction, Light and Power Company (Belg. v. Spain)*, 1970 I.C.J. 3 (Feb. 5), the Court said:

   > ". . .[A]n essential distinction should be drawn between the obligations of a State towards the international community as a whole, and those arising vis-à-vis another State in the field of diplomatic protection. By their very nature the former are the concern of all States. In view of the importance of the rights involved, all States can be held to have a legal interest in their protection; they are obligations *erga omnes*."

   Examples: Some examples given by the Court of *erga omnes* obligations owed by every state to every state are the prohibitions or acts of aggression, genocide, slavery, and race discrimination. The Restatement (Third) also includes Section 902, defining customary law obligations with respect to human rights and protection of the environment.

   b. **International crimes:** Related to the concept of obligations, *erga omnes* is the concept of state responsibility for international crimes. Article 19 of the Draft Articles on State Responsibility defines an international crime as an international obligation "so essential for the protection of fundamental interests of the international community that its breach is recognized as a crime by that community as a whole. . . ." Examples given generally correspond to the Restatement's examples of obligations *erga omnes*. The Draft Articles differentiate international crime from other illegal acts ("delects") as entailing all the legal consequences of an illegal act plus "such rights and obligations as are determined by the applicable rules accepted by the international community as a whole." Other states must not aid the offending state in maintaining the crime. It continues to be controversial whether customary international law recognizes the distinction between international crimes and delects for state responsibility.

5. **Remedies:** Breach of international obligations may give rise to the following remedies:

a. **Collective sanctions:** Acts of aggression or gross violations of human rights are often countered by means of collective sanctions. Collective sanctions are imposed by the international community in reaction to its collective interests or common concerns, and they include severance of diplomatic relations, trade boycotts, and cessation of air or sea traffic. The U.N. Security Council may adopt collective sanctions as a non-military enforcement measure under article 41 of the U.N. Charter. For example, collective sanctions were imposed against Southern Rhodesia (Zimbabwe) in 1970.

b. **Restitution:** Restitution is a form of reparation for an injury and is designed to put the injured party back in the same state in which it would have been had the wrongful conduct or omission not taken place. Restitution may be accomplished through performance of the failed obligation, revocation of an unlawful act or abstention from further wrongful conduct.

c. **Indemnity:** Under international law, indemnity is the term for monetary compensation, and it is the most common form of reparation. Indemnity should compensate all damages resulting from a wrongful act or omission, including ascertainable lost profits. Highly speculative lost profits are not awarded. Punitive damages were awarded in one arbitration decision (*The I'm Alone*, 3 Int'l Arb. Awards 1618 (1923)), but international tribunals have generally rejected claims for punitive damages.

d. **Satisfaction:** This form of reparation is appropriate for situations in which there has been no material injury. Forms of satisfaction include official regrets and apologies, formal or judicial declaration of the illegality of an act, and punishment of guilty minor officials.

e. **Self-help, retorsions and reprisals:** *See* p. 141-142, 147-148, *infra*.

6. **Implementing obligations of reparation:** Reparation may be sought through diplomatic channels or through agreed upon procedures of dispute settlement. *See* p. 101-113, *infra* (discussing International Dispute Settlement). Regardless of the nature of the procedure, there are several common requirements:

a. **Standing:** Parties may present a claim only if possessing a "legal interest." (Consider here the discussion of *erga omnes* obligations on p. 61, *supra*.) Some international conventions permit any party to the convention to bring a claim if both parties to the dispute have agreed to a provision to that effect.

   b. **Laches:** International tribunals have discretion to decide whether or not there has been undue delay in bringing a claim. Some tribunals deny remedies on the basis of undue delay, and others find that the principle of laches is inapplicable in international law.

   c. **Negotiations as a pre-requisite:** Many international agreements and tribunals require the parties to enter into negotiations, consultations, or "diplomacy" before submitting their claim to adjudication. The ICJ in the *North Sea Continental Shelf Cases, supra*, stated that the negotiations must be meaningful and entered into with the purpose of reaching an agreement.

   d. **Exhaustion of local remedies:** A state submitting a claim on behalf of its nationals for denial of rights in another state must first exhaust available remedies in the violating state. Exceptions have been made in cases in which the injured individual had minor and transitory connections with the violating state (such as being a passenger in its national airlines) or was injured by a space object or missile of the foreign state.

   e. **Consent to third party settlement:** Both parties to a claim must consent, expressly or impliedly, to its submission to a tribunal. Consent may be implied by the submission of arguments on the merits free of reservations on the issue of jurisdiction.

VIII. HEADS OF STATE, GOVERNMENT OFFICIALS, DIPLOMATS, AND OFFICIALS OF INTERNATIONAL ORGANIZATIONS: ROLES AND STATUS IN INTERNATIONAL LAW

A. **Heads of state:** Until the 19th century the heads of state had the power to fully represent their states in foreign affairs, but today most are considered organs of the state and are limited in their powers by the states' constitutions. Many heads of state now are competent to proclaim war, declare peace, receive diplomatic representatives and possibly ratify international agreements. Under modern international law, a head of state may be *held personally responsible for certain international crimes* such as genocide, crimes against peace, crimes against humanity, and war crimes. The Charter of the International Military Tribunal at Nuremburg, after World War II, established this principle, and is discussed *infra* at p. 155.

B. **Government:** Foreign political acts of a government and statements of a prime minister (or its functional equivalent) made on behalf of the state are binding on the state. A person in the position of a prime minister (or its equivalent) is considered competent by other states to represent his state without inquiry into his actual authority.

C. **Secretary of State/Minister of Foreign Affairs (or the functional equivalent):** The Secretary of State (or its functional equivalent) is a state's key figure with respect to its foreign affairs. He is in charge of the foreign service, holds talks and negotiations, supervises the drafting of foreign policy acts and execution of international agreements, and generally safeguards the interests of the state and its nationals abroad. His acts and statements *are binding upon the state* and third countries need not inquire into his actual authority.

D. **Diplomatic agents:** Diplomatic agents are persons empowered to represent a state in a foreign state or in an international organization. Every sovereign state has the right to send and receive diplomats. In the case of a federal state that right is reserved for the central government.

1. **Types of diplomats:** Regular diplomats are permanent representatives in foreign states. Extraordinary diplomats serve temporarily in order to carry out a special mission, usually in connection with international congresses, international conferences, and sessions of international organizations.

2. **Heads of mission:** Heads of mission are technically divided into three classes (ambassadors or *nuncios*; envoys, ministers or internuncios; and *charges d'affaires*), but the only distinctions which can be drawn on the basis of class relate to precedence and etiquette.

3. **Diplomatic corps:** Traditionally, the diplomatic corps in a state consisted only of all the heads of missions, but the modern trend is to include all diplomats.

4. **Appointment of a diplomatic mission:** Permanent diplomatic relations are established by an international agreement followed by the exchange of diplomatic representatives. Agreement is the term signifying *a state's consent to the foreign state's appointment of a head of mission,* as well as the appointment of military, naval and air attaches. Following receipt of the agreement, there is a formal ceremony in which the new head of mission presents a document called the letters of credence. The letters of credence include the nature of his appointment, his name, the subject matter of the particular mission, and an expression of the desire to foster good relations.

5. **Diplomatic immunities and privileges:** From ancient times down to the present, diplomats have had an *independent and spe-*

cially protected status. The privileges and immunities of diplomats have been established both as a matter of customary law and treaty law. The immunities and privileges apply only from the moment the diplomat enters the host country and only for the period in which he is, in fact, a diplomat. For discussion of diplomatic immunity, *see* p. 84, *infra*.

6. **Termination of a diplomatic mission:** Diplomatic missions with a particular purpose are terminated with the completion of that job. Diplomatic agents in more permanently established missions generally serve for a specific term, but their tour of duty may be cut short by death, recall or request by the host country.

E. **Consuls:** Consuls are authorized to protect the interests of their state in a foreign state with respect to administrative, legal, economic and cultural affairs. Consuls generally have no political function and are therefore distinguished from diplomats, who do have a political function. However, a consul may take on a political role if serving in a foreign state in which his state has no diplomatic mission. A common and important function of consuls is to oversee the growth of trade, economic, scientific and cultural relations between the two states. The consul is also charged with administrative duties such as the issuance of passports, visas and other travel documents.

Consulars *enjoy immunities and privileges*, but to a lesser extent than do diplomats. For a comparison of the immunities and privileges of consuls and diplomats, *see* pp. 84-86, *infra*.

F. **Officials of international organizations:** The proliferation of international organizations following World War II has given rise to increasing numbers of international officials. The status of these officials is regulated by treaties, such as the U.N. Charter and the U.N. Convention on Privileges and Immunities, setting forth applicable privileges and immunities. *See* p. 87, *infra* (discussing the immunities granted to international organizations).

CHAPTER 5

STATE JURISDICTION

I. DEFINITION OF JURISDICTION

Jurisdiction can be defined as ***the authority to affect legal interests.*** More specifically under international law, jurisdiction is understood to be the allocation of power and authority among the states.

A. Types of jurisdiction: Three interdependent types of jurisdiction are recognized:

1. the right to prescribe or apply laws to persons and activities;

2. the right to enforce those laws through application of sanctions;

3. and the power of courts to exercise jurisdiction over a particular person or object.

B. Civil and criminal jurisdiction: International law in this context is most important for the restrictions it imposes on state jurisdiction over criminal matters. International law appears to impose few, if any, restraints on a state's exercise of civil jurisdiction other than sovereign and diplomatic immunity. As stated in *S.S. Lotus (Fr. v. Turk.)* [1927] P.C.I.J. (ser. A) No. 10 at 21:

> "Far from laying down a general prohibition to the effect that States may not extend the application of their laws and the jurisdiction of their courts to persons, property, and acts outside their territory, it leaves them in this respect a wide measure of discretion which is only limited in certain cases by prohibitive rules; as regards other cases, every State remains free to adopt the principles which it regards as best and most suitable."

The comments to the Restatement (Third), however, say that its limitations on jurisdiction apply to civil as well as criminal jurisdiction.

C. Extraterritorial jurisdiction: A topic of much controversy in international law is the exercise of extraterritorial legislative jurisdiction. The United States' extraterritorial claim of jurisdiction in antitrust and drug enforcement, for example, is very contentious.

II. INTERNATIONAL JURISDICTION PRINCIPLES

International jurisdictional principles are concerned primarily with the states' right to prescribe or enforce its laws. Five bases for such jurisdiction with respect to crimes are recognized. It is a widely accepted principle of international law that *the exercise of jurisdiction on any basis must be reasonable.*

A. **The territorial principle:** The territorial principle is a fundamental and universally accepted basis for jurisdiction, the principle being that *an essential attribute of a state's sovereignty is to have jurisdiction over all persons and objects within its territory.*

   1. **"Pure" territoriality:** The pure territoriality principle is applied when acts or offenses *are commenced within the state's territory*, regardless of whether or not they were also concluded or consummated there. This principle of jurisdiction is particularly applicable to conspiracies to commit crimes in foreign states.

   2. **"Objective" territoriality:** The objective territoriality principle is applied to offenses or acts *commenced outside the state's territory, but completed within the state's territory;* or causing *serious and harmful consequences to the social and economic order within the state's territory.*

      Example: The *Lotus* case is often cited for recognition in international law of the principle of objective territoriality. Negligence occurring on board a French ship, the Lotus, had the effect of causing injury on the Turkish ship (a "piece" of Turkish territory). *See also United States v. Aluminum Co. of America,* 148 F.2d 416 (2d Cir. 1945).

   3. **The "effects" doctrine in U.S. law:** American federal courts and the Restatement (Third) have adopted a broad interpretation of the objective territoriality principle based upon effects within a state's territory. Jurisdiction is sometimes exercised *on the basis of reprehensible effects or consequences alone, no matter how minimal or attenuated.* Such broad claims to jurisdiction have been criticized by many states and may be contrary to international law in allowing a state's territorial jurisdiction to be virtually limitless. *See* p. 74, *infra* (discussing the application of the "effects" test by U.S. courts).

B. **Active nationality principle based on nationality of the defendant:** The state of a person against whom proceedings are taking place may exercise jurisdiction based *on the nationality of the defendant.*

1. **Nationality of individuals:** The right of states *to regulate the conduct of its nationals everywhere and thus assert nationality as a basis for jurisdiction is widely accepted.* International law requires that a state must have a *genuine link with the person* to assert jurisdiction based on nationality, Nottebohm (*Liech. v. Guat.*), 1955 I.C.J. 4 (April 6). Nationality is otherwise a question of each state's domestic law, and jurisdictional conflicts often arise when a person is a national of more than one state.

2. **Nationality of corporations:** Jurisdiction based on the nationality of corporations is controversial because "nationality" of a corporation is also determined in different ways by different states. Nationality may be determined by state of incorporation, by the location of the principal place of business, or by the nationality of those owning or controlling the corporation.

3. **Nationality of vessels:** The nationality of a vessel is determined by the flag it flies, but international law requires a "genuine link" between the vessel and the state. Article 5 of the 1958 Convention on the High Seas and article 91 of the 1982 LOS Convention.

4. **Nationality of aircraft and spacecraft:** The nationality of an aircraft is determined by its place of registration under the 1944 Chicago Convention on International Civil Aviation. The state of registration may be changed, but registration may not exist in more than one state at a time. A spacecraft likewise is under the jurisdiction of the state in which it is registered under article 8 of the Outer Space Treaty.

5. **Extent of the territory to which jurisdiction applies:** The applicable territory to be used as a basis for exercising jurisdiction includes the land within the state's boundaries, the coastal zones as specified in the law of the sea, and the airspace above the lands and territorial waters.

C. **Protective principle:** A state may exercise jurisdiction over crimes *which threaten its security and integrity or its vital economic interests.* The reasoning behind the protective principle is that an offense may have extremely grave consequences in one state, but may otherwise go unpunished if the state where the offense was actually committed does not itself consider the conduct to be unlawful. The objection to this basis for jurisdiction is that it is subject to abuse, with each state free to determine what crimes threaten its security. The Restatement (Third) limits protective jurisdiction to conduct generally recognized as criminal by states in the international community. Crimes generally recognized as being detrimental to a state's interests and within protective jurisdiction include espionage, counterfeiting a state seal or currency, and violations of immigration or customs laws.

D. Universality principle: The international community considers some offenses *to be so serious that they are subject to the jurisdiction of all states*. Crimes clearly subject to universal jurisdiction are piracy on the high seas, slave trade, and war crimes. U.S. law and multilateral conventions also treat torture, genocide, aircraft piracy, some criminal acts against diplomats, and other crimes as subject to universal jurisdiction. It is unclear, however, whether customary international law recognizes these and other crimes as universal crimes. *See generally Demjanjuk v. Petrovsky*, 776 F.2d 571 (6th Cir. 1985), *cert. denied*, 475 U.S. 1016 (1986) (war crimes and crimes against humanity); *Filartiga v. Pena-Irala*, 630 F.2d 876 (2d Cir. 1980) (torture is a universal crime).

E. Passive personality principle based on nationality of the victim: An injured person's state may assert *the victim's nationality as a basis for exercising jurisdiction*. This principle is not widely accepted for ordinary crimes, so that the principle often overlaps with jurisdiction predicated on universal crimes.

F. Jurisdiction based on agreement: In addition to the five basic principles of jurisdiction, there exists the possibility that *states can confer jurisdiction through international agreements*. The Restatement (Third) provides that a state has jurisdiction to prescribe and enforce a rule of law in the territory of another state to the extent provided by international agreement with the other state.

1. **An example of such an agreement** exists between Cuba and the United States with respect to Guantanamo. The U.S. recognizes Cuba's continuing "ultimate sovereignty" over the leased area, but Cuba conferred upon the U.S. "complete jurisdiction and control over and within" the leased areas.

2. **Jurisdiction over the armed forces** taking part in NATO (the North Atlantic Treaty Organization) is also determined by a series of multilateral and bilateral treaties.

G. Conflicts of state jurisdiction: The various bases of jurisdiction frequently result in overlapping state jurisdiction. Although the problem is somewhat mitigated by the requirement of reasonableness in asserting jurisdiction, the possibility of conflicts remains. *See* p. 75, *infra.*

III. EXTRADITION

Extradition is the ***process by which an individual charged or convicted of a serious crime in one state (the requisitioning state) and found in a second state (the asylum state) is returned to the requisitioning state for trial or punishment***. Extradition arises from bilateral and multilateral treaties and many issues of extradition are matters of treaty interpretation.

A. **Obligation to extradite:** In the absence of a treaty there is ***no obligation to extradite***. A state may volunteer to extradite an individual without the existence of a treaty but is obliged to extradite only by the terms of a treaty. The practice of the United States and the general modern trend is to disallow extradition in the absence of an applicable treaty.

B. **Extraditable offenses:** Treaties employ one of two methods for specifying the grounds for extradition. The treaty may rely solely on the requirement of double criminality or it may list the indictable offenses for which extradition is available. In either case, treaties often prohibit extradition if prosecution of the offender would be barred in either state by the statute of limitations.

   1. **Double criminality:** Treaties often provide that extradition is available for any conduct which is an offense in both the requisitioning state and the asylum state punishable by a specified minimum term of imprisonment.

   2. **List of extraditable offenses:** A second method of listing extraditable offenses has fallen into disfavor, because it is considered clumsy and results in treaties being outdated as new crimes emerge.

C. **Nationals of the asylum state:** State treaties sometimes provide that a state may not or cannot extradite its own nationals. A consequence of the latter type of treaty is that criminals may escape punishment altogether if their own state fails to prosecute them. Some treaties with such an exception obligate the asylum state to prosecute its own nationals for the crime if it refuses to extradite.

D. **Process of requesting extradition:** Although the process of requesting extradition varies, there are common characteristics. Requests for extradition are often initiated along diplomatic channels. The request is then subject to a judicial determination followed by consideration in the executive branch, which has some discretion in the final determination.

E. Standard treaty limitations on extradition: Extradition treaties may include exceptions under which extradition by the asylum state is not required.

1. **Discrimination:** Extradition will not be granted if it would subject the fugitive to prosecution based on race, nationality, political opinion or other similar grounds that would prejudice the process.

2. **Lack of probable cause:** The request for extradition must include sufficient *prima facie* evidence of guilt attributable to the fugitive whose extradition is sought. This limitation is commonly found in treaties of English-speaking states. More generally, extradition does not apply to persons merely suspected of having committed an offense. Nor may extradition be utilized to obtain a person's presence as a witness or for the purpose of enforcing a civil judgment.

3. **Political offenses:** Most treaties today exempt from extradition political offenses in either mandatory or discretionary terms. The exemption for political offenses is widely accepted by non-socialist states but the term itself is subject to several interpretations. While there is no generally agreed upon definition of political offenses, there are a few offenses which are generally recognized as not being political offenses, such as assassination of heads of state, war crimes, and genocide.

   a. **Purely political offenses:** Purely political offenses are acts directed against the state which lack the essential characteristics of a common crime. Examples are treason, sedition, rebellion and espionage. Such acts are done with the purpose of damaging a political regime as such.

   b. **Related political offenses:** Related political offenses are common crimes motivated by political goals. There are three approaches to related political offenses, requiring varying degrees of connection between the crime and the political act.

      i. **The "Political Incidence" approach (the Anglo-American approach):** This approach requires the criminal offense to be committed in the course of a dispute between a governing party and another party with political aims. The motive and purpose of the crime must be to further the aims of the party. Application of the test in U.S. courts has been inconsistent. Compare *Eain v. Wilkes*, 641 F.2d 504 (7th Cir. 1981), cert. denied, 454 U.S. 894 (1981) (extradition of PLO member for marketplace bombing) with *Matter of Mackin*, 668 F.2d 122 (2d Cir. 1981) (denied extradition of IRA member for attempted murder of British soldier); and *Quinn v.*

Robinson, 783 F.2d 776 (9th Cir. 1986), *cert. denied*, 479 U.S. 882 (1986) (extradition of IRA member for murder of London police constable because relevant political uprising was in Northern Ireland, not Great Britain).

ii. **The "Political Objective" Approach (the Franco-Belgian approach):** Under this approach, the means used to achieve the political objective may not be unlimited; the means used must relate to the political objective; and a degree of proportionality must exist between the political objective and the crime for which extradition is sought.

iii. **The "Predominant Motive" Approach (the Swiss approach):** This approach demands a close and direct link between the crime and the political act, thus making it more likely for a fugitive to be extradited. A crime is a political offense if it was committed in the course of preparing to perpetrate a purely political offense; there must be a direct link between the act and the political goal; and the common law criminal element must be proportional to the political goal.

iv. **Treaty exceptions for acts of terrorism:** There is an emerging trend in extradition treaties to exempt from treatment as political offenses, and this require extradition for, acts of terrorism as defined by the relevant treaty. Such exceptions have been recognized in bilateral treaties (*e.g.*, the 1985 Supplementary Extradition Treaty between the U.S. and the United Kingdom) and in regional treaties (*e.g.*, the European Convention on Suppression of Terrorism). Use of this exception in extradition treaties has been criticized, particularly when done on a state-by-state basis (thus singling out certain political movements for less favorable extradition treatment) and when the extraditable offenses are broadly defined to include crimes against military and other non-civilian targets.

4. **Doctrine of specialty:** The requisitioning nation cannot prosecute the extradited person for offenses other than those stated as the grounds for extradition. American extradition treaties expressly include such a provision, and the Supreme Court has also ruled that the doctrine of specialty may be implied from the "manifest scope and object of the treaty."

   a. **Re-extradition to third state:** The doctrine of specialty may also prevent a state from extraditing the accused to a third state without first offering him the "right to return."

b. **Exceptions:** The requisitioning state may prosecute the extradited person for offenses committed after extradition. Other offenses committed before extradition may also be prosecuted if the accused first has a reasonable opportunity to depart the country.

5. **Territorial jurisdiction:** Extradition treaties often rely on the principle of territorial jurisdiction so that the crime for which extradition is being requested must have been committed within the territorial jurisdiction of the requisitioning state. Difficulties often arise when a state is requesting extradition based on non-territorial jurisdictional grounds.

6. **Other non-extraditable crimes:** A mandatory or discretionary exception for crimes of a religious, fiscal, or military nature is often included.

F. **Methods employed to avoid the safeguards of extradition treaties:** There are two principal methods used to avoid the safeguards of extradition treaties: *deportation* and *abduction*.

1. **Deportation (also referred to as "disguised extradition"):** A potential asylum state may avoid the terms of an extradition treaty by either denying the fugitive permission to enter the state initially or by deportation as an undesirable alien.

2. **Abduction:** States occasionally recover fugitives by abduction from the asylum state. Although abduction is generally considered an affront to the sovereignty of the asylum state and widely considered a violation of individual human rights, U.S. courts nevertheless accept jurisdiction of defendants brought before them by such illegal means. *See, e.g., Kerr v. Illinois*, 119 U.S. 436 (1886) (kidnapping by nongovernmental party); *United States v. Alvarez-Machain*, 112 S.Ct. 2188 (1992) (kidnapping by government agents). Illegal recovery of a fugitive, however, will not be ignored by U.S. courts if the abduction, in addition to being illegal, was performed in a violent, brutal and inhumane manner. *See United States v. Toscanino*, 500 F.2d 267 (2d Cir. 1974).

IV. JURISDICTIONAL PRINCIPLES IN UNITED STATES LAW

A. **The role of international law:** The jurisdictional principles of international law and U.S. domestic law affect one another and may be limiting factors on one another. The international law principles of jurisdiction, *see* pp. 67-69, *supra*, sometimes restrict the exercise of national jurisdiction. Conversely, U.S. due process considerations of fairness expressed by tests such as "minimum contacts" and "purposeful availment" may place restrictions on jurisdiction that would be acceptable under international law.

1. **Federal legislation:** Courts may also be confronted with conflicts between customary international law principles of jurisdiction and federal legislation. Article VI of the U.S. Constitution makes federal legislation binding upon the courts. U.S. courts have upheld federal legislation even when it causes the courts to violate international law jurisdictional principles. *United States v. Aluminum Co. of America*, 148 F.2d 416 (2d Cir. 1945); *The Over the Top*, 5 F.2d 838 (D. Conn. 1925). U.S. courts do try, however, to interpret federal legislation consistently with the international principles of jurisdiction. *The Charming Betsy*, 6 U.S. (2 Cranch) 64 (1804).

2. **Conflicts of laws:** Conflicts between domestic courts may arise over which state should exercise jurisdiction over a dispute, which state's law should apply, and whether to enforce a judgment of a foreign court. Conflict of laws, sometimes referred to as private international law, is not really part of public international law at all. Each state has developed its own legal rules as a matter of comity to resolve such conflicts, and therefore this section only addresses U.S. law governing conflicts.

B. **U.S. grounds for jurisdiction:** United States courts rely on several bases to assert jurisdiction.

1. **The "conduct" and "effects" tests in U.S. law for claiming jurisdiction:** Under the widely accepted "pure" territorial principle, *see* p. 67 *supra*, U.S. law is applied to ***conduct taking place in U.S. territory***, regardless of where the effects are felt. The controversial effects test of U.S. law, *see* p. 67 *supra*, is an extension of the objective territoriality principle. The effects test has been applied in anti-trust, securities trading, export controls, and environmental protection with U.S. courts finding that conduct between foreign companies on foreign soil could nevertheless subject them to U.S. jurisdiction if there are effects in the U.S. (*Timberlane Lumber Co. v. Bank of America Nat'l Trust & Saving Ass'n*, 549 F.2d 597 (9th Cir. 1976)), and perhaps even if only an intent to affect U.S. trade is shown. *United States v. Aluminum Co. of America*, 148 F.2d 416 (2d Cir. 1945).

2. **The protective principle in U.S. law:** U.S. courts rely mostly on the territorial basis for jurisdiction but have applied the protective principle of international law for jurisdiction in a few cases. The

protective principle is recognized in the Restatement (Third) § 402 which states that:

> "Subject to § 403 a state has jurisdiction to prescribe law with respect to . . . certain conduct outside of its territory by persons not its nationals that is directed against the security of the state or against a limited class of other state interests."

The Comments give as examples "espionage, counterfeiting of the state's seal or currency, falsification of official documents, as well as perjury before consular officials, and conspiracy to violate the immigration or customs laws."

C. Conflict of laws under U.S. law: Several states may have grounds for jurisdiction of a single case. "Comity" is the term used to describe *judicial restraint practiced in order to avoid or resolve such conflicts* of jurisdictions. It is not a hard and fast rule of law but rather stems from the notion that a state should treat others as it would wish to be treated. Comity has been used by U.S. courts to refuse jurisdiction in deference to another state. Lack of reciprocity, on the other hand, has been used to justify a refusal to enforce a foreign court's judgment. In determining whether jurisdiction should be exercised, the Restatement lists as factors to be balanced: the *vital national interests* of each state; *nationality* of the persons subject to concurrent jurisdiction; ability to *enforce* the judgment; the extent to which the required conduct is to take place *in another state*; *hardship* to the parties from possibly conflicting national decisions; the existence of *justified expectations*; and *consistency* with international traditions. The Restatement (Third) also concludes that customary international law requires jurisdiction be exercised only in a reasonable manner with deference to another state if its interests are clearly greater, although it has been widely questioned whether customary international law does impose such a limitation.

1. *Forum non conveniens:* The doctrine of *forum non conveniens,* an exercise of comity, is an often utilized method for settling problems of concurrent jurisdiction. It is defined by the Restatement (Second) of Conflict of Laws § 84: "A state will not exercise jurisdiction if it is a seriously inconvenient forum for the trial of the action provided that a more appropriate forum is available to the plaintiff." (emphasis added) The Supreme Court has stated that *forum non conveniens* determinations should be at "the sound discretion of the trial court", balancing "all relevant public and private interest factors." *Piper Aircraft Co. v. Reyno,* 454 U.S. 235 (1981); *see also In re Union Carbide Corporation Gas Plant Disaster at Bhopal,* 809 F.2d 195 (2d Cir. 1987) (upholding district court judgment as revised

that Union Carbide must submit itself to the jurisdiction of Indian courts because all relevant events had taken place in India and the public interests of India were much greater than the public interests of the U.S.).

2. **Reciprocity distinguished:** U.S. courts have refused to enforce proper foreign judgments on the grounds that the foreign states have failed to give effect to U.S. judgments. *See, e.g., Hilton v. Guyot*, 159 U.S. 113 (1895). This reciprocity requirement for enforcement of a foreign judgment, generally disfavored today, is more a political tool than a legal principle.

3. **Sovereign compulsion:** The sovereign compulsion defense is designed to prevent unfairness to private parties subject to the conflicting commands of several states. The defense most often has been applied in situations when production of foreign-based documents in a court proceeding would violate the law of the foreign state in which they are located. The Restatement of Foreign Relations (Third) § 441, entitled "Foreign State Compulsion," gives further guidelines for resolving conflicting demands on parties, stating that:

    a. A person generally may not be required by a state

        i. to do an act in another state that is prohibited by the law of that state or by the law of the state of which he is a national; or

        ii. to refrain from doing an act in another state that is required by the law of that state or by the law of the state of which he is a national.

    b. A person of foreign nationality may generally be required by a state

        i. to do an act in that state even if it is prohibited by the law of the state of which he is a national; or

        ii. to refrain from doing an act in that state even if it is required by the law of the state of which he is a national.

V. IMMUNITIES FROM JURISDICTION

Both international law and municipal law grant immunities from jurisdiction. Municipal laws can create additional immunities not existing under international law, but municipal law restrictions on the immunities granted by international law may result in violations by the state of its international obligations. Of the three types of jurisdiction (legislative, judicial and enforcement), the subject of immunities is most concerned with judicial and enforcement jurisdiction. However, the view is widely accepted that denial of immunity from judicial jurisdiction also implies denial of immunity from legislative jurisdiction.

A. Sovereign immunity: States are generally not subject to the jurisdiction of other states.

1. Absolute theory: Until about 1900, a state's immunities were very broad. Absolute immunity is based on the notion that all sovereign states are equal and are not subject to each other's authority. *The Schooner Exchange v. M'Faddon*, 11 U.S. 116 (1812). Even absolute immunity did not extend to litigation involving a state's interest in property or other immovables abroad, or its interests in the administration of an estate in a foreign state's territory.

2. Restrictive theory: The modern view holds that a state may be subject to a foreign jurisdiction when it engages in commercial activity. A distinction is made between "commercial" activity or property (*acta gestionis*) and "public" activity or property (*acta imperii*). The U.S. first adopted the restrictive theory in 1952 in the so-called Tate letter from the State Department to the Justice Department.

a. Approach of third world states: The approach of the former Soviet Union and other third world states was to adhere to the absolute theory. Although the absolute theory was espoused, in actual practice the communist states concluded international agreements allowing their trade missions to be subject to foreign jurisdiction.

b. "Nature" test and "Purpose" test: One of two tests is employed to determine whether or not a state's activity is a commercial activity. Some states look to the nature of the activity while others consider the purpose of the activity. For example, under the "nature" test a state-owned bank extending credits to encourage investment in its country is engaged in a commercial activity. Under the "purpose" test, however, the activity may be regarded as governmental because the bank's activities are serving a public policy interest.

c. Exceptions: In addition to the "commercial exception," modern law supports the traditional denial of immunity for claims to property or other immovables acquired by gift of succession, as well as claims in non-commercial torts cases.

3. Foreign Sovereign Immunities Act (FSIA): The Foreign Sovereign Immunities Act of 1976 essentially codified the restrictive theory of immunity.

4. Exceptions to immunity: A state is presumptively immune unless an exception applies. Immunity does not apply under the following statutory exceptions: waivers of immunity, commercial activities, expropriation claims, property claims, non-commercial torts, maritime liens, counterclaims and international agreements. The party claiming immunity bears the burden of demonstrating that no exception applies. *Arango v. Guzman Travel Advisors Corp.*, 621 F.2d 1371 (5th Cir. 1980).

   a. Jurisdiction through application of FSIA: Jurisdiction over a foreign state in federal or state courts of the United States may only be obtained through application of the FSIA. *Argentine Republic v. Amerada Hess Shipping Corp.*, 488 U.S. 428 (1989). "Foreign state" is defined under the FSIA to include its political subdivisions (including local governments), agencies and instrumentalities. Agency or instrumentality is in turn defined as a separate legal entity which is either an organ of or owned by a foreign state and which is neither a citizen of one of the United States or of any third nation. Foreign Sovereign Immunities Act § 1603(b).

   b. Waivers of immunity: Waivers of immunity may be explicit or implicit and may not be withdrawn except in a manner consistent with the original terms of the waiver. F.S.I.A. § 1605(a)(1). Explicit waivers occur as a result of treaties or contacts with private parties, and waiver may be implied from a state's conduct. Common examples of conduct implying a waiver are the filing of a general appearance, signing of arbitration clauses, forum selection clauses, choice-of-law clauses, and assertion of counterclaims.

   c. Commercial activities: The FSIA codifies the commercial exception to immunity denying immunity in any case "in which the action is based upon a commercial activity. . . ." The commercial activity must either be carried on in the United States or have a direct effect in the U.S. F.S.I.A. § 1605(a)(2). The Act defines "commercial activity" as a "regular course of commercial conduct or a particular commercial transaction or act," with the nature of the activity, rather than its purpose, determining characterization as either a commercial or public/governmental activity. F.S.I.A. § 1603(d).

      i. Examples of commercial activity are purchasing supplies and equipment for its armed forces, issuing letters of credit, and contracting for repairs on embassy buildings.

ii. Activities considered non-commercial are those arising from a state's mere participation in foreign assistance programs of organizations such as the Agency for International Development (AID).

iii. "Commercial activity carried on in the United States" is in turn defined as commercial activity "carried on by such state and having substantial contact with the United States." F.S.I.A. § 1603(e). In *Saudi Arabia v. Nelson*, 113 S.Ct. 1471 (1993), a U.S. citizen sued Saudi Arabia alleging that he was tortiously detained and tortured for a critical report he had written as an employee of a government-controlled hospital. The Court concluded that his suit was not "based upon" his employment but upon the tortious conduct, and that the tortious conduct itself was not "commercial activity."

d. Expropriation claims: Sovereign immunity does not apply when "rights in property taken in violation of international law are in issue." F.S.I.A. § 1605(a)(3). The phrase "taken in violation of international law" refers to nationalization or expropriation of property without proper compensation and arbitrary or discriminatory takings.

e. Property rights: Sovereign immunity does not apply in any case "in which rights in property in the United States acquired by succession or gift or rights in immovable property situated in the United States are in issue." F.S.I.A. § 1605(a)(4). Rights in property include leaseholds, easements, servitudes and security interests in land. The denial of immunity extends to all property, including property used for diplomatic or consular purposes.

f. Non-commercial torts: Sovereign immunity does not apply when a foreign state or one of its agents is subject to a tort claim for money damages. Possible tort actions include personal injuries, death, and property damage. This tort exception to immunity does not apply if the conduct at issue was the discharge of a discretionary function or the claims are for "malicious prosecution, abuse of process, libel, slander, misrepresentation, deceit or interference with contract rights." F.S.I.A. § 1605(a)(5)(B).

i. Discretionary acts are acts requiring the exercise of judgment, rather than the mere carrying out of orders.

ii. This provision is generally inapplicable to torts or injuries occurring outside the U.S.

g. Maritime liens: Sovereign immunity does not apply to suits brought in admiralty to enforce a maritime lien against a foreign state-owned vessel or cargo when the lien suit is based on commercial activity by the state. F.S.I.A. § 1605(b) and (c).

h. Counterclaims: A foreign state which is subject to a counterclaim is denied immunity if it would also have been denied immunity had the claim been brought as a direct claim against the state, or the counterclaim arises from the same transaction or occurrence giving rise to the foreign state's claim. F.S.I.A. § 1607.

i. Attachment, arrest and execution: The FSIA also provides immunity for the property of foreign states from attachment, arrest and execution. F.S.I.A. § 1609. The exceptions to this immunity are generally the same as the exceptions to immunity from jurisdiction. *See* F.S.I.A. § 1610(a). Some forms of state property are immune without exception. F.S.I.A. § 1611.

j. International agreements: The FSIA states that "[s]ubject to existing international agreements . . . a foreign state shall be immune . . . except as provided in sections 1605 to 1607. . . ." It is unclear whether "international agreements" refers only to treaties or whether it is broad enough to encompass nonimmunity as established by custom.

k. Extent of liability under FSIA: A foreign state denied sovereign immunity is liable to the same extent as a private party, except that it will not generally be liable for punitive damages. An exception to the exception is made when a state's laws award only punitive damages in wrongful death actions, in which case the foreign state is liable for them but only to the extent that the award reflects actual or compensatory damages. F.S.I.A. § 1606.

B. Act of State Doctrine: The Act of State doctrine is not a rule of sovereign immunity and, in fact, is not even a rule of international law. It is a ***domestic court-made doctrine***, but because it is related to the concept of sovereign immunity it is often discussed in that context. It is a doctrine which protects the sovereignty of states by judicial deference to the public acts of a foreign state done on that state's territory. Courts accord such deference to avoid the adjudication of delicate international political issues. While the doctrine of sovereign immunity looks to the limits of a court's jurisdiction, the Act of State doctrine functions more like a choice-of-law rule by which courts defer to a foreign state's prescriptive authority within its own territory. Furthermore, while sovereign immunity may be employed only by "foreign states," the Act of State doctrine is available to private litigants. In the U.S., recent cases have focused on the doctrine as an outgrowth of separation of powers in foreign relations between the executive and judicial branches.

1. **Basic doctrine in the U.S.:** The U.S. has applied the Act of State doctrine since the late 1800s. The development of the Act of State doctrine has given rise to several exceptions which have decreased the scope of the doctrine.

   a. **Early cases:** The early version of the Act of State doctrine was developed by the courts in several cases ranging between the late 1800s and early 1900s.

      i. In *Underhill v. Hernandez*, 168 U.S. 250 (1897), an American citizen seeking damages resulting from detention by the armed forces of Venezuela was denied relief on the grounds that "the courts of one country will not sit in judgment on the acts of the government of another, done within its own territory." *See also Oetjen v. Central Leather Co.*, 246 U.S. 297 (1918) (Hides sold to a Texas leather company following their seizure from a Mexican citizen as a military levy could seek remedy only in the courts of Mexico or through diplomatic channels).

      ii. In *Bernstein v. Van Heyghen Freres Societe Anonyme*, 163 F.2d 246 (2d Cir. 1947) cert. denied, 332 U.S. 772 (1947), the court applied the Act of State doctrine and refused to return to a Jewish plaintiff property which had been seized by Nazi officials. Later, the same case (*Bernstein v. N.V. Nederlandsche-Amerikaansche, Stoomvaart-Maatschappij*, 210 F.2d 375 (2d Cir. 1954)) gave rise to the so-called Bernstein exception. This rule of exception provided that the Act of State doctrine was inapplicable in the face of explicit statements from the State Department that such judicial restraint was not required.

   b. **Recent Supreme Court decisions:** Court decisions from 1964 to the present combined with congressional action have resulted in poorly defined parameters for the Act of State doctrine based on vague notions of separation of powers in foreign relations between the executive and judicial branches.

      i. **The height of the Act of State Doctrine:** In *Banco Nacional de Cuba v. Sabbatino*, 376 U.S. 398 (1964), the Cuban government had expropriated a Cuban sugar company (C.A.V.) owned by U.S. nationals. The dispute before the courts regarded the distribution of the proceeds and Sabbatino, essentially acting on behalf of the expropriated U.S. owners, argued that the proceeds belonged to him rather than the Cuban government. According to Cuban law, however, the proceeds were the property of the Cuban government. The Supreme Court, applying the Act of State doctrine, refused jurisdiction and stated that the courts "... will not examine the validity of a taking of property within its own territory by a foreign sovereign government ... in the absence of a treaty or other unambiguous agreement regarding controlling legal principles, even if the complaint alleges that the taking violates customary international law." *Banco Nacional*, 376 U.S. at 428. The Court asserted that the Act of State doctrine was premised upon the "distribution of functions between the judicial and political branches of the Government on matters bearing upon foreign affairs." *Banco Nacional*, 376 U.S. at 427. Congress reacted by passing the Sabbatino Amendment to the Foreign Assistance Act of 1961 (also called the Second Hickenlooper Amendment) which stated that courts were required to adjudicate claims to property taken in violation of international law. The lower courts have narrowly construed the amendment to cases in which the property is physically present in the U.S.

ii. **Decline of the doctrine:** *First National City Bank v. Banco Nacional de Cuba*, 406 U.S. 759 (1972), like the Sabbatino case, involved the expropriation of property by Cuba. The State Department notified the Court that it need not apply the Act of State doctrine. The Court did not in fact apply the doctrine, but only three of the five justices in the minority regarded this outcome as an application of the Bernstein exception. In the course of *Alfred Dunhill of London, Inc. v. Republic of Cuba*, 425 U.S. 682 (1976) the State Department wrote a "Bernstein" letter suggesting an end to the application of the Act of State doctrine under any circumstances. The Court nevertheless rejected the State Department's suggestion even while refusing to apply the Act of State doctrine to the repudiation of debts owed by Cuban-nationality cigar companies. The results of this case, as well as the First National City Bank case, leave unclear the current status of the Bernstein exception. In *W.S. Kirkpatrick & Co. v. Environmental Tectonics Corp.*, 493 U.S. 400 (1990) the Supreme Court ruled on the Act of State doctrine for the first time since 1976. The Court concluded by stating that the Act of State doctrine requires U.S. courts to deem as valid "the acts of foreign sovereigns taken within their own jurisdictions." *Kirkpatrick*, 493 U.S. at 401. The Act of State doctrine was found to be inapplicable because "no foreign sovereign act [was] at issue" in a suit against a Nigerian citizen by an unsuccessful bidder for disbursing bribes to obtain a government contract for another bidder.

2. **Exceptions to the Act of State Doctrine:**   The development of the Act of State Doctrine has given rise to the *treaty* exception, the *commercial activity* exception, and the *situs of property* exception. Furthermore, the Act of State doctrine cannot be pleaded to defend against charges of war crimes, crimes against peace or crimes against humanity.

   a. **Treaty law exception:**   This exception was referred to in the *Sabbatino* case and applied in *Kalamazoo Spice Extraction Co. v. Provisional Military Government of Socialist Ethiopia,* 729 F.2d 422 (6th Cir. 1984). Many treaties call for the "prompt payment of just and effective compensation" when property is expropriated by one of the nations party to the treaty. The State Department suggested in *Kalamazoo Spice* that the judiciary need not abstain from adjudication because the applicable treaty had provided the "controlling legal standard for compensation." It remains unclear, however, whether or not this "treaty exception" applies in every case involving a similar treaty or only in those cases in which the court receives a special letter from the Executive Branch permitting adjudication.

   b. **Commercial activity exception:**   This exception is analogous to the commercial activity exception to sovereign immunity. The Act of State doctrine is inapplicable to "the repudiation of a purely commercial obligation owed by a foreign sovereign or by one of its commercial instrumentalities." *Alfred Dunhill of London, Inc. v. Republic of Cuba,* 425 U.S. 682 (1976).

   c. **The situs of the property:**   The "situs" of the property at issue is important because the Act of State doctrine applies only to acts of a foreign state done on its own territory and not to seizure of property located in the U.S. The situs of the property presents a difficult issue with respect to intangible property, and it remains unclear whether the situs is to be determined by federal law or by the applicable state (of the United States) law. *See Callejo v. Bancomer,* 764 F.2d 1101 (5th Cir. 1985) (federal law applied to determine that the situs of certificate of deposits was Mexico because the CDs were issued in Mexico and called for payment in Mexico).

3. **Act of State doctrine in anti-trust cases:**   Application of the doctrine is especially controversial in anti-trust cases, in which the defendant may be liable for treble damages. Defendants raise the Act of State doctrine to shift blame for damages incurred by the

plaintiff to the conduct of a foreign state. This defense has met with varying success. *See Hunt v. Mobil Oil Corp.*, 550 F.2d 68 (2d Cir.), *cert. denied*, 434 U.S. 984 (1977).

4. **Doctrine in other states:** Although international law does not require application of the Act of State doctrine as practiced by United States courts, the courts of many other states do, in fact, recognize a similar doctrine.

C. **Immunity of state representatives:** Just as diplomatic and consulate premises enjoy special protection, so also do various state representatives.

1. **Head of State:** The immunity of heads of state relies on both sovereign immunity and diplomatic immunity. A suit against the head of state is often treated like a suit against the state itself for purposes of immunity. Heads of state traveling abroad also enjoy the privileges and immunities accorded to diplomats. Not yet well-developed are issues pertaining to former heads of state and other government officials, such as cabinet ministers.

2. **Diplomatic representatives:** Diplomats have enjoyed personal immunity (personal inviolability) from the times of ancient Greece to modern-day codification of custom in the widely adopted Vienna Convention on Diplomatic Relations. Diplomatic privileges and immunities are regarded as indispensable to the diplomat's performance of duties. Diplomats (and their family members) enjoy broad protection from arrest or detention, as well as immunity from criminal laws and civil and administrative jurisdiction. Art. 31, ¶ 1.

   a. **Specific protections and limitations under the Vienna Convention:** The Vienna Convention, also enacted as U.S. federal statutory law in 22 U.S.C. § 254(a-e) (1982), provides that diplomats are:

      i. *not required to give evidence*. Art. 31, ¶ 2.

      ii. *immune from personal service*. Art. 35.

      iii. *excused from paying most taxes* and social security provisions. Arts. 33-34.

      iv. *excused from customs duties and inspections*. Art. 36.

      The Convention provides that diplomats do *not* enjoy immunity with respect to:

      i. actions involving *purely personal property*;

      ii. estate administration in the host state in which the diplomat is involved in a *non-official capacity*; or

iii. any other commercial or professional conduct in which the diplomat is functioning *outside his official duties*. Art. 31 ¶¶ a-c.

The U.S. legislation extends its protection to diplomats of states even for states which are not parties to the Vienna Convention. 22 U.S.C. § 254(b).

b. The Iranian hostages case: The protections granted diplomats both by customary international law and its subsequent codification in the Vienna Convention on Diplomatic Relations were strongly reaffirmed by the I.C.J. in the case concerning *United States Diplomatic and Consular Staff in Tehran (U.S. v. Iran)*, 1980 I.C.J. 3 (May 24). The Court found that Iran had breached its fundamental international law obligations and that these rules of diplomatic immunity could not be violated even in the alleged extraordinary circumstances.

c. Convention on the Prevention and Punishment of Crimes Against Internationally Protected Persons: The treaty requires states to prosecute or extradite for prosecution anyone who commits, attempts to commit, or threatens to commit a violent crime against any head of state, diplomatic agent, or consular official. The U.S. has implemented the Convention in 18 U.S.C. § 112 (1982).

d. Administrative, technical and service staff of a diplomatic mission: Such staff have complete immunity from criminal jurisdiction, but immunity from civil and administrative jurisdiction only with respect to their official acts.

3. **Status of embassies and consulates:** Diplomatic mission and consular post properties are not considered an extension of the foreign state's territory. Although such diplomatic premises are within the territory of the receiving state they do enjoy special protection, related to the issue of sovereign immunity. Diplomatic and consulate premises are "inviolable, and are immune from any exercise of jurisdiction by the receiving state that would interfere with their official use." Restatement (Third) of Foreign Relations § 466. *See also 767 Third Avenue Associates v. Permanent Mission of Republic of Zaire to United Nations*, 988 F.2d 295 (2d Cir. 1993), *petition for cert. filed*, (U.S. May 24, 1993) (No. 92-1896) (Zaire mission to U.N. immune from eviction for its failure to pay rent).

a. The host state is to refrain from search, seizure, attachment or any other form of enforcement jurisdiction which interferes with the official use of the premises. Vienna Convention on Diplomatic Relations, art. 22.

b. Furthermore, the host state is obliged to protect the diplomatic premises from interference by private parties. Art. 22. The U.S., for example, has enacted statues prohibiting congregation within 500 feet of diplomatic premises.

c. Authorities of the territorial state are not permitted to enter the building and other premises of a diplomatic mission unless they have gained the permission of the head of the mission. In fact, the territorial state is further obliged to prevent any unlawful entry by others. Art. 22.

d. Diplomatic missions are generally exempt from all taxes of the host country. Arts. 23, 28.

e. Correspondence, records, and documents of the mission are inviolable. Art. 24. Diplomatic mail may not be opened or detained by the host country. Art. 27.

f. The host country is obliged to make all necessary facilities available for the proper functioning of a diplomatic mission. Art. 25.

g. Diplomatic agents enjoy freedom of travel within their host country, but may be barred from designated zones related to national security interests. Art. 26.

h. Diplomatic missions have the right to use all suitable means of communications, with the exception of radio transmitters for which they must seek special permission. Art. 27.

i. Diplomatic agents may not be arrested or subject to coercive measures. *See* p. 84, *supra.* Diplomats' dwellings, correspondence and other property are likewise inviolable. Art. 30.

4. Consuls: Historically, consuls were granted only very limited immunity because they were often merchants in addition to consuls. More recently, a consulate position is often a career in itself, and states have negotiated specific immunities for their consulates. Consular immunity has been codified under the Vienna Convention on Consular Relations. Under the Convention, consulars are immune from arrest or detention except for serious crimes or as directed by court decisions, and consular archives are inviolable. The primary difference between diplomatic and consular immunity is that consuls enjoy immunity only with respect to their official acts. Diplomats enjoy a much broader "personal" immunity.

5. Special missions: In recognition of "itinerant envoys, diplomatic conferences and special missions sent to a State for limited purposes" the General Assembly has approved a Convention on Special Missions. Although more than 20 countries (not including the U.S.) have ratified it, the Convention is not yet in force. Under the

Restatement (Third), immunity for special missions is covered by the general provisions of diplomatic immunity.

6. **Representatives to international organizations:** U.N. civil servants are protected under the Convention on the Privileges and Immunities of the United Nations, which generally grants immunities similar to those enjoyed by diplomats and consuls. Two limitations are that U.N. representatives are immune from legal process only with respect to their official acts, and only their personal luggage is free from customs duties. Protection for international civil servants is provided in the U.S. under the International Organizations Immunities Act, 22 U.S.C. § 258 *et seq.*

D. **Immunity of international organizations, their agents, officials, and invitees:** As international organizations become increasingly influential in world affairs, they require some of the same immunities required by states in order to carry out their functions. International organizations, however, have not been established long enough to have enjoyed a prolonged history of immunity similar to sovereign and diplomatic immunity. Consequently, immunity of international organizations has been established by treaty rather than by customary law, and not all states have been eager to extend broad protections. The General Convention of the Privileges and Immunities of the United Nations is an example of such a treaty. It provides the following immunities to the U.N.:

1. immunity from *all legal process*;

2. *inviolability of premises, assets, archives and official papers*;

3. *exemption from direct taxes* and customs duties;

4. *exemption for staff from income tax* on salaries; and

5. *diplomatic immunity for the Secretary-General and Assistant Secretaries-General*. Other staff members have limited immunities.

CHAPTER 6

INTERNATIONAL ORGANIZATIONS

International organizations usually refer to public or intergovernmental organizations, in contrast to private or nongovernmental organizations (NGOs) such as Amnesty International or the Red Cross. International organizations are established by treaties and governed by international law. *Advisory Opinion on Reparation for Injuries Suffered in the Service of the United Nations*, 1949 I.C.J. 174 (April 11).

I. THE UNITED NATIONS

The United Nations (U.N.) is a public organization of states that was established by intergovernmental cooperation on October 24, 1945. The fundamental purpose of the U.N. was to implement a system of collective security and discourage states from the use of unilateral force. Now, however, much of the U.N.'s efforts are directed toward economic and development concerns of impoverished states.

A. The U.N. Charter: The U.N. Charter entered into force on October 24, 1945. The U.N. has over 150 members, with most states of the world as members (a few notable exceptions are Switzerland, the Koreas, and Taiwan).

1. **Purposes:** The four purposes of the United Nations are described in Article 1 as to: (1) *"maintain international peace and security,"* which includes using "collective measures for prevention and removal of threats to the peace" and peaceful means for the settlement of international disputes according to international law; (2) *"develop friendly relations among states"*; (3) *achieve international cooperation* in solving economic, social, cultural and humanitarian problems; and (4) be a *center for states* to use to attain these common goals. U.N. Charter art. 1 (emphasis added).

2. **Principles:** Article 2 lists seven guiding principles for the U.N. and its members. First and foremost is the principle of sovereign equality of all member states. Further, members are required to:

   a. fulfill their *obligations under the Charter*;

   b. *settle disputes by peaceful means*;

   c. *refrain from the threat or use of force* against the territorial integrity of political independence or "in any other manner inconsistent with the Purposes of the United Nations"; and

d. give the U.N. *"every assistance"* in any action it takes. U.N. Charter art. 2, ¶¶ 2-5 (emphasis added).

e. The organization will also seek to hold *non-member states* to these principles insofar as to maintain international peace and security. U.N. Charter art. 2, ¶ 6.

f. Finally, the U.N. is *not authorized to intervene* in matters which are essentially within the domestic jurisdiction of a state, although this provision does not apply to enforcement measures under Chapter VII. U.N. Charter art. 2, ¶ 7.

   Note: Article 2(7) has had little impact on U.N. action. First, resolutions phrased in general terms and not identifying any specific state or states is not considered "intervention" and, more significantly, many areas once considered "domestic" concerns are now considered matters of international concern (*e.g.*, widespread human rights violations).

3. Revision of the Charter: Under article 108, the Charter can be amended by a two-thirds vote of the General Assembly, and ratification by the constitutional processes of two-thirds of the members of the U.N., including all permanent members of the Security Council.

B. Nature and function of the U.N.: The U.N. has organizational *personality* (legal capacity) and *immunity* in the international system.

1. Legal capacity: Article 104 specifically states that "the Organization shall enjoy in the territory of each of its Members such legal capacity as may be necessary for the exercise of its functions and the fulfillment of its purposes." The International Court of Justice in an advisory opinion, *Advisory Opinion on Reparations for Injuries Suffered in the Service of the United Nations*, 1949 I.C.J. 174 (April 11), outlined the scope of the U.N.'s legal capacity, filling in the gaps left by the Charter. The Court addressed the issue of whether the U.N. can sue a responsible government to obtain reparation for harm done to the organization itself or one of its agents in the performance of his duties. The Court stated that, without question, the U.N. has the requisite international personality endowing it with the legal capacity to bring international claims for harm done to the organization itself. It further held that the U.N. can bring claims for reparations for harm done to an agent fulfilling his or her duties, even if the agent is a national of the defendant state, and even if the defendant state is a non-member. The Court reasoned that although these powers are not specifically mentioned in the Charter, they are "conferred upon it by necessary implication as being essential to the performance of its duties," and that "the effective working of the Organization — the accomplishment of its task" requires that states strictly adhere to the principle in article 2, ¶ 5 of the Charter requiring "every assistance" to the U.N. by its members.

2. **Immunity:** The United Nations and its representatives and officials enjoy privileges and immunities in the territory of its members necessary to fulfill its purposes, the same immunity that is normally enjoyed by foreign governments. *See* pp. 84-86, *supra* (discussing immunities granted to foreign government representatives).

C. **Membership:** Membership in the United Nations is governed by provisions in the Charter.

1. **Original and other members:** There were fifty-one original member states which either participated in the United Nations Conference on International Organization at San Francisco or previously signed the Declaration by United Nations of January 1, 1942, and then signed the Charter and ratified it according to their domestic constitutional procedures. The Charter was signed by a majority of its signatories on October 24, 1945, thereby officially establishing the United Nations. Since its inception, membership in the U.N. has increased dramatically, doubling by 1965, and tripling by 1985. Most new members are former colonies that achieved independence after World War II.

2. **Admission to membership:** According to article 4, ¶ 1, membership is open to "all other peace loving states which accept the obligations contained in the present Charter" and are able and willing to carry them out. A state wishing to join must submit a request to the Security Council, which then may submit a recommendation for membership to the General Assembly. The General Assembly then decides by a two-third vote whether or not to admit a state. Note, however, that the Security Council is not required to recommend a state for membership, and may effectively keep states from joining. Indeed, the Soviet Union has kept South Korea from joining the U.N. by vetoing its proposals for membership.

3. **Suspension:** A member-state against which preventive or enforcement action has been taken by the Security Council may have its membership suspended by the General Assembly upon recommendation of the Security Council. U.N. Charter art. 5. This provision has never been applied.

4. **Expulsion:** If a member persistently violates the principles of the Charter, it may be expelled from the organization by the General Assembly, also upon recommendation by the Security Council. U.N. Charter art. 6. This provision has never been applied.

5. **Withdrawal:** There is no provision in the Charter for voluntary withdrawal by a state.

6. **Credentials:** Which governmental representatives are entitled to represent a member state of the U.N. is a question of credentials. Determination of credentials is considered a procedural question subject to the less demanding voting requirements for procedural questions in the Security Council and General Assembly. *See* pp. 92-93, *infra* (discussing the voting procedures of the General Assembly and the Security Council). Sometimes the question of credentials is difficult to differentiate from admission (*e.g.*, the question of representation/admission of China after the communists gained control of mainland China in 1949).

D. **Charter supremacy and the Lockerbie Case:** Under article 103, if a Charter obligation conflicts with any other treaty obligation, the Charter prevails. In the *Lockerbie Case* (*Libya v. United States*), Libya, based on the Montreal Convention, resisted extradition requests from the United States, France, and the United Kingdom for Libya nationals suspected of causing the explosion of a Pan Am flight in 1988 over Lockerbie, Scotland. While Libya's request for provisional relief was pending, the Security Council acting under Chapter VII ordered Libya to comply with the requests. While acknowledging the Court's continuing authority despite Security Council action, the Court denied Libya's request for provisional relief on the grounds that, whatever the merits of Libya's claims under the Montreal Convention, decisions of the Security Council are binding on U.N. members and under article 103 take precedence over any conflicting treaty obligation.

E. **The U.N. organs:** There are six principal organs to the U.N.: the *General Assembly*, the *three Councils*, the *Secretariat*, and the *International Court of Justice*.

1. **The General Assembly:** The General Assembly is composed of all member states of the U.N.

   a. **Sessions:** The General Assembly meets in regular annual sessions and may also meet in special sessions if required. Special sessions are convened by the Secretary General of the General Assembly at the request of the Security Council or of a majority of the members of the U.N. The General Assembly adopts its own rules of procedure and elects a President for each session.

   b. **Functions and powers:** The General Assembly is essentially a *global forum* for the exchange and debate of ideas. It may address any questions or matters within the scope of the Charter and may make recommendations to the Security Council or the U.N. on any such questions or matters, U.N. Charter art. 10, except "disputes" or "situations" that the Security Council is considering. U.N. Charter art. 12. Specifically, the General Assembly may consider matters concerning international peace and security and may make recommendations about such matters to the members, concerned states, or the Security Council. The functions of its various commissions and committees include: making and consideration of reports of international events, supervision of Trusteeship Council, approval of budgets and application for membership, participation in the selection of judges for the International Court of Justice, supervision of Trusteeship Council, and the appointment of the Security General of the U.N.

c. **Limitations on its powers:** The most important limitation on the General Assembly's powers is in article 11, ¶ 2. It provides that any question of international peace and security "... on which action is necessary shall be referred to the Security Council. ..." The ICJ has interpreted article 11, ¶ 2 to apply only to *enforcement* action. *See* pp. 139-140, *infra*.

d. **Voting:** Each member of the General Assembly has one vote. Decisions on "important" questions are made by a two-thirds majority of members present and voting. Important questions according to article 18, ¶ 2 include: recommendations concerning international peace and security; the election of non-permanent members of the Security Council, members of the Economic and Social Council and members of the Trusteeship Council; admission of new members; suspension and expulsion of members; questions relating to the operation of the trusteeship system, and questions relating to the budget. Decisions on other questions are made by a majority of members present and voting, including determination of which questions other than those in article 18(2) will require a two-thirds majority.

Note: A member who is behind in financial contributions to the U.N. by at least two years may not vote unless the General Assembly has determined that the failure to pay is due to conditions beyond the control of the member. U.N. Charter art. 19.

e. **Legal status of Assembly resolutions:** Although the General Assembly does seek to encourage the progressive development of international law and its codification, its "recommendations" are just that and not legally binding upon members as a matter of Charter law. On the law-making effect of General Assembly resolutions generally under international law, *see* p. 89, *supra*.

2. **Security Council:** The Security Council is the U.N. organ with primary responsibility for the maintenance of international peace and security. U.N. Charter art. 24, ¶ 1.

    a. Composition: The Security Council consists of fifteen member states. The five permanent members are: the People's Republic of China, France, the Soviet Union (now Russia), the United Kingdom, and the United States. The other ten member states are rotating members elected by the General Assembly for a term of two years, with due regard to "equitable geographic distribution." U.N. Charter art. 23. Each member of the Council has one representative.

    b. Functions and powers: The Security Council has primary responsibility for the maintenance of international peace and security. U.N. Charter art. 24. Specifically, the Council's powers include: pacific settlement of disputes under Chapter VI; action with respect to threats to the peace, breaches of the peace, and acts of aggression under Chapter VII; using regional arrangements for the maintenance of international peace under Chapter VIII; and certain aspects of the international trusteeship system under Chapter XII. U.N. Charter art. 24, ¶ 2. Decisions of the Security Council are legally binding upon members. U.N. Charter art. 25. The Council is required to submit annual reports to the General Assembly for its consideration, and special reports when necessary. It adopts its own rules of procedure and selects its president. Unlike the General Assembly, the Security Council is expected to function continuously, with members represented at all times. U.N. Charter art. 28.

    c. Voting: Under article 27, each member of the Security Council has one vote. Decisions on "procedural" matters require an affirmative vote by nine members. Decisions on "all other matters" require an affirmative vote of nine members, "including the concurring votes of the permanent members. . . ."

    It is this requirement of the concurring votes of which each permanent member creates their right to *veto* any nonprocedural decision brought forth on any nonprocedural matter, effectively preventing the decision from passing.

    d. Abstention: Despite the requirement of the "concurring" votes of the permanent members, in practice a refusal to vote (or abstention) by a permanent member is not treated as a veto. Article 27 also requires that "a party to a dispute" being evaluated by the Council under Chapter VI (for peaceful settlement of disputes) abstain from voting, but in practice, states do not do so even when clearly involved in a dispute under consideration.

  e. **"Double veto":** Article 27 gives no guidance on procedural versus nonprocedural matters. In the early years of the Council, the Soviet Union treated determination of the procedural/nonprocedural nature of a resolution as itself a nonprocedural vote subject to a veto, and then would veto the substance of the resolution (thus the "double veto"). This procedural manipulation was soon overcome in practice by another procedural maneuver. The presidency of the Council is held by each member for one month. The president could rule that the procedural/nonprocedural issue is itself procedural and not subject to veto; presidential rulings are final unless reversed by a procedural veto (*i.e.*, nine votes, with no state having a veto power).

3. **The Economic and Social Council (ECOSOC):** The ECOSOC is established under Chapter X and consists of 54 members of the U.N. elected by the General Assembly. Each member has one vote and decisions are made by a simple majority. Its primary responsibilities are to make studies, reports, and cultural matters and to prepare draft conventions for submission to the General Assembly on matters within its competence. It has established a number of subsidiary organs, including the U.N. Commission on Human Rights.

4. **Trusteeship Council:** The Trusteeship Council under Chapter XII is responsible for administering trusteeship territories that are not yet self-governing. The Council consists of members who administer trustee territories, permanent members of the Security Council, and as many other members as the General Assembly elects as necessary to ensure that the Council is equally divided between members which administer and those which do not. Each member has one vote, and decisions are rendered by a majority of the members present and voting. Its importance has greatly diminished as the trust territories have become independent.

5. **International Court of Justice:** The International Court of Justice (ICJ) is the principal judicial organ of the U.N., U.N. Charter art. 92, and the successor to the Permanent Court of International Justice for the League of Nations. It functions in accordance with a statute annexed to the Charter. All members of the U.N. are parties to the Statute of the International Court of Justice, and a state which is not a member of the U.N. may become party to the Statute by the General Assembly upon recommendation by the Security Council. U.N. Charter art. 93. *See* p. 108, *infra* (discussing nonmember states becoming parties to the Statute).

6. **Secretariat:** The Secretariat is composed of a Secretary-General and any required staff of the organization. U.N. Charter art. 97. The Secretary-General is elected by the General Assembly upon recommendation by the Security Council (subject to the veto power), and is the chief administrative officer of the U.N. The Secretary-General is required to submit annual reports to the General Assembly on the work of the organization, and may be required to perform other functions as requested by the Security Council, General Assembly, ECOSOC, and the Trusteeship Council. Under article 99, the Secretary-General "may bring to the attention of the Security Council any matter which in his opinion may threaten the maintenance of international peace and security." This agenda-setting power is potentially very significant as the basis for more expansive substantive responsibilities for the position.

F. **Legislative activities of the General Assembly and the International Law Commission:** The General Assembly created the International Law Commission (ILC) in 1947 to assist in fulfilling the Assembly's legislative duties under article 13, ¶ 1(a) of the U.N. Charter. The ILC is composed of leading international lawyers. The General Assembly has delegated authority to the ILC to research international law and draft conventions. The ILC has drafted many multilateral conventions which codify existing international customary law as well as create new law. When such conventions are adopted by the General Assembly and receive broad support, they often become a generally accepted statement of international law in the area. The legislative activities of the General Assembly, as delegated to the ILC, have contributed significantly to the body of international law.

G. **Specialized agencies:** Specialized agencies are organizations that are related to the U.N. through article 57 of the U.N. Charter.

1. **Defined:** Article 57 defines specialized agencies as those "established by intergovernmental agreement and having wide international responsibilities, as defined in their basic instruments, in economic, social, cultural, educational, health, and related fields. . . ." The Economic and Social Council reaches agreement with qualifying organizations to grant special agency status and coordinates the activities of the special agencies. The agreements differ for each agency but usually involve regular reporting to the Economic and Social Council and agency consideration of recommendations from the General Assembly.

2. **Examples:** Some of these specialized agencies are the International Monetary Fund (IMF), the International Bank for Reconstruction and Development (World Bank), the United Nations Educational, Scientific, and Cultural Organization (UNESCO), the

Food and Agriculture Organization (FAO), World Health Organization (WHO), International Labor Organization (ILO), the Universal Postal Union (UPU), and the International Civil Aviation Organization (ICAO).

3. **Membership:** Membership in specialized agencies is not limited to members of the U.N. Some organizations only admit U.N. members, but most agencies attempt to expand their own membership to as many nations as possible. Conversely, a few members of the U.N. are not members in all of the specialized agencies.

4. **Legislative activities:** By making recommendations and drafting conventions, specialized agencies have developed international law in many areas. Like the General Assembly, specialized agencies generally do not have the authority to enact binding legislation. Some agencies such as the UPU and ICAO have developed regulations and standards that have been widely accepted. In certain situations, WHO can enact health regulations that are binding on member states. Other organizations, as the ILO, have drafted a number of widely adopted treaties. These activities have contributed significantly to the body of international law in newly developing areas.

II.   **REGIONAL ORGANIZATIONS**

Regional organization is a term of art under the U.N. Charter that refers to international associations established under Chapter VIII. Each of these institutions is created through an agreement between the member states that outlines the structure, functions and authority of the organization. "Regional organization" is not defined in the U.N. Charter. Unlike other international organizations, however, regional organizations are concerned with problems within a specific region. Some handle only specific concerns such as economic, military or political issues, while others deal with any matter that concerns the nations in that region.

A. **Basic characteristics:** Some regional organizations are loose associations of member states with little or no legislative authority. These organizations may only provide a forum for nations to meet and discuss matters of common interest. Other regional organizations have legislative power and take significant actions in fulfilling their mandates. The organizations with the most legislative authority are supranational organizations. *See* p. 98, *infra*.

B. Major organizations: The Organization of American States (OAS), Council of Europe, and the Organization of African Unity (OAU) are three of the most prominent regional organizations.

1. **The Organization of American States:** The OAS was created in 1948 to promote unity and cooperation among nations in the Western Hemisphere. One of the primary influences on the formation of the OAS was the Cold War. As a result, its charter emphasized security through a common defense.

2. **The Council of Europe:** The Council of Europe was created in 1949 to promote unity in Europe after World War II.

3. **The Organization of African Unity:** The OAU was formed in 1963 as a loose association of African nations. The many conflicting points of view held by the member states were reflected by the limited power given to the OAU in its charter. Each nation retained autonomy as recognized by the OAU charter.

C. Functions: The primary function of each of these regional organizations is to promote cooperation between the member states. The specific areas, methods and extent of cooperation, however, differ among regional organizations.

1. **The Organization of American States:** The OAS has concentrated its efforts on responding to political developments and furthering political cooperation. The OAS charter outlines the functions of the organization as strengthening security, ensuring peaceful settlement of disputes, coordinating common defense and promoting economic, social and cultural development. Although the OAS has drafted a number of treaties, it has been less successful than the Council of Europe in winning the acceptance of those treaties. The OAS has made some progress in the area of regional human rights, including the establishment of the Inter-American Court of Human Rights in 1969.

2. **The Council of Europe:** The Council of Europe has focused on economic cooperation through the European Communities and has developed a number of agreements in many areas. These agreements have resulted in significant cooperation between the member states and increased power for the European Communities.

3. **The Organization of African Unity:** The OAU Charter is primarily concerned with noninterference and peaceful resolution of disputes among member states. The OAU has promoted African unity on issues including human rights, but has played a limited role in dealing with regional conflicts.

D. Relationship to U.N.: Chapter VIII of the United Nations Charter describes the relationship between the U.N. and regional organizations. Article 52, ¶ 1 in the U.N. Charter allows U.N. members to participate in any regional arrangement with principles consistent with the U.N. The United Nations encourages its members in regional organizations to attempt to settle "local disputes" in those organizations before referring them to the Security Council. U.N. Charter art. 52, ¶ 2. Regional organizations have a duty to inform the Security Council of any actions the organization is undertaking or contemplating for the maintenance of international peace and security. U.N. Charter art. 54. Regional organizations must seek Security Council authorization for any enforcement action. U.N. Charter art. 53.

1. **Jurisdictional issues:** Chapter VIII is unclear concerning regional jurisdiction and the often overlapping authority of the Security Council. Although it has been argued that regional organizations have primary or exclusive jurisdiction over regional matters, *see* U.N. Charter art. 52, ¶ 2. Neither of these arguments has been accepted given the Security Council's "primary" responsibility for the maintenance of international peace and security. *See* U.N. Charter art. 52, ¶ 4 and art. 24. The U.N. Security Council, however, has chosen to defer to regional organizations in a number of instances. The Security Council also may choose to exercise concurrent jurisdiction, but these decisions are founded more on pragmatic considerations than any legal requirements in the U.N. Charter.

2. **Collective self-defense organizations distinguished:** Occasionally, the term regional organization has been loosely applied to collective defense arrangements under article 51 of the U.N. Charter. Collective self-defense refers to the aid of other states coming to the defense of an attacked state, and is discussed at p. 142, *infra*.

III.   SUPRANATIONAL ORGANIZATIONS

Supranational organizations are a relatively new development in international law. The concept of supranationality involves an association with its own structures, sovereign rights and authority independent from the member states. Member states submit themselves and their citizens to the law-making power of the organization through treaties with the other member states. Supranational organizations result in a division of power between the individual member states and the organization in which member states have forfeited some aspects of their sovereignty but still actively participate in the law-making powers of the organization.

Example: The European Community is the quintessential example of a supranational organization, which resulted from the unification of three organizations. The European Coal and Steel Community (ECSC) formed in 1952 was the first European organization with supranational characteristics. In 1958, the European Economic Community (EEC) and the European Atomic Energy Community (Euratom) were created with similar institutions and powers. These three organizations were subsequently merged into the European Community with common institutional structures; however, each of the original treaties is still applicable to the three Communities.

A. **Mandate:** The European Communities were established to promote unity and economic integration among the member states. This general goal was accompanied by several specific aims to be achieved by the Communities. The Communities were to promote free movement of goods and capital and freedom of movement for persons between the member states. Ultimately, these steps were to lead to the complete integration of the economic policies of the member states into one Community policy. The new common market would have uniform external tariffs and no internal trade barriers. Progress toward these goals slowed in the late 1970s and early 1980s, so the Single European Act (SEA) in 1987 amended all three original treaties, establishing 1992 as the deadline for creation of the integrated market. The SEA also expanded the areas of authority of the Communities to foreign policy and the environment. The 1991 Maastricht Treaty, if ratified, sets a 1999 deadline for economic union, gives Parliament a new veto power, and makes new strides in political union, defense policy, immigration, and other social issues.

B. **Structure:** The treaties establishing the European Communities provide the institutional structure for the organization. These agreements created four institutions to utilize the power held by the European Community: the Commission, the Council of Ministers, European Parliament, and the European Court of Justice. The Commission comprises persons appointed collectively by the member states, and each must be a national of one of the member states. No more than two can be nationals of the same member state. The Commission makes its decisions in private and is not intended to represent the individual interests of the member states. These interests are represented by the Council which consists of one representative from each of the member states. The European Parliament was created to represent the peoples of the Community and is comprised of representatives elected in direct elections. Seats in the Parliament are not allotted according to population but according to party. The European Court of Justice has thirteen judges appointed for six-year terms and six assistants that issue advisory opinions in each case. The Court ensures compliance with European Community policies and reviews actions by the other institutions under the treaties that created them.

C. **Community law and domestic law:** The treaties signed by the member states in the European Community are treated as the ***constitution of the Community*** and are ***binding*** on each of the nations and individuals. Regulations, directives and decisions created by the institutions of the European Community in accordance with the treaties are also directly applicable to member states and citizens. The European Court of Justice has held that these Community laws are superior to any conflicting domestic laws. The Court of Justice has made this determination in previous cases and continues to decide questions of Community law and enforcement. The Court has used two theories to support this conclusion.

1. **The institutional theory:** The institutional theory states that member states have given up their sovereignty in certain specified areas in favor of the Community; therefore, they have given up the power to enact conflicting laws in these areas.

2. **The political theory:** Under the political theory, the states have limited their sovereignty granting power to the Community, so any laws of an individual member state that contradict Community laws are not valid. This power of the Community to enact laws that supersede the laws of the member states and apply them directly to the citizens is a primary difference between supranational and other regional organizations. The lack of complete control of the legislative process by the individual member states is another important characteristic.

CHAPTER 7

INTERNATIONAL DISPUTE SETTLEMENT

I. DISPUTE DEFINED

Under international law "dispute" has a specific meaning which goes beyond a mere difference of views. A dispute is *a contest of some specificity, the resolution of which has some practical effect on the relations between the parties*. The ICJ accepts only "disputes", which are defined as "a disagreement on a point of law or fact, a conflict of legal views or interests between two persons." *Mavrommatis Palestine Concessions* (*Greece v. Gr. Brit.*) (1924) P.C.I.J. (Ser. A) No. 2, at 11.

II. THE ROLE OF THE U.N.

The U.N. Charter includes several provisions outlining methods of dispute settlement. Article 2, ¶ 3 requires members to engage in *peaceful settlement* of disputes. Article 33 of the Charter calls for peaceful settlement of disputes through "negotiation, enquiry, mediation, conciliation, arbitration, judicial settlement, resort to regional agencies or arrangements, or other peaceful means of their own choice." Several organs of the U.N. are engaged in dispute settlement. In addition to the ICJ, disputes may be brought before the General Assembly and the Security Council.

A. General Assembly: Articles 10, 11, 12 and 14 deal with the ability of the General Assembly to hear disputes. Any member-state, as well as any non-member state which is party to the dispute and agrees to the obligations of pacific settlement imposed by the U.N. Charter, may bring disputes to the General Assembly. The General Assembly is limited to establishing fact-finding missions and making recommendations. Although the actions of the General Assembly may have significant political influence, states are under no legal obligation to cooperate with the fact-finding missions or to follow recommendations.

B. Security Council: Consideration of a dispute by the Security Council may be requested by any member of the U.N., article 35, ¶ 1, by any non-member which is party to the dispute and agrees to the obligation of peaceful pacific dispute settlement, article 35, ¶ 2, by the General Assembly, article 10, 11 ¶¶2-3, and by the Secretary General, article 99. The Security Council has discretion to deny the request or accede to it by placing the dispute on its agenda. Once on the agenda, only the

Security Council may remove it. Under Chapter VI, the Security Council has investigative powers and may make recommendations. The recommendations of the Security Council under Chapter VI exert great political influence but create no legal obligations. Recommendations are substantive and subject to the veto power.

III. OTHER TREATY OBLIGATIONS OF PEACEFUL SETTLEMENT

Before the U.N. Charter came into force, there were many separate bilateral treaties calling for conciliation and arbitration. Since the entry into force of the U.N. Charter, the treaties calling for peaceful dispute settlements are primarily regional treaties such as the European Convention on the Peaceful Settlement of Disputes (1957) and the African states' Protocol on Conciliation and Arbitration. In addition, treaties on everything from opium production to anti-ballistic missiles include provisions for peaceful settlement of disputes, ranging from a simple reference to the obligation imposed by the U.N. Charter to complex schemes outlining varying procedures and methods depending on the nature of the dispute.

IV. NON-JUDICIAL METHODS

Methods of non-judicial dispute resolution are negotiation, inquiry, mediation/good offices, and conciliation. Each method may be used alone or in any combination with the other methods. Many international institutions today provide dispute-resolution processes which combine negotiation, inquiry, mediation and conciliation and, as a final resort, adjudication.

A. **Negotiation:** Negotiation is a face-to-face discussion between the disputing parties. It is a traditional and commonly employed method, and usually the first step in the peaceful resolution of disputes. In fact, international courts such as the ICJ *require* parties to enter into "meaningful" negotiations before presenting the matter for adjudication. Negotiations are not bound by rules of procedure and are frequently carried out through diplomatic channels or handled by "competent authorities" representing appropriate government departments and ministries. In addition, recurring problems may be addressed by joint commissions specifically created to negotiate.

B. Inquiry: Inquiry is the attempt to clarify the facts pertinent to a dispute in the hopes that agreement on factual matters will facilitate a final resolution. A group of individuals or an institution may be designated as impartial fact-finders.

C. Mediation: Mediation, unlike negotiation, involves the intervention of an outside party. This method is commonly employed when the negotiations have reached a dead-lock and a third-party is required to break the impasse and to assist the parties in reaching an acceptable solution. Mediation may be sought by the disputing parties themselves or may be offered by outside parties. The third-party mediator becomes an active participant and is expected to informally present proposals for a solution based on information supplied by the disputing parties. The benefit of mediation is that it provides the disputing parties with the possibility of solutions without binding them to the mediator's suggestions. Furthermore, disputing parties may find it politically easier to make necessary concessions through a third party as opposed to making concessions in the course of direct negotiations.

D. Good offices: An outside party is said to contribute "good offices" when the intervention in a dispute is more passive than that of a mediator. A third-party contributing "good offices" usually does nothing more than simply encourage a resumption of the negotiations or provide an additional channel of communication.

E. Conciliation: This method of dispute settlement also involves the intervention of a third-party and is a link between mediation and arbitration. Conciliation has been described as the process of settling a dispute by referring it to a commission of persons whose task it is to elucidate the facts and to make a report containing proposals for a settlement, but without the binding character of an award or judgment. Conciliation is a more formal process than mediation and involves independent investigation of factual matters but does not result in legally binding solutions, as does arbitration. Although approximately 200 conciliation commissions have been formed and conciliation is provided for in the Vienna Convention on the Law of Treaties and the Vienna Convention of Succession of States in respect of Treaties, it is not a commonly employed method of dispute settlement.

V. QUASI-JUDICIAL METHODS/ARBITRATION

Arbitration, unlike any of the five methods discussed above, results in ***legally binding settlements***. The settlement is reached on the basis of law by a group of judges appointed by the parties. Arbitral panels may be used to settle not only disputes between states, but are widely used to settle commercial disputes between a state and a private party or between private parties. Many states have passed domestic legislation to facilitate arbitration and have ratified bilateral treaties and conventions utilizing arbitration as a means of settling disputes.

A. Advantages of arbitration: Arbitration has several advantages over both the other non-judicial means of dispute settlement and adjudication:

1. It is *more conclusive* than the other forms of non-judicial dispute settlement because the decisions of the arbitral panels are binding upon the parties.

2. The disputing parties retain *greater control* in the arbitration process than they retain in the judicial process because they appoint the arbitrators. In making such appointments, the parties may select people with specialized knowledge of the matters at issue.

3. Parties may *designate the procedures and the laws* to be applied. The selected procedures are usually less cumbersome than those applied in the courtroom and the arbitration process can therefore be less time consuming.

4. Arbitration is *less formal* and *less contentious* than adjudication. This is especially important for maintaining commercial relationships.

5. Both the arbitration proceedings and decisions can be kept *confidential*, a great advantage in disputes regarding sensitive matters.

B. Disadvantages of arbitration: Arbitration also has its disadvantages:

1. If the parties do not specify procedures, arbitration may be a *very cumbersome* and *time-consuming* process.

2. Arbitration panels *do not have the authority of courts* to conduct discovery or subpoena witnesses.

3. The *parties themselves pay for the entire cost* of the arbitration, which includes compensation for the arbitrators as well as administrative costs. However, if the arbitration is conducted efficiently these costs are often less than the costs of litigation.

C. Types of international arbitral clauses: There are several types of international arbitral clauses.

1. **Clause inserted in treaty:** An arbitration clause may be inserted in a treaty dealing with one or more substantive issues to provide a method of settling disputes arising from the treaty. Such

arbitration clauses are common in commercial treaties and in international civil aviation agreements.

2. **Treaty itself establishes settlement method:** The treaty itself may exist solely to establish a method of resolving either certain categories of disputes or all disputes which may arise between the parties. Two-well known examples are the Hague Convention for the Pacific Settlement of International Disputes and the General Act for the Pacific Settlement of International Disputes.

3. **"After-the-fact" arbitral agreements:** Arbitral agreements may be concluded after the dispute has arisen. Such "after-the-fact" arbitral agreement is often concluded when the parties have been unsuccessful with the other methods of dispute settlement. An example is the Iran-U.S. Claims Tribunal.

D. **Consent to arbitrate and the *compromis*:** Unless the parties to a dispute have previously consented to submit to arbitration through an arbitral clause or arbitration convention, there is **no international law requirement to arbitrate**. Parties may, subsequent to the rise of a dispute, consent to arbitrate. A single instrument may express this consent and provide details of the arbitration process itself. On the other hand, the consent may be expressed in one document followed by a subsequent agreement dealing with the details of the arbitration. The subsequent agreement is called the *compromis d'arbitrage* and it outlines the constitution of the arbitral panel, the rules of procedure, the issues to be decided and the binding nature of the arbitral decision.

E. **Composition of the arbitral tribunal:** An arbitral tribunal may be established on an ad hoc basis or as a continuing institution, and it usually has a tripartite structure. Each party selects a member independently and then the third member is selected by a joint decision of the parties. Should the parties fail to agree on a selection, the final member is chosen by an outside party, such as the Secretary-General of the Permanent Court of Arbitration at the Hague. Some arbitral tribunals, such as the Iran-U.S. Claims Tribunal, have nine members but the tripartite structure is maintained.

F. **Choice of location:** Choice of location can be important because some countries' laws provide that their courts have jurisdiction over arbitration proceedings. Those courts may review arbitral awards reached within their country and may sometimes entertain interlocutory appeals. To avoid the jurisdiction of a party's courts, arbitration in a neutral country is advisable.

G. **Rules of arbitration/ad hoc vs. institutional arbitration:** Parties may choose between the established sets of rules for arbitration or may develop their own "ad hoc" rules. With the exception of the United

Nations Commission on International Trade Law Arbitration (UNIC-TRAL) the set of rules listed below have accompanying institutions. The institutions may be used to actually conduct the arbitration or may assist by advising on all aspects of the arbitration, such as organization of the panel or the unique problems of conducting arbitration in particular countries. The principal established sets of arbitration rules are:

1. **Rules of the International Centre for the Settlement Investment Disputes (ICSID):** This Centre is affiliated with the World Bank and it deals with investment disputes. The United States is a signatory to this Convention.

2. **Rules of Conciliation and Arbitration of the International Chamber of Commerce (ICC):** Both the ICC Rules and the Court of Arbitration are very widely used, especially in the area of trade.

3. **Rules of the United Nations Commission on International Trade Law Arbitration (UNCITRAL):** This set of rules governs the Iran-United States Claims Tribunal.

4. **Commercial Arbitration Rules of the American Arbitration Association (AAA):** The AAA promotes both domestic and international arbitration in many fields.

H. **Applicable law:** The *compromis* usually sets forth the governing rules to be applied by the arbitrators and those rules in turn stipulate the choice of law. The ICSID, for example, provides for application of the law of the host country "(including its rules on the conflict of laws) and such rules of international law as may be applicable," unless the parties have agreed otherwise. Arbitral panels look to the decisions of the ICJ and other permanent courts as well as other contemporary arbitral decisions for evidence of international law.

I. **Arbitral award:** As a general rule ***arbitral awards are binding*** on the parties and ***are not subject to appeal***. However, parties to a dispute may derogate from this rule and permit judicial review by a court such as the ICJ. According to the United Nations Convention on the Recognition and Enforcement of Foreign Arbitral Awards, other circumstances providing a ***defense against enforcement*** of the arbitral award are:

1. the arbitral tribunal ***exceeded its powers***;

2. the enforcement of the award is ***contrary to*** the ***public policy*** of the forum country;

3. the award resulted from arbitration of matters considered ***incapable of settlement*** by arbitration under the laws of the forum country;

4. the *defendant* proves that he was *"not given proper notice*...or was *otherwise unable to present his case*." (Article V(1)(b)) (emphasis added); and

5. the award is in *"manifest disregard"* of the law.

The U.N. Model Rules of Arbitral Procedure provide *additional bases for challenging the validity* of an arbitral award:

1. *corruption* on the part of a member of the arbitral panel;

2. *failure to state the reasons* for the award;

3. *serious departure from a fundamental procedural rule*;

4. the agreement to arbitrate or the compromis are a *nullity*; or

5. the *tribunal exceeded its powers*.

The New York Convention of the Recognition and Enforcement of Foreign Arbitral Awards provides the following *defenses to enforcement* of the arbitral award:

1. the parties to the agreement were under some *incapacity*;

2. the *agreement is invalid* under the applicable law of the arbitration or under the law of the country where the award is to be made;

3. the *defendant* was *not given proper notice* or was *otherwise unable to present its case*;

4. the award *exceeds the powers* of the tribunal;

5. the composition of the arbitral tribunal was *not in accordance with agreement* of the parties or of the law in the country in which the arbitration took place;

6. the award is not binding because it has been *set aside* or *suspended* by a competent authority in the country in which the award was to be made;

7. the subject of the arbitration is *not capable of settlement* by arbitration according to the laws of the country where the award is to be recognized and enforced;

8. recognition and enforcement of the award are *contrary to* the *public policy* of that country.

J. **The role of the ICJ:** Article 36, ¶ 1 of the Statute of the International Court of Justice sets forth the ICJ's role as a public international arbiter, stating that the Court has jurisdiction in "all cases which the parties refer to it." A *compromis* may confer jurisdiction of particular legal questions to the ICJ and indicate the rules of law to be applied by the

Court. The ICJ, however, differs from other arbitration tribunals in that its membership is preestablished.

VI. THE INTERNATIONAL COURTS

There are five generally recognized international courts. They are: the International Court of Justice, Court of Justice of the European Communities, Benelux Court of Justice, European Court of Human Rights, and the Inter-American Court of Human Rights.

A. **The International Court of Justice:** The International Court of Justice (ICJ), successor to the Permanent Court of International Justice, is the ***principal judicial organ*** of the United Nations. Its Statute is annexed to the United Nations Charter. All members of the United Nations are automatically parties to the ICJ Statute, and under certain circumstances parties not members of the U.N. may appear before the Court and may also be parties to the Statute. U.N. Charter art. 93. Being a party to the statute does not mean that the state has submitted itself to the Court's jurisdiction. The ICJ hears relatively few cases because only states may be parties in contentious proceedings before the Court. Stat. of the I.C.J. art. 34, ¶ 1. States must consent to jurisdiction. This limitation is further compounded by the fact that historically states often have chosen to settle disputes through political and diplomatic channels rather than through the ICJ. Regional international courts, on the other hand, have been more frequently utilized for international law claims of private parties. Nevertheless, the cases the ICJ has decided have had a major impact on the development of international law.

1. **Structure and composition:** Article 3, ¶1 of the Statute requires that the Court, with its seat in The Hague, be composed of fifteen judges elected by both the Security Council and the General Assembly. Judges serve for nine-year periods but may be, and often are, re-elected. The terms are staggered so that elections for five of the fifteen judges take place every three years. In practice, several considerations, including the following, determine the composition of the court. For instance, members of the Security Council almost always have a judge on the court. Judges are elected with regard for distribution. A balanced distribution, as exemplified in the 1986 Court, was four judges from Western Europe, two judges from Eastern Europe, three judges each from Africa and Asia, two judges from Latin America and one judge from the U.S. No more than one national of a state may sit as a judge at any one time. Stat. of the I.C.J. art. 3, ¶ 1. If a state appearing before the Court does not have

one of its own nationals as a judge, it may appoint an ad hoc judge to ensure that its views will be fully considered. This practice is not easily reconciled with the view of judges as impartial decision-makers. *See* Stat. of the I.C.J. art. 20.

2. **Contentious and advisory jurisdiction:** The Court may only hear cases *governed by international law*. Stat. of the I.C.J. art. 38. The ICJ has two types of jurisdiction: contentious jurisdiction and advisory jurisdiction. Contentious jurisdiction is based on either the express or implied consent of the parties, and only states party to the ICJ Statute may be parties in a contentious case. Decisions in contentious cases are binding on the parties. The Court also may issue non-binding, advisory opinions at the request of bodies so authorized by the U.N. Charter. Article 36 provides three ways for a state to consent to the jurisdiction of the ICJ. First, states may refer an existing dispute on an ad hoc basis. Second, a treaty may provide that any disputes arising from it be settled by the ICJ. Stat. of the I.C.J. art. 36. Third, the ICJ may have jurisdiction under the so-called "optional clause" of art. 36, ¶ 2.

3. **Compulsory jurisdiction under the optional clause:** Article 36, ¶ 2 provides that states which are parties to the present Statute may at any time declare that they recognize as compulsory *ipso facto* and without special agreement, in relation to any other state accepting the same obligation, the jurisdiction of the Court in all legal disputes concerning: the interpretation of a treaty; any question of international law; the existence of any fact which, if established, would constitute a breach of an international obligation; and the nature or extent of the reparation to be made for the breach of an international obligation. As of 1986, 56 states had made declarations under article 36, ¶ 2, but only 44 of the declarations were still in force. In 1986, in response to *Nicaragua v. United States*, *infra*, the United States withdrew its acceptance of the Court's compulsory jurisdiction under article 36(2), but remains a party to many treaties conferring jurisdiction to the Court under article 36, ¶ 1.

   a. **Reciprocity:** A state accepting the jurisdiction of the ICJ, under the optional clause of article 36, ¶ 2, does so only with respect to other states which have made a similar declaration. Thus a respondent state may assert not only whatever reservations it has declared on the Court's compulsory jurisdiction, but also any reservations of the petitioner state. *See Case of Certain Norwegian Loans (Fr. v. Nor.)* 1957 I.C.J. 9 (July 6).

   b. **Nicaragua v. United States:** In 1946, when the U.S. accepted the ICJ's jurisdiction under art. 36, ¶ 2, it accepted jurisdiction for a period of five years and "thereafter until the expiration of six months after notice may be given to terminate this declaration." In 1984, however, the U.S. sought to amend the declaration to exclude disputes with Central American states, with the amendment to take effect immediately. In *Military and Paramilitary Activities in and Against Nicaragua (Nicar. v. U.S.)*, 1984 I.C.J. 392 (Nov. 26), the ICJ agreed with Nicaragua and ruled that the U.S. was bound to its original six-months notice provision and was thus precluded from escaping the ICJ's jurisdiction on such short notice. The Court so held even though Nicaragua's declaration had no advance notice requirement. The Court refused to apply reciprocity to excuse compliance with a state's own declaration "whatever its scope, limitation, or conditions." The Court appears to require that reasonable notice of withdrawal be given. Moreover, withdrawal precludes future cases but not cases which have already been started. Nottebohm (*Liecht. v. Guat.*) 1953 I.C.J. 111 (April 6).

4. **Duration of declaration under article 36, ¶ 2:**   Some declarations state no time limits, while others remain in effect for specific periods (usually five or ten years) and often include automatic renewal clauses. Many declarations include a right to terminate effective upon receipt by the U.N.'s Secretary-General of a notice of withdrawal.

5. **Reservations to compulsory jurisdiction:**   Article 36, ¶ 3 authorizes reservations conditioned on other states accepting the Court's compulsory jurisdiction or for a certain time. In fact, a wide variety of reservations have been utilized.

   a. **Disputes to be settled by other means:** The most common reservation is to exclude disputes which the parties had already agreed to settle in other tribunals or by other means.

   b. **Disputes within domestic jurisdiction:** Another common reservation is the so-called self-judging reservation, such as the "Connally Amendment," a reservation to the United State's acceptance of compulsory jurisdiction from 1946 to 1986. This reservation excluded from the jurisdiction of the ICJ "disputes with regard to matters which are essentially within the domestic jurisdiction of the United States of America as determined by the United States of America." It has been argued (most notably by ICJ judge and eminent scholar Hersch Lauterpacht) that such clauses violate article 36, ¶ 6, which provides that the ICJ, rather than domestic courts, shall determine whether or not it has jurisdiction over a dispute.

    c. Disputes under multilateral treaties: Other reservations exclude disputes arising under a multilateral treaty "unless all parties to the treaty affected by the decision are also parties to the case before the Court", or "unless all parties to the treaty are also parties to the case before the Court."

    d. Specific disputes: Also excluded may be specific disputes, such as those concerning law of the sea issues and territorial disputes.

6. Reservations for national security and self-defense: A number of states have modified their acceptance of compulsory jurisdiction to exclude matters related to national security and defense. The ICJ itself, however, does not adhere to the view that such matters are *ipso facto* unsuitable for adjudication in its Court.

7. Effect and enforcement of judgments: Article 94 of the United Nations Charter and article 59 of the Statute provide that judgments of the ICJ are **binding** upon the parties. Article 94 authorizes the Security Council to "make recommendations or decide upon measures to be taken to give effect to the judgment." Recommendations under Chapter VI or enforcement measures under Chapter VII are substantive and subject to the veto power. When Nicaragua sought enforcement of the ICJ decision against the United States, the United States vetoed the proposed resolution. *See* 25 I.L.M. 1352 (1986).

8. Advisory jurisdiction: Article 65 of the ICJ Statute authorizes the Court to give advisory opinions "on any legal question at the request of whatever body may be authorized by or in accordance with the charter to the United Nations to make such a request." Article 96 of the U.N. Charter authorizes the General Assembly or the Security Council to request advisory opinions, as well as "[o]ther organs of the United Nations and specialized agencies, which may at any time be so authorized by the General Assembly." Examples of other authorized bodies are the International Labor Organization, the World Health Organization, the International Bank for Reconstruction and Development (World Bank), the International Monetary Fund and the International Atomic Energy Agency.

9. Legal effect: Although advisory opinions are legally **non-binding**, they are, nevertheless, very influential in the development of international law. Some international agreements do provide that disputes arising from the agreement will be submitted to the ICJ for an advisory opinion which will be "accepted as decisive by the parties." The Convention on the Privileges and Immunities of the United Nations is one such example.

10. **Preliminary relief:** The ICJ under article 41 may provide preliminary relief "if the circumstances so require . . . to preserve the respective rights of either party." Examples include the preliminary prohibition on mining of Nicaraguan harbors in *Nicaragua v. United States*, and the preliminary order against Yugoslavia to take measures to prevent genocide in *Bosnia v. Yugoslavia*.

B. **Other international courts:** Since World War II there have been a growing number of regional and specialized tribunals, particularly in Western Europe. Three regional courts sitting in Europe are: the Court of Justice of the European Communities, the Benelux Court of Justice, and the European Court of Human Rights.

   1. **Court of Justice of the European Communities:** Also known as the European Court of Justice, this 13-judge court is the ***sole judicial organ of the European Community***, which, as of 1993, includes Belgium, Denmark, France, Germany, Greece, Ireland, Italy, Luxembourg, Netherlands, Portugal, Spain and the United Kingdom.

      a. **Functions:** The European Court of Justice was established to ensure that the laws of the EC are enforced, to act as referee between disputing member-states and between the Community institutions and the member-states, and to guard against infringement of individual rights by the Community institutions.

      b. **Structure:** Thirteen judges are appointed for staggered six year terms and are eligible for re-appointment. Traditionally, there is a judge from each member state with an additional judge appointed to complete the bench with an odd number. The Court may sit in plenary session, the quorum for a full court being seven; or it may sit in Chamber of three or five judges to consider preliminary rulings or actions instituted by individuals. The judges issue a single "judgment of the court" and have been sworn to uphold the secrecy of their deliberations. The judges are thus protected from the pressure of national interests. In addition to the judges, the European Court of Justice has six advocates general, whose function it is to make "reasoned submissions on cases brought before the Court of Justice, in order to assist the Court..."

      c. **Jurisdiction:** The European Court of Justice has only the jurisdiction conferred on it by the treaties. There is a fundamental division between direct actions, which are those actions initiated in the European Court of Justice, and actions begun in a national court but referred to the Court of Justice for a preliminary ruling. Direct actions begin and end in the European Court of Justice and are usually the result of an agreement between the parties assigning disputes to the Court of Justice. On the other hand, actions begun in national courts also end in national courts, which apply the preliminary ruling obtained from the Court of Justice. The Court of Justice issues preliminary rulings only when requested to do so by a national court seeking clarification of Community law before coming to its own decision.

d. Precedence: Although there is no legal doctrine of *stare decisis* in the European Court of Justice, the Court often follows earlier decisions. Instances in which prior rulings have not been followed are often the result of changed circumstances or changed opinions amongst the judges. In such instances, the Court does not follow the common law practice of formally overruling the earlier decision, but rather ignores it altogether.

e. Sources of law: The European Court of Justice relies on ***primary legislation***, ***secondary legislation***, and ***international agreements*** concluded by the Community. Primary legislation includes the Community's constitutive treaties with all their amendments, protocols, etc. Secondary legislation consists of the laws created by the Community institutions.

f. The Court of First Instance: The Single European Act called for the addition of this new court to relieve the European Court of Justice of its heavy caseload. It has a more limited jurisdiction than the Court of Justice, but otherwise has similar structures and procedures.

2. Benelux Court of Justice: This court is modeled after the European Court of Justice and was established by Belgium, the Netherlands and Luxembourg. Its primary function is to ensure uniformity of the interpretation of the many Benelux treaties.

3. European Court of Human Rights: This court, established under the European Convention on Human Rights, enforces European human rights law, and is discussed at p. 132, *infra*.

CHAPTER 8

THE RIGHTS OF INDIVIDUALS — INTERNATIONAL LAW OF HUMAN RIGHTS

I. STATUS OF INDIVIDUALS

Under modern international law of human rights, *individuals are protected without regard to their status as nationals or aliens*. This approach is in sharp contrast to the traditional concept of international law as governing relations between states. The law governing a state's obligations to an alien was established within this traditional framework of international law regulating the relationship between states, but not the relationship between states and individuals. Thus an offense to an alien was considered an offense only against the alien's native state. The modern international law of human rights, however, makes nationality irrelevant.

II. BRIEF HISTORY

Historically, a state's treatment of individuals in its territory was considered a domestic affair, and not a matter of international law.

A. Traditional concept: An early exception, dating as far back as Roman times, was recognition of a state's obligations to aliens. *See* p. 51, *supra* (discussing the recognition of states and governments). By the late 19th century there were many "minority" treaties concluded by European governments to protect ethnic minorities with which they identified in other states. The only clear early example of an internationalization of individual rights was with respect to slavery. Several major countries abolished slavery in the 19th century; the unacceptability of slavery became an international standard; and slave trade became illegal. In a related matter, the doctrines of humanitarian intervention and humanitarian rules of war have roots traceable to the 17th and 18th centuries.

B. Early twentieth century: A major recognition of an international law of individual human rights came with the establishment of the International Labor Organization (ILO) after World War I. The ILO set forth basic universal standards for labor and social welfare and has since promulgated over a hundred conventions. A number of the peace treaties after World War I provided protection to national, religious, linguistic and ethnic minorities in Central and Eastern Europe. These treaties focused on group rights — a minority's right to its own schools, language, and religions — and freedom from discrimination. The Covenant of the League of Nations also created a mandate system by which the population of the colonies formerly under German and Turkish control were to be protected.

C. Post-World War II: The modern concept of international human rights law is the result of the world's reaction to the Holocaust and other Nazi atrocities during World War II. Nazi war criminals were tried for violating international law before the Nuremberg tribunal, the establishment of which demonstrated that human rights were a matter of international concern rather than a matter left solely to each state. *See* p. 155, *infra*. This modern concept of international human rights law was also key to the formation of the United Nations in 1945, having as one of its principal purposes the promotion and protection of human rights. U.N. Charter art. 1, ¶ 2; art. 3.

D. Current status: Although the basic concept of international human rights law is now firmly established, its relatively recent emergence results in a body of law characterized by evolving ideas, institutions and procedures.

III. HUMAN RIGHTS AND THE UNITED NATIONS

The United Nation's Charter in 1945 was a departure from earlier treaties remedying the problems of particular abuses or particular groups because it was the first attempt to provide comprehensive protection for all individuals. In 1946, the U.N. established a Commission on Human Rights to draft human rights treaties, and in 1948 the U.N. General Assembly passed the Universal Declaration of Human Rights. In the decades since its foundation, the U.N. has continued to promote and protect human rights and has drafted treaties for global adoption dealing with many aspects of human rights. In addition to the Charter, the Universal Declaration of Human Rights, together with the subsequent International Covenant on Civil and Political Rights, the International Covenant on Economic, Social and Cultural Rights and the Optional Protocol to the Civil and Political Covenant form the so-called "International Bill of Human Rights."

A. The U.N. Charter: The two main provisions of the U.N. Charter concerning human rights are articles 55 and 56. These articles are the foundation of modern human rights law.

1. **Article 55:** Article 55 states that "the United Nations shall promote ... universal respect for, and observance of, human rights and fundamental freedoms for all without distinction as to race, sex, language or religion."

2. **Article 56:** Article 56 states that "all members pledge themselves to take joint and separate action in cooperation with the Organization for the achievement of the purposes set forth in article 55."

3. **Implementation:** The Commission on Human Rights was established in 1946 to draft treaties implementing articles 55 and 56 and these two articles have been the main source of subsequent human rights treaties. The language of article 56 may suggest that the member states are obliged to a progressive rather than present fulfillment of the goals set forth in article 55. The imprecision of articles 55 and 56 has led one United States court to find that they are not self-executing and do not confer any rights on individuals. In *Sei Fuji v. California*, 242 P.2d 617 (1952), the California Supreme Court held that the U.N. Charter lacked the mandatory quality and precision required to create enforceable rights as a matter of United States law.

B. **The Universal Declaration of Human Rights:**   In 1948, the U.N. General Assembly passed the Universal Declaration of Human Rights. The rights delineated fall into two general categories: ***civil and political rights***, and ***economic, social and cultural rights***. This declaration was intended to define the rights protected by articles 55 and 56 of the U.N. Charter. As a resolution of the General Assembly, it is not per se legally binding. At the time of its passage, many of the 48 states which voted to pass the declaration regarded it as a statement of aspirations rather than a legal obligation. There is, however, an argument to be made that since 1948 it has become ***binding as a new rule of customary international law***. Those finding a legal obligation point to a 1968 U.N. resolution proclaiming the Declaration to constitute "an obligation for the members of the international community." Clearly, some of the rights listed have evolved into customary international law.

1. **Civil and political rights:**   The provisions dealing with civil and political rights include prohibition of slavery; torture; discrimination on grounds of race, gender, religion, language, political opinion, nationality, ethnicity, birth or other status; and prohibition of arbitrary arrests or interferences with privacy. Protected rights are: the right to a fair trial, the right to marry, the right to own property, the right to political asylum, the freedoms of religion and expression, freedom of movement, freedoms of peaceful assembly and association, establishment of free elections and equal access to public positions. Political and civil rights are the ***foundation of democratic***

political systems and have been the focus of human rights development in those countries.

2. **Economic, social and cultural rights:**　Communist and developing countries have pushed for greater recognition of these rights, which include the right to social security, full employment, fair work conditions, education, health care, an adequate standard of living, and participation in the community's cultural life.

3. **Limitations on human rights:**　Most human rights documents contain exceptions to the protections provided as necessary to maintain public order and preserve the security of the state. Accordingly, the Universal Declaration allows limitations "for the purpose of securing due recognition and respect for the rights and freedoms of others and of meeting the just requirements of morality, public order and the general welfare in a democratic society." U.N. Charter art. 29, ¶ 2. Such limitations are uncertain in scope and often subject to abuse.

C. **The U.N. human rights covenants:**　The two groups of rights set forth in the Universal Declaration of Human Rights were the basis for the General Assembly's adoption in 1966 of two treaties: the International Covenant on Civil and Political Rights (with the Optional Protocol to the Civil and Political Covenant) and the International Covenant on Economic, Social and Cultural Rights. Both entered into force in 1976 after ratification by 35 states.

1. **The International Covenant on Civil and Political Rights:** This instrument deals, in greater detail, with the same political and civil rights protected by the Declaration of Human Rights.

   a. **Rights protected:**　In addition to the many individual rights protected by the Declaration, the Covenant includes two "rights of peoples" or group rights: the ***right of self-determination*** and the ***right of all peoples to freely dispose of their natural wealth and resources***. Article 27 also provides that ethnic, religious, and linguistic minorities "shall not be denied the right, in community with the other members of their own group, to enjoy their own culture, to profess and practice their own religion, or to use their own language." Interestingly, neither Covenant includes the right to property included in the Universal Declaration.

   b. **Limitations:**　*See* p. 129, *infra* (discussing and listing the limitations under this covenant).

2. **The International Covenant on Economic, Social and Cultural Rights:**　This Covenant, like the one on civil and political rights, amplifies the rights set forth in the Universal Declaration.

    a. Rights protected: In addition to elaboration on the economic, social, and cultural rights in the Universal Declaration, the Covenant also guarantees two collective rights: the *right of self-determination* and the *right of all peoples to freely dispose of their natural wealth and resources*.

    b. Limitations: The legal obligations of the Covenant are much less precise and demanding than those in the Covenant on Civil and Political Rights. Article 2 only requires states to "take steps . . . to the maximum of its available resources . . . with a view to achieving progressively" the rights in the Covenant. Moreover, the state may limit rights "for the purpose of promoting the general welfare in a democratic society." U.N. Charter art. 4.

    c. Review of compliance: Review of compliance is also more limited than in the other Covenant. Implementation is limited to review of state reports by the Economic and Social Council, which has established an expert committee to review reports.

D. The role of specialized agencies of the U.N.: A number of specialized agencies, particularly U.N. commissions, the International Labor Organization (ILO), the United Nations Economic and Social Council (UNESCO), and the Commission on Human Rights, have been active in the area of developing human rights law.

IV. FUNDAMENTAL HUMAN RIGHTS

    Many of the rights discussed below are addressed by specific U.N. treaties and resolutions. Although those instruments are emphasized here, support for these fundamental rights can often be found in other international agreements, as well as regional human rights conventions.

A. The right of peoples to self-determination: The principle of self-determination is the *right of people in a territory to decide the political and legal status of that territory*. The concept has its political origins in the American Declaration of Independence (1776) and has been invoked throughout the 19th and 20th centuries by nationalist movements as the basis for their right to establish independent states. In 1945, the concept of self-determination was incorporated into the U.N. Charter.

    1. The U.N. Charter: Although the U.N. Charter incorporates the concept of self-determination, the general principles of "self-determination of peoples" referred to in the Charter lack concrete definition. The main provisions referring to self-determination are in articles 1, ¶ 2, 55, 73, and 76, ¶ b. Article 1, ¶ 2 states one purpose of the Charter is the promotion of "equal rights" and "self-determination of peoples." Article 55 states that the U.N. promotes solutions to international economic, social, health and related problems with a view to creating stability and friendly relations amongst nations "based on the respect for the principle of equal rights and self-determination of peoples." Article 73 is aimed at U.N. members assuming responsibility for the administration of non-self-governing territories. Such members are to assist in the development of self-government through the establishment of free political institutions. Chapter XII states that a basic objective of the international trusteeship system established for the trust territories after World War II is to promote "progressive development towards self-government or independence as may be appropriate to the particular circumstances of each territory and its peoples and the freely expressed wishes of the peoples concerned." U.N. Charter art. 76, ¶ b.

2. **Other U.N. documents:** The U.N. General Assembly has contributed to the development of the principle of self-determination. In 1960, the U.N. General Assembly adopted the Declaration on the Granting of Independence to Colonial Countries and Peoples, viewed as the basis for the U.N. policy of decolonization. As discussed above, *see* p. 117, *supra*, the International Covenants on Civil and Political Rights and on Economic, Social and Cultural Rights also provided for the right of all peoples to self-determination. The most comprehensive and authoritative treatment of the principle of self-determination is the U.N. Declaration on Principles of International Law Concerning Friendly Relations and Cooperation Among States.

B. **Defining a "people":** " For a group to be characterized as a "people" there must exist the proper objective and subjective elements. The objective element is the existence of an ***ethnic group*** linked by some ***common history***. The common history is often, but not always, expressed by a common language, religion, or territory. The subjective element is the group's ***own identification of itself as a "people."*** The group maintains the desire to live together and uphold common traditions.

C. **Legal status of principle of self-determination:** Despite its inclusion in several U.N. documents, the uncertainty of its legal status results from the lack of concrete definition, as well as its conflict with the well-established principle of sovereignty. The law of decolonization and the right of the inhabitants of an established state to determine their own government are well-accepted, but there is little or no agreement on: the right of groups to secede from states of which they form a part, reunification of peoples in divided states, or the right of minorities to preserve their own separate identities within a state.

D. Rights of indigenous peoples: Indigenous peoples have asserted a right to self-determination to prevent their complete absorption into states dominated by non-aboriginal populations. Indigenous peoples may be seeking to secede to form their own states, or to retain control over their own communities and land. Recognition of such a right of self-determination for indigenous peoples presents conflicts with respect to territorial claims and competition between the sovereignty of the state and the traditional institutions of the indigenous people. The emphasis on integration and assimilation in the Convention Concerning the Protection and Integration of Indigenous and Other Tribal and Semi-Tribal Populations in Independent Countries is disfavored by many indigenous leaders.

E. Civil and political rights: These rights are defined and protected under the International Covenant on Civil and Political Rights, discussed at p. 117, *supra*.

F. Economic, social and cultural rights: These rights are defined and protected under the International Covenant on Economic, Social and Cultural Rights, discussed at p. 117, *supra*.

G. Prohibition of slavery: An early development in the internationalization of human rights was the widespread prohibition against slavery. During the 19th century, major countries abolished slavery resulting in the development of an international standard prohibiting slavery and outlawing the slave trade. This antislavery movement eventually led to the adoption of the Slavery Convention of 1926 and the Protocol amending that Convention. The prohibition against slavery is a ***fundamental norm as a matter of customary international law*** and the norm is recognized as *jus cogens* from which no decognition is permitted.

H. Genocide: The 1948 Convention on the Prevention and Punishment of the Crime of Genocide was adopted by the General Assembly in response to the atrocities of the Holocaust in World War II. Genocide is a crime for which individuals are punishable under international law. *Convention on the Prevention and Punishment of the Crime of Genocide*, Dec. 9, 1948, 78 U.N.T.S. 277.

    1. Definition: Article 2 defines genocide as acts "committed with the intent to destroy, in whole or in part, a national, ethnical, racial or religious group, as such." Prohibited acts include killing members of the group, inflicting serious mental or bodily harm, inflicting living conditions calculated to destroy the group, imposing birth control measures to prevent births within the group, and forcibly transferring children of the group to another group. Under both the Convention and customary international law, genocide is a crime which states undertake to prevent and to punish.

2. **Punishable acts:** Article 3 makes punishable: genocide, conspiracy to commit genocide, direct and public incitement to commit genocide, complicity in genocide, and attempt to commit genocide.

3. **Jurisdiction:** Given the absence of an established international tribunal for genocide or criminal court, punishment is left to the domestic courts of states. Genocide is generally acknowledged as a *universal crime punishable in any state.*

I. **Crimes against humanity:** The Nuremburg Tribunal was established after World War II to punish Nazi leaders in accordance with international law. *See* p. 155, *infra.* The Nuremberg Charter, charging Nazi leaders with "crimes against humanity" invoked the customary law of human rights and was an important step in the development of international human rights law. "Crimes against humanity" were defined as "murder, extermination, enslavement, deportation, and other inhumane acts committed against any civilian population, before or during the war, or persecutions on political, racial or religious ground . . . whether or not in violation of the domestic law of the country where perpetrated." *Agreement for the Prosecution and Punishment of the Major War Criminal of the European Axis*, art. 6, 59 Stat. 1544, 1547-1548. Crimes against humanity can be committed in peacetime as well as war. *See* p. 155, *infra.*

J. **Prohibitions of discrimination:** Racial, sexual, and religious discrimination have been prohibited in certain international treaties.

1. **Racial discrimination:** The principal treaties are the Convention on the Elimination of All Forms of Racial Discrimination, and the International Convention of the Suppression and Punishment of the Crime of Apartheid. The first convention entered into force in 1969, and the Apartheid Convention entered into force in 1976.

a. **International Convention on the Elimination of All Forms of Racial Discrimination:** This convention defines "racial discrimination" as "any distinction, exclusion, restriction or preference based on race, colour, descent of national or ethnic origin which has the purpose or effect of nullifying or impairing the recognition, enjoyment or exercise, on an equal footing, of human rights and fundamental freedoms in the political, social, cultural or any other field of public life." *International Convention on the Elimination of All Forms of Racial Discrimination*, opened for signature Mar. 7, 1966, art. 1, 660 U.N.T.S. 195 [hereinafter *Race Convention*]. State parties must eliminate racial discrimination, (art. 2), and are permitted in some circumstances to take special measures to secure advancement of racial or ethnic groups. Art. 1. States are also obligated to prevent, prohibit and eradicate the practice of apartheid in their territories. Art. 3. The enforcement machinery of this Convention goes beyond the usual reporting mechanisms for implementation. A Committee on the Elimination of Racial Discrimination has jurisdiction to hear complaints by one state against another, as well as individual petitions if the state has agreed to be subject to such petitions. Arts. 11, 14. The action it can take, however, is limited to reports and recommendations.

b. **The International Convention on the Suppression and Punishment of the Crime of Apartheid:** This convention defines apartheid as a *crime against humanity*, involving "inhuman acts committed for the purpose of establishing and maintaining domination by one racial group of persons over any other racial group of persons and systematically oppressing them." "Inhuman acts" include denial of life and liberty through murders, infliction of serious bodily or mental harm, and arbitrary arrests and imprisonment; certain suppressive or divisive legislative measures; and forced labor. *International Convention on the Suppression and Punishment of the Crime of Apartheid*, Nov. 30, 1973, art. II, 13 I.L.M. 50 (1974). Liability extends to conspiracy to commit, aiding and abetting, and direct incitement of the inhuman acts listed in article II. A person charged with the offense may be tried by any state party or before an international penal tribunal yet to be established, and implementation consists of periodic reports to a group of experts.

2. **Sexual discrimination:** The first international document to recognize equal rights without regard to sex was the U.N. Charter. The Convention on the Elimination of All Forms of Discrimination Against Women, which was adopted by the General Assembly in 1979 and entered into force in 1981, focuses on the status of women and provides an extensive bill of rights for women including the right to equal education, health care, and equality before the law.

a. **General protections:** "Discrimination against women" is defined as "any distinction, exclusion or restriction made on the basis of sex which has the effect or purpose of impairing or nullifying the recognition, enjoyment or exercise by women, irrespective of their marital status, on a basis of equality of men and women, of human rights and fundamental freedoms in the political, economic, social, cultural, civil or any other field." *Convention on the Elimination of All Forms of Discrimination Against*

Women, Dec. 18, 1979, art. 1, U.N.G.A. Res 34/180 (xxxiv) [hereinafter *Sex Discrimination Convention*]. Under article 3 of the Convention on the Elimination of All Forms of Discrimination Against Women, "[s]tate Parties shall take in all fields, in particular in the political, social, economic and cultural fields, all appropriate measures, including legislation to ensure the full development and advancement of women, for the purpose of guaranteeing them the exercise and enjoyment of human rights and fundamental freedoms on a basis of equality with men." Special measures designed to achieve equality between men and women shall not be considered discrimination, but shall be discontinued when the objective of equality has been achieved. *Sex Discrimination Convention*, art. 4, U.N.G.A. Res 34/180 (xxxiv). State parties must take all "appropriate measures" "(a) To modify the social and cultural patterns of conduct of men and women, with a view to achieving the elimination of prejudices and customs and all other practices which are based on the idea of the inferiority or the superiority of either of the sexes or on stereotyped roles for men and women. (b) To ensure that family education includes a proper understanding of maternity as a social function and the recognition of the common responsibility of men and women in the upbringing and development of their children." *Sex Discrimination Convention*, art. 5, U.N.G.A. Res 34/180 (xxxiv).

b. **Review of compliance:** Implementation is reviewed through submission of periodic reports by state parties to the Committee on the Elimination of Discrimination Against Women. *Sex Discrimination Convention*, U.N.G.A. Res 34/180 (xxxiv).

3. **Religious discrimination:** Of more recent origin than the other discrimination prohibitions, the prohibition against discrimination on religious grounds is embodied in the 1981 U.N. General Assembly resolution entitled Declaration on the Elimination of All Forms of Intolerance and of Discrimination Based on Religion or Belief. Passed in accordance with the U.N. Charter, it affirms the fundamental freedom of all thought, conscience, and religion; the elimination of discrimination; and the right of children to have religious education. Freedom of religion is subject only to "such limitations as are prescribed by law and are necessary to protect public safely, order, health or morals or the fundamental rights and freedoms of others." Art. 1, ¶ 3. States have an affirmative duty to enact or rescind legislation in order to prevent or eliminate discrimination based on religious beliefs. Art. 4. Among other specific rights, the Declaration acknowledges the right of parents to have access to religious education and the right to teach a religion or belief in suitable

places. Arts. 5, 6. Nothing in the Declaration, however, is to restrict or derogate from any right in the Universal Declaration on Human Rights or the International Covenants on Human Rights. Art. 8.

K. Freedom from torture: There are ***no justifications for torture*** or exceptions to its prohibition. *Convention Against Torture and Other Cruel, Inhuman or Degrading Treatment or Punishment*, entered into force June 26, 1987, art. 2, ¶¶ 2, 3, U.N. Doc. E/CN. 4/1984/72, 23 I.L.M. 1027 [hereinafter *Torture Convention*]. States must adopt measures to prevent torture in their jurisdiction, and ensure that torture, complicity, and attempts to commit torture are criminal offenses. Art. 2, ¶ 1; art. 4.

1. **Definition of torture:** The Convention Against Torture and other Cruel, Inhuman or Degrading Treatment or Punishment, which entered into force in 1987 defines torture as ". . . any act by which severe pain or suffering, whether physical or mental, is intentionally inflicted on a person for such purposes as obtaining from him or a third person information or a confession, punishing him for an act he or a third person has committed or is suspected of having committed, or intimidating or coercing him or a third person, or for any reason based on discrimination of any kind, when such pain or suffering is inflicted by or at the instigation of or with the consent or acquiescence of a public official or other person acting in an official capacity. It does not include pain or suffering arising only from, inherent in or incidental to lawful sanctions." *Torture Convention*, art. 1, ¶ 1.

2. **Committee against torture:** Implementation of articles 2(1) and 4 is monitored through periodic state reports to a Committee Against Torture. If a state consents, the Committee can hear interstate complaints and individual complaints. *Torture Convention*, arts. 21, 22. If no solution is reached, the Committee issues a report to the parties involved. The Committee also has the unusual power to initiate inquiries, unless a state has declined to recognize this Committee function at the time of its signature on ratification. Arts. 20, 28.

L. Rights of refugees: The principal international instruments concerning refugees are the 1951 Geneva Convention Relating to the Status of Refugees, the 1957 Hague amendments to that convention, and the 1967 Protocol Relating to the Status of Refugees. At present, customary international law ***does not appear to recognize a right to asylum***, although this rule has been the subject of much criticism.

1. **Definition of a refugee:** The 1951 Geneva Convention defines a refugee as a person who "owing to well-founded fear of being perse-

cuted for reasons of race, religion, nationality, membership of a particular social group or political opinion, is outside the country of his nationality and is unable or, owing to such fear, is unwilling to avail himself of the protection of that country; or who, not having a nationality and being outside the country of his former habitual residence as a result of such events, is unable, or owing to such fear, is unwilling to return to it." *Geneva Convention Relating to the Status of Refugees*, July 28, 1951, art. 1, § A, ¶ 2, 189 U.N.T.S. 137. In *INS v. Elias-Zacarias*, 112 S. Ct. 812 (1992), the Supreme Court held that a Guatemalan native had failed to show persecution on account of political opinion based on his resistance to recruitment by a guerilla movement because he was afraid the government would retaliate against him or his family.

2. **State's obligation to refugees:** The Convention aims to secure the best possible treatment of refugees lawfully within a state, and its provisions address many topics, including access to courts, employment, housing and education. Refugees illegally within a state must be given a reasonable time to resettle. The Convention and subsequent instruments do not, however, guarantee any right of entry into a country, or impose any duty on the state to admit refugees. The ***state has a right to grant asylum***, but the ***individual has no right to demand asylum***. Articles 13 and 14 of the Universal Declaration of Human Rights and the General Assembly's 1967 Declaration on Territorial Asylum recognize the "right to leave any country, including [one's] own" and the "right to seek and to enjoy in other countries asylum from persecution." Those rights, however, are not coupled with a corresponding state obligation to grant asylum. The principle of *nonrefoulement* prohibits return of the refugee to the state of persecution, and an admitted refugee may only be deported for reasons of state security.

3. **The *Haitian Refugees* Case:** In *Sale v. Haitian Centers Council, Inc.*, 113 S. Ct. 2549 (1993), the U.S. Supreme Court held that neither domestic immigration law or Article 33 of the Refugee Convention, prohibiting return of a refugee to the state of persecution, applied extraterritorially to interception upon the high seas.

4. **Diplomatic asylum:** Diplomatic asylum is the ***granting of refuge by a state in its embassies, ships, or aircraft in the territory of another state***. Once diplomatic asylum is granted, there is a right of safe conduct from the foreign state. Beyond that, the rules of asylum are generally based on treaty rather than customary international law.

V. NEWLY EMERGING RIGHTS AND FUNDAMENTAL RIGHTS RECOGNIZED AS CUSTOMARY INTERNATIONAL LAW

Many of the rights recognized in international agreements above are also recognized as customary international law. An early invocation of human rights as part of customary international law was found in the Nuremberg Charter, charging Nazi leaders with "crimes against humanity." A more recent acknowledgment of the rights recognized in customary law is found in *Filartiga v. Pena-Irala*, 630 F.2d 876, 884, 890 (2d Cir. 1980) (". . . we conclude that official torture is now prohibited by the law of nations."). "[T]he torturer has become — like the pirate and slave trader before him — *hostis humani generis*, an enemy of all mankind."

A. **Restatement § 702:** The comments following this section indicate that it is a list of human rights generally accepted as customary law. The comments further state that the list is neither complete nor closed and other rights may have also reached the status of customary law. "A state violates international law if, as a matter of state policy, it practices, encourages or condones genocide, slavery or slave trade, the murder or causing the disappearance of individuals, torture or other cruel, inhuman or degrading treatment or punishment, prolonged arbitrary detention, systematic racial discrimination, or consistent patterns of gross violations of internationally recognized human rights."

B. **Creation of customary human rights law:** The Reporter's Notes to Restatement § 701 suggest that customary human rights law is established in a manner different from other customary law, because historically human rights have been a matter between a state and its own individuals. According to the notes, customary human rights law may be established through: virtually universal adherence to the U.N. Charter; virtually universal adherence to the Universal Declaration of Human Rights; widespread participation of states in preparation and adoption of international human rights agreements; widespread support for United Nations General Assembly resolutions applying international human rights principles; and frequent invocation and application of international human rights principles in both domestic practice and diplomatic practice.

C. **The evolution of new rights:** Human rights law is constantly evolving from recognition of rights in treaties, U.N. resolutions, and domestic state practice to the level of custom and *jus cogens*. Many protections originate in internal domestic law, with gradual recognition as general principles of international law if common to most legal systems. A few examples of more recently developed rights include the rights in the 1989 Convention on the Rights of the Child and the right to development in the 1986 General Assembly Resolution on the Right to Development.

VI. ENFORCEMENT OF HUMAN RIGHTS LAW IN THE U.S. COURTS

As of 1986, the only comprehensive human rights treaties ratified by the United States were the Refugee Protocol and the Convention on the Political Rights of Women. The Genocide Convention was ratified in 1986 with a number of reservations, declarations, and understandings. The Genocide Convention Implementation Act is 18 U.S.C. § 1091. In 1990, the United States Senate ratified the Torture Convention, but stated that the President should not ratify the Convention until implementing legislation had been passed. In 1992, Congress passed the Torture Victim Protection Act, 28 U.S.C. § 1350 (1992), which creates a civil action for damages from torture. The Act does not implement the Torture Convention which requires criminal sanctions for violations. Also in 1992, the United States ratified the International Covenant on Civil and Political Rights, but as of 1993 had not passed any implementing legislation. As of June, 1993, the United States had not ratified the International Covenant on Economic, Social and Cultural Rights, the Race Convention, the American Convention on Human Rights, the Apartheid Convention, the Convention on Elimination of All Forms of Discrimination Against Women, or the Convention on the Rights of the Child. Because the United States has failed to ratify so many human rights treaties, or to implement non-self-executing treaties, enforcement of human rights law in United States courts is largely dependent on *incorporation of custom by courts into United States law* (*see* p. 43 *supra*) and *specific legislative provisions*, such as the Alien Tort Statute (28 U.S.C. § 1350). The Alien Tort Statute confers district court jurisdiction over any "civil action by an alien for a tort only, committed in violation of the law of nations or a treaty of the United States."

Example: In *Filartiga v. Pena-Irala*, 630 F.2d 876 (2d Cir. 1980), the Second Circuit Court of Appeals held that *freedom from torture was part of customary international law* for which § 1350 provides federal jurisdiction. *See also Trajano v. Marcos,*

978 F.2d 493 (9th Cir. 1992) (reaffirming the *Filartiga* approach).

Example: In contrast, the D.C. Circuit Court of Appeals in *Tel-Oren v. Libya Arab Republic*, 726 F.2d 774 (D.C. Cir. 1984), took a much more restrictive approach to § 1350. In *Tel-Oren*, the plaintiffs sued the alleged perpetrators of an attack on a civilian bus in Israel. The three-judge court dismissed the case with three separate opinions. Judge Robb held the case involved a nonjusticiable political question. Judge Edwards endorsed *Filartiga*, but concluded that non-state, politically motivated acts of terrorism were not prohibited by customary international law. Judge Bork concluded that the Alien Tort Statute only provided jurisdiction over alien tort suits for which *international law* recognizes an individual cause of action (such as violation of safe conducts, piracy, and infringement of the rights of ambassadors).

VII. DEROGATION FROM PROTECTION OF RIGHTS

Agreements ensuring protection of fundamental human rights often allow derogation from the rights in times of "*public emergencies*." A wide margin of appreciation is given to countries to determine whether such a "public emergency" exists in their state. Human rights conventions with derogation clauses include the International Covenant on Civil and Political Rights (article 4), Convention Relating to the Status of Refugees (article 9), Convention Relating to the Status of Stateless Persons (article 9), European Convention for the Protection of Human Rights and Fundamental Freedoms (article 15), and the European Social Charter (article 30). The derogation provisions of the Covenant on Civil and Political Rights and the European Convention serve as key examples, demonstrating the necessary circumstances and limitations to derogation.

A. **The International Covenant on Civil and Political Rights:** There are limitations on, and procedures regulating derogation under this Convention.

1. **Requirements for derogation:** Article 4 provides derogation from the Covenant's obligations under the following circumstances. It must be a "time of public emergency which threatens the life of the nation." The existence of such dire circumstances must be "officially proclaimed." Derogation is permitted "only to the extent

strictly required by the exigencies of the situation." The measures may not be "inconsistent with their other obligations under international law." The measures may not "involve discrimination solely on the ground of race, colour, sex, language, religion or social origin."

2. **Limitations to derogation under the Covenant:** Certain rights may not be derogated from, even in times of public emergency. Article 4, ¶2 states that no derogation is permitted from the rights accorded by articles 6, 7, 8 (¶¶ 1 and 2), 11, 15, 16, and 18.

   a. Article 6 protects the inherent right to life, prohibits genocide, restricts death penalty to only the most serious crimes, requires rights to seek pardon or commutation of death penalty, and prohibits death penalty for persons under 18 and pregnant women.

   b. Article 7 prohibits torture and cruel, inhuman or degrading treatment of punishment.

   c. Article 8, Paragraph 1 prohibits slavery and slave trade. Paragraph 2 prohibits holding anyone in servitude.

   d. Article 11 prohibits imprisonment for failure to fulfill contractual obligation.

   e. Article 15 prohibits conviction for act or omission not a criminal offense under either national or international law at time it was committed. Also prohibits imposition of a heavier penalty than was applicable at time crime was committed.

   f. Article 16 guarantees each person everywhere a right to recognition as a person before the law.

   g. Article 18 protects rights of religious freedoms and prevents imposition of religion.

3. **Procedure:** Article 4, ¶ 3 requires a state availing itself of the right of derogation to follow specific steps. For instance, a state must immediately inform other state parties to the Covenant of the provisions from which it has derogated, using the U.N. Secretary-General as intermediary; it must provide the reasons for derogation; and it must communicate the date on which it terminates the derogation.

B. **European Convention for the Protection of Human Rights and Fundamental Freedoms:** The derogation provision of the European Convention is similar to that of the Covenant on Civil and Political Rights.

1. **Requirements for derogation:** Article 15, ¶ 1 permits derogation: "[i]n time of war or other public emergency threatening the life of the nation"; "[o]nly to the extent strictly required by the exigen-

cies of the situation;" and "[p]rovided such measures are not inconsistent with its other obligations under international law." European Convention for the Protection of Human Rights and Fundamental Freedoms, Nov. 4, 1950, art. 15, ¶ 1, Europ. T.S. No. 5 [hereinafter European Human Rights Convention]. The European Court of Human Rights has given states a wide "margin of appreciation" in determining whether the first condition exists, but has been more demanding in determining whether the second condition has been satisfied.

2. **Limitations to derogation:** Article 15, ¶ 2 prohibits derogation from articles 2, 3, 4 (paragraph I) and 7.

   a. Article 2 protects right to life, except for executions resulting from conviction of a crime for which the death penalty is provided by law. Deprivation of life does not violate this article if it occurs as a result of self-defense; in the course of attempts to make a lawful arrest or prevent escape from lawful detention; or from lawful action taken to quell riots or insurrections.

   b. Article 3 prohibits torture or inhuman or degrading treatment or punishment.

   c. Article 4 prohibits slavery or servitude.

   d. Article 7 prohibits ex post facto criminal law.

3. **Procedure:** Article 15, ¶ 3 requires the derogating party to fully inform the Secretary-General of the Council of Europe of measures taken and the reasons therefor and further inform the Secretary-General when derogation has ceased and provisions of the Convention are once again fully executed.

4. **Clauses of limitation:** A number of the rights enumerated in the European Convention on Human Rights also have their own clauses of limitation, which allow restrictions on the right as necessary to protect national security, safety, and health or morals.

VIII. REGIONAL HUMAN RIGHTS LAW AND INSTITUTIONS

Regional human rights regimes operate in Western Europe, the Americas and Africa. Asia is not yet represented by a regional system and the Permanent Arab Commission on Human Rights has focused mostly on the rights of Palestinian Arabs in Israeli-occupied territories. The significance of the regional regimes, particularly the European system, is attributed to three factors. First, the relative homogeneity of socio-economic, cultural, political, and juridical characteristics permits the members of a regional system to act in concert with one another, thus facilitating the promotion and protection of human rights. Second, the geographic proximity of states within a region results in more or less common interests and an interdependence between them. Third, the relative homogeneity and geographic proximity facilitate the actual process of investigating and remedying human rights violations.

A. **The European system of human rights law:** European human rights law is contained primarily in the European Convention for the Protection of Human Rights and Freedoms and subsequent protocols for civil and political rights, and the European Social Charter for Economic and Social Rights.

1. **The European Convention on Human Rights:** The organization and content of the European Convention is similar to the International Covenant on Civil and Political Rights. As of 1995, 30 states were bound by the Convention's terms, including every member of the Council of Europe. The European Convention and its protocols include: the right to life; freedom from torture and inhuman treatment; freedom from slavery, servitude or forced labor; rights to a fair and public hearing to determine civil rights and criminal charges; freedom of expression and religion; rights of privacy; rights of assembly and association; and freedom from discrimination. Protocols that have entered into force in the last decade prohibit capital punishment in time of peace and double jeopardy. The Convention differs from the International Covenant by failing to recognize a people's right of self-determination or make any reference to the rights of people belonging to ethnic, religious or linguistic minorities. The Convention also differs by not making any reference to the rights of the child or to prohibitions on war propaganda or propaganda inciting discrimination.

2. **The European Social Charter:** In addition to the European Convention's protection of political and civil rights, there is promotion and protection of economic and social rights under the European Social Charter, which has been ratified by approximately half of the states in the Council of Europe. The Charter's recognition of economic, social and cultural rights includes: the right to work, the right to fair compensation, the rights of children, the rights of employed women to protection, and the right to social and medical assistance. States have some latitude in selecting which of the enumerated rights they will accept. European Social Charter, Oct. 18, 1961, art. 20, Europ. T.S. No. 35. Its lack of adjudicative machinery (implementation is through a reporting system like many human

rights treaties) makes it less prominent than the Convention in the enforcement of human rights in Europe.

B. The institutions of the European regime: The European Convention of Human Rights has established an effective human rights regime, enforcing rights through the European Commission of Human Rights, the European Court of Human Rights, and the Committee of Ministers of the Council of Europe.

   1. **European Commission of Human Rights:** The Commission is composed of a number of members equal to the number of state parties to the Convention. As of 1995, there were 30 states bound by the terms of the convention. The Commission is vested with both compulsory and optional jurisdiction.

      a. **Compulsory jurisdiction:** It may hear cases filed by one state against another state as long as both states have ratified the Convention. *European Human Rights Convention*, art. 24, Europ. T.S. No. 5.

      b. **Optional jurisdiction:** The Commission has optional jurisdiction with respect to individual petitions. The optional jurisdiction is invoked only if a state has ratified the Convention and declared its acceptance of the Commission's right to hear individual petitions. *European Human Rights Convention*, art. 25, Europ. T.S. No. 5. Most states have made such a declaration.

   2. **European Court of Human Rights:** The Court is comprised of a number of members equal to the membership of the Council of Europe. The Court's jurisdiction is optional and is not invoked by mere ratification of the Convention. Most state parties have made the necessary special declaration accepting the jurisdiction of the Court. Cases may be referred to the Court by states, the Commission, or individuals, and the Court's judgments are final and binding. The Court is vested with the power to award damages. The Court also has limited authority to issue advisory opinions. Decisions of the Court are enforced by the Committee of Ministers.

   3. **Committee of Ministers of the Council of Europe:** The Committee is made up of one representative for each member state of the Council of Europe. It appoints the members of the Human Rights Commission and decides those cases which the Commission fails to settle and which are not referred to the European Court within three months after the Commission's report.

C. The process of implementation and enforcement: The process discussed below is the adjudicative process under the European Convention, followed by a brief description of the reportorial system under the European Social Charter.

1. **Human Rights Commission:** Consideration of claims submitted by either states or individuals begins with the Commission. The Commission's work involves three stages. The Convention permits a state to submit a complaint on behalf of a non-national individual.

   a. **Stage 1:** The Commission considers the admissibility of the case, determined by whether the petition presents a *prima facie* case for violations of specific provisions of the Convention and by whether all available domestic remedies have already been exhausted. An inadmissible case is closed, while admissible cases proceed.

   b. **Stage 2:** The Commission ascertains the facts and attempts to resolve the case with a friendly settlement. Reports on friendly settlements are sent to the states concerned and to the Council of Europe for publication.

   c. **Stage 3:** Finally, the Commission prepares a report regarding unsettled cases, including findings of facts and its opinions with regard to violations of the Convention. This report is submitted to the Committee of Ministers of the Council of Europe. During the three month period following submission of the report to the Committee, the Commission or any interested state party may refer cases to the Court, provided the Court has jurisdiction.

   Note: Prior to the entry into force of Protocol 9, adopted in 1990, individual claims could come before the Court only through submission by the Commission because only states or the Commission could bring cases before the Court.

2. **Committee of Ministers:** Cases not submitted to the Court within three months are decided on by the Committee of Ministers, and states are obliged to take measures to satisfy the decision of the Committee. The Commission typically leaves to the Committee only those cases in which the Commission believes there has been no violation of the Convention. The Committee can find a violation of the Convention only by a two-thirds vote, short of which it decides to take no action.

3. **European Court of Human Rights:** The European Court of Human Rights is the judicial organ of the Council of Europe, an organization distinct from the European Community. As of 1995, every state which is a party to the European Convention had accepted the jurisdiction of the Court. The member most frequently before the Court has been the United Kingdom which has no constitution and no formal domestic guarantee of individual rights, which often forces individuals to seek protection for individual rights in tection for individual rights in this forum. The number of judges is

equal to the number of members to the Council and there is usually one judge from each member state. No two judges can be nationals of the same state. Judges serve for staggered nine-year terms, with one-third of the judges being elected every three years.

Note: Before reaching the Court, a case is first dealt with by the Commission of Human Rights. Admissible complaints are first investigated by the Commission, which then attempts to negotiate a settlement. If the negotiations fail, the Commission sends a report to the Committee of Ministers, another organ of the Council of Europe. In the three-month period following issuance of the report, the case may be referred to the Court but only by the Commission or the interested member-state. The case may be referred to the Court by the Commission, the interested member-state, or an individual applicant pursuant to a state's acceptance of Protocol 9 (see above). If a case has not been otherwise referred to the Court, the final determination is made by the Committee of Ministers.

4. **The European Social Charter:** The Charter does not provide an adjudicative process similar to that of the European Convention. Rights are promoted and protected primarily by reportorial means. *European Social Charter*, arts. 21-29, Europ. T.S. No. 35. State parties "undertake to consider the economic, social and cultural rights enumerated [in the Charter]" and to pursue such aims with appropriate measures. States report on their progress in biennial reports submitted to the Council of Europe's Secretary-General. The reports are examined by the Committee of Experts; then passed on with the Committee of Expert's conclusions to the Governmental Social Committee and finally to the Council's Consultative Assembly. The Committee of Ministers may, on the basis of reports and consultation with the foregoing bodies, make necessary recommendations to the state.

D. **Inter-American system — human rights law:** Outside of Europe the most developed regime of human rights law is in the Americas. The primary sources for human rights law in the Americas are the Charter of the Organization of American States (OAS) and the 1969 American Convention on Human Rights.

1. **OAS Charter:** The original OAS Charter itself made little mention of human rights and provided no machinery for the protection of human rights. An enumeration of substantive rights was embodied in the American Declaration of the Rights and Duties of Man, but until 1960 the Declaration served only as a nonbinding resolution of the OAS. In 1960, however, the OAS formed the Inter-American Commission on Human Rights to promote respect for human rights. In 1970, the Commission was elevated to the status of an

organ of the OAS in order to further implementation of the American Declaration. The American Declaration is similar to the European Convention on Human Rights and includes: the rights to life, liberty and security of one's person; equality before the law, religious freedom; freedom of expression, special protection for pregnant women and children; freedom of movement; right to an education, etc.

2. **The American Convention on Human Rights:** The second source of Inter-American human rights law is the 1969 American Convention on Human Rights, which entered into force in 1978 and has been signed but not ratified by the U.S. The American Convention is similar to the European Convention and has a similar institutional structure. The American Convention focuses on protection of political and civil rights such as the right to life, freedom from torture and inhuman treatment, prohibition of *ex post facto* criminal laws, freedom of association, right to participate in free elections, etc. Unlike the Declaration, the American Convention does not include the right to an education or other economic and social rights. Rather, the economic and social rights are to be achieved "progressively by legislation or other appropriate means." *American Convention on Human Rights*, Nov. 22, 1969, art. 26, 9 I.L.M. 673 (1970). The Inter-American Commission, established originally under the OAS Charter, has also been incorporated into the institutional framework established by the American Convention.

E. **Institutions of the Inter-American system:** The two organs responsible for supervising implementation and enforcement of human rights are the Inter-American Commission on Human Rights and the Inter-American Court of Human Rights.

1. **Inter-American Commission on Human Rights:** The Inter-American Commission is an organ of both the OAS and the American Convention on Human Rights. It consists of seven members elected for four-year, once-renewable terms by the OAS General Assembly to "represent all member countries."

   a. **Functions under the OAS Charter:** Its principal function under the OAS is to ensure compliance by OAS member states to their obligations under the OAS Charter. Note that states, such as the U.S., which have not ratified the Convention are nevertheless obliged under the Charter to promote human rights. In addition to receiving individual communications, preparing country studies, and reporting on the status of human rights in various states, the Commission may investigate human rights conditions without awaiting formal individual or interstate complaints.

b. Functions under the Convention: The Commission's principal function under the Convention is to consider charges of violations of the rights guaranteed by the American Convention on Human Rights. The American Convention differs from other international human rights regimes by making the right of individual petition mandatory and interstate petitions optional. Thus, the Commission has authority to deal with individual petitions against any state which has ratified the Convention, but may only consider interstate claims if both states have made a special declaration in addition to ratification.

2. Inter-American Court of Human Rights: The Court is composed of seven judges elected by state parties to the American Convention to six-year, once-renewable terms. The judges are not elected by the OAS General Assembly, because the Court was not established under the OAS Charter, as was the Commission. Only state parties and the Commission have the right to bring cases before the Court, which has both contentious and advisory jurisdiction.

a. Contentious jurisdiction: Under its contentious jurisdiction, the Court has authority to decide claims that a state party violated rights guaranteed by the American Convention. Contentious jurisdiction is optional and cases may be filed by or against only those states which have accepted such jurisdiction.

b. Advisory jurisdiction: The Court's authority is broader under its advisory jurisdiction than under its contentious jurisdiction. It may render opinions interpreting not only the American Convention but also other human rights treaties of the inter-American regime. All OAS member states and all OAS organs may invoke the advisory jurisdiction of the court.

F. Process of implementation and enforcement: As in the European system, claims of human rights violations are first considered by the Commission and then referable to the Court.

1. The Commission: Claims of violations may be brought before the Commission by individuals or organizations, and the complainant need not have been a victim of the violation. All domestic remedies must have first been exhausted, and the complaint must state a *prima facie* case. Rejections by the Commission at this stage are not appealable. Following admission of a case, the Commission investigates the facts of the case and encourages negotiation of a friendly settlement. If the parties fail to reach a settlement, the Commission then prepares a report with its factual findings and recommendations and submits it to the parties. During the three months following submission of the report, the Commission's recommendations may be accepted, or the case may be referred to the Court. If neither occurs, the Commission is then authorized to make final determinations and require the defendant state to adopt certain measures by established deadlines. Compared to its European counterpart, however, the Commission's reports and subsequent resolutions have thus far shown little legal effectiveness.

2. **The Court:** Either the Commission or state parties to the Convention which have accepted the Court's jurisdiction may refer cases to the Court. The Court issues final and binding judgments on the parties and also has the authority to award damages, render declaratory decrees, and occasionally enter preliminary injunctions.

G. **African regional system — human rights law:** The primary source of law is the African Charter of Human and People's Rights, which entered into force in 1986. Thirty members of the Organization of African Unity thus far have ratified the Charter, which differs significantly from the European and American human rights regimes. It guarantees economic, social and cultural rights as well as political and civil rights; it is concerned with the rights of "peoples" as well as individuals; and it proclaims the duties as well as rights of individuals. The recent emergence of the African human rights system means that many provisions of the Charter have yet to be interpreted and applied. The Charter also differs significantly from the European and American human rights regime, because it ***does not provide a human rights court***. The Charter does, however, establish an African Commission on Human and People's Rights to consider state and individual petitions. The Charter places a relatively strong emphasis on friendly settlements and negotiations.

IX. INTERNATIONAL HUMANITARIAN LAW

A. **Generally:** International humanitarian law attempts to place limitations upon the conduct of warfare in order to prevent unnecessary suffering of civilians and combatants. This is more fully discussed at p. 148, *infra*.

CHAPTER 9
THE LAW OF ARMED CONFLICT

I.   ARMED CONFLICT GENERALLY

The law of armed conflict is that area of international law which governs the circumstances under which a state may use military force as a means of coercion. In addition, once armed hostilities have commenced, the humanitarian law of armed conflict attempts to minimize human suffering by placing limitations upon the means by which force may be exerted and the targets against which such force may be directed. Early international legal scholars referred to this area of law as the law of war, and divided it into two sections — *jus ad bello*, the law leading up to war, and *jus in bello*, the law during war. This section addresses only hostilities of an international character. The law relating to civil conflict is addressed on p. 158, *infra*.

A. Definition of war and armed conflict: The terms "war" and "armed conflict" are extremely difficult to define. Some scholars define war narrowly, reserving it for circumstances in which one or more of the states involved in hostilities has actually declared war. Others define the term more broadly, to encompass any armed hostilities carried on between states or even between citizens in the same state. Armed conflict is an equally elusive term. Some scholars use the term "armed conflict" to refer to hostilities which in some fashion fall short of an all-out, formally declared war, while others use it to refer to any state of armed hostilities, including declared wars. For the purposes of this text, the two terms will be used interchangeably to mean any armed conflict beyond isolated and sporadic acts of violence between the armed forces of states.

Note: This definition excludes armed hostilities of an internal nature, or civil wars, which will be dealt with in the final section of this heading. During the 19th century, a state had to declare war before international law would recognize its existence. As late as 1907, the Hague Convention provided that a nation should not begin hostilities without "previous and explicit warning" in the form of a declaration of war or an ultimatum. However, in recent years many states have engaged in hostilities without a formal declaration of war. In any event, whether war is formally declared is a question of decreasing importance because the applicability of the Geneva Conventions is not restricted to declared wars and the U.N. Charter speaks in terms of the use of force, rather than in terms of war.

B. Legal prohibitions against international armed conflict: During the 19th Century, every sovereign state was considered to have the right to wage war. After the devastation of World War I, the Charter of the League of Nations provided for a three month "cooling off" period before a state could commence hostilities as well as imposing certain other limitations on the ability of a state to wage war. In the Kellogg-Briand Pact of 1928 (or Treaty of Paris) the signatory states *renounced war* as an instrument of national policy and agreed that disputes were to be settled only by pacific means.

1. **The U.N. Charter's requirements of first resort to peaceful means:** The Charter requires members to settle their disputes by *peaceful* means. U.N. Charter, art. 2, ¶ 3; Art. 33, discussed in p. 101 *supra*. If settlement fails, the parties to a dispute must refer a dispute which is a threat to peace to the Security Council. Art. 37, ¶

   a. **U.N. peacekeeping functions:** The Security Council has very broad powers to carry out its peacekeeping functions. *See Advisory Opinion on Namibia*, 1971 I.C.J. Rep. 16. The General Assembly also has the authority to recommend peaceful settlement. *See* U.N. Charter, arts. 11, 12. The Security Council has the primary responsibility for maintaining international peace and security. Art. 24. When the veto has prevented the Security Council from acting, the General Assembly has used its secondary authority to maintain peace.

   b. **Peacekeeping forces and the Certain Expenses case:** In 1956, the General Assembly under the Uniting for Peace Resolution (discussed *infra*) sent troops (United Nations Emergency Forces I, or UNEF I) to supervise a cease-fire after Israel, France, and the United Kingdom had attacked Egypt. In 1960, the Security Council sent troops (the United Nations force in the Congo, or ONUC) to the Congo to restore order after Belgium deployed troops in the Congolese civil war. UNEF I was deployed in Egypt with its consent; ONUC was deployed with the consent of the Congolese government (although it was far from clear who the government was). Several countries, including the Soviet Union and France, refused to pay the expenses of the forces, arguing that these "peacekeeping forces" were unauthorized under the Charter and, thus, their expenses were not expenses of the U.N. within the meaning of article 17. In an advisory opinion requested by the General Assembly, the ICJ concluded that both forces were not "enforcement action" within the meaning of Chapter VII because the troops have been deployed with consent. *Advisory Opinion on Certain Expenses of the United Nations*, 1962 I.C.J. 151 (Jul. 20). Despite the decision, several countries continued to refuse to pay and were threatened (but not sanctioned) with loss of voting privileges under article 19. Expenses of peacekeeping forces, as well as of enforcement actions, continues to be a troublesome issue.

c. **Enforcement action distinguished:** Enforcement action within the meaning of Chapter VII, involving deployment of troops, differs from peacekeeping forces in that enforcement action is imposed without consent of the state against which such action is directed.

2. **The U.N. Charter prohibition against the use of force:** Article 2, ¶ 4 of the U.N. Charter provides that:

> All Members shall refrain in their international relations from the threat or use of force against the territorial integrity or political independence of any state, or in any other manner inconsistent with the Purposes of the United Nations.

Article 2, ¶ 4 is recognized as *customary international law*. It should be noted that article 2, ¶ 4 bans not only the use of *force*, but the *threat of force*. While it is clear that this provision bans most uses of force, there has been considerable debate as to whether article 2, ¶ 4 constitutes an absolute ban on the use of force except as expressly permitted by the Charter. The viewpoints summarized below represent the two extremes of this debate; many scholars have adopted views somewhere in between these extremes.

a. **The restrictive reading:** Scholars supporting the restrictive reading argue that the words of article 2, ¶ 4 must be given their plain, common-sense meaning. Under this approach, article 2, ¶ 4 prohibits only the use of force which is directed against the territorial integrity or political independence of any state. This interpretation would allow a state to use force against another state for other purposes — for example, protect itself against possible attack or protect the lives of nationals or their property in another state because in both instances the primary purpose would not be to impinge on the territorial integrity or political independence of the second state. This interpretation also opens the door to recognition of humanitarian intervention, by which a state may forcibly intervene in the domestic affairs of another state in order to rectify gross deprivation of human rights. Even assuming the restrictive reading is appropriate, the final phrase of article 2, ¶ 4, which limits the use of force to actions that are consistent with the purposes of the United Nations, may impose limits on a state's ability to use force. Critics of this view point to this last phrase as indicating that any use of force not expressly authorized by the Charter is inconsistent with the Charter's purpose to promote and maintain international peace and security.

b. **The expansive reading:** Scholars supporting the expansive reading contend that the language in article 2, ¶ 4 should be interpreted in light of the *travaux prèparatoires*, which indicate that the phrase "use of force against the territorial integrity or political independence of a state" was not intended to be restrictive but, on the contrary, was intended to provide more specific guarantees to small states. Additionally, they point out that the provision must be viewed in light of the presumption against self-help and use of force which underlies the Charter, as indicated in the final phrase of the article. Under this view, article 2, ¶ 4 should be given an expansive reading, prohibiting all use of force except as expressly permitted by the U.N. Charter.

The decision of the ICJ in the *Corfu Channel case* (*U.K. v. Alb.*), 1949 I.C.J. 4 (Apr. 9), lends support to this reading of article 2, ¶ 4. After British warships were struck by mines while engaging in innocent passage through Albanian territorial waters, the United Kingdom sent warships to sweep the waters for mines, a form of intervention into Albanian territory. In response to the United Kingdom's asserted justifications of self-help, necessity, or anticipatory self-defense, the Court concluded: The court can only regard the alleged right of intervention as the manifestation of a policy of force, such as has, in the past, given rise to most serious abuses and such as cannot, whatever be the present defects in international organization, find a place in international law. Intervention is perhaps still less admissible in the particular form it would take here; for, from the nature of things, it would be reserved for the most powerful States, and might easily lead to perverting the administration of international justice itself. The United Kingdom's agent, in his speech in reply, has further classified "Operation Retail" among methods of self-protection or self-help. The Court cannot accept this defence either. Between independent states, respect for territorial sovereignty is an essential foundation of international relations. The Court recognizes that the Albanian Government's complete failure to carry out its duties after the explosions, and the dilatory nature of its diplomatic notes, are extenuating circumstances for the action of the United Kingdom Government. But to ensure respect for international law, of which it is the organ, the Court must declare that the action of the British Navy constituted a violation of Albanian sovereignty.

C. Threat or use of force authorized by the U.N. Charter: Even within the U.N. Charter, the article 2, ¶ 4 *prohibition on the use of force is not absolute*. There are only a few instances in which nonconsensual use of force is expressly authorized by the Charter.

1. **Article 51 self-defense:** Article 51 of the U.N. Charter provides in part that:

   > Nothing in the present Charter shall impair the inherent right of individual or collective self-defence if an armed attack occurs against a Member of the United Nations, until the Security Council has taken measures necessary to maintain international peace and security.

   a. **Scope of article 51:** As with the prohibition against the use of force, the exclusivity of the right of self-defense as defined by article 51 has been the subject of considerable debate.

      i. **Exclusivity:** There is disagreement as to whether article 51, with its apparent requirement that an armed attack already have occurred, provides the exclusive justification for self-defense or whether states retain some customary right to self-defense that might be broader in scope than that contained in article 51. Proponents of exclusivity argue that allowing states to define broadly what may trigger a right of self-defense undermines the purpose of the Charter to maintain peace.

      ii. **Anticipatory self-defense:** There is disagreement as to whether or not a state may, under article 51 or under customary international law, justify the use of force in anticipatory self-defense when an attack is imminent. Assuming such a right exists, there is great uncertainty as to how imminent the attack must be. The requirements for a valid act of self-defense are discussed at p.143, *infra*.

         Examples: In 1981, when Israel attacked a nuclear reactor under construction in Iraq it claimed would be used to make nuclear weapons, Israel's justification was anticipatory self-defense. The Security Council condemned Israel's action but imposed no sanctions. In 1986, the U.S. asserted anticipatory self-defense to justify the bombing of Libya after an attack against U.S. soldiers in West Berlin which the U.S. claimed was sponsored by Libya.

      iii. **Right of collective self-defense:** If a state is entitled to use force in self-defense under article 51, other states are entitled to come to the defense of the attacked state in collective self-defense. There is some question as to whether a state may exercise the collective right of self-defense without an explicit request for assistance from the state on whose behalf the right is being exercised. In *Nicaragua v. United States*, the ICJ concluded that the U.S. was not entitled to come to the defense of El Salvador, Honduras, and Costa Rica because at the time it had not been requested to do so.

    iv. Duration of right of self-defense: It is unclear whether the right of a state to act in self-defense comes to an end as soon as the Security Council has taken action. It is clear that self-defense does not justify reprisals; once the threat has been terminated, the state may not continue to use force to retaliate for the attack.

    v. Targets for which a state may assert self-defense: An attack triggering self-defense may be upon a state's territory, its armed forces, or state vessels or aircraft. Attacks upon a state's nationals or private property abroad may justify counter-attack only if protection of nationals is recognized under international law. *See* p. 147, *infra* (discussing protection of nationals and property).

  b. Necessity and proportionality requirements for self-defense: The requirements for a valid act of self-defense were stated by Daniel Webster over 150 years ago in the *Caroline* case and reaffirmed in *Nicaragua v. United States*, 1986 ICJ Rep. 14. These requirements apply whether a nation is acting in self-defense against an attack which has already occurred or acting in anticipatory self-defense. First, there must be a "***necessity of self-defense, instant, overwhelming, leaving no choice of means, and no moment of deliberation.***" Second, the actions justified by the necessity of self-defense "***must be limited by that necessity and kept clearly within it***." These two requirements are often referred to as the ***requirements of necessity*** and ***proportionality***.

  c. What constitutes an armed attack: The concept of an "armed attack" prerequisite to the exercise of self-defense is clarified by three United Nations General Assembly resolutions: the Definition of Aggression, the Declaration on the Inadmissibility of Intervention in the Domestic Affairs of States and the Protection of Their Independence and Sovereignty, and the Declaration on Principles of International Law Concerning Friendly Relations and Co-operation Among States in Accordance with the Charter of the United Nations. The Declaration on the Inadmissibility of Intervention and the Declaration on Principles of International Law prohibit armed intervention against another state and reaffirm the Charter's requirement that international disputes be resolved by peaceful means, the use of force being a last resort. The Definition of Aggression clarifies the meaning of "aggression" for purposes of Chapter VII enforcement action, but is helpful in determining what constitutes an armed attack. The resolution is discussed on p. 146, *infra*.

2. **Enforcement actions by the U.N.:**   Chapter VII of the U.N. Charter sets forth the authority of the Security Council to act with respect to "threat[s] to the peace, breach[es] of the peace, or act[s] of aggression." U.N. Charter art. 39. These critical terms are not defined in the Charter. If the Security Council finds that such circumstances exist, it may take enforcement action in accordance with articles 41 and 42 of the Charter in order "to maintain or restore international peace and security." Before resorting to such measures, the Security Council may take provisional measures. Art. 40. All member states are bound by such decisions. Art. 25. Action taken under Chapter VII is subject to the veto power.

   a. **Definition of aggression:**   The General Assembly Resolution Definition of Aggression is a clarification of the United Nations Security Council's jurisdiction over "any threat to the peace, breach of the peace, or act of aggression." Article 1 defines aggression as "the use of armed force by a State against the *sovereignty, territorial integrity or political independence* of another State, or in any other manner inconsistent with the Charter of the United Nations. . . ." Article 2 provides that the first use of armed force by a state in contravention of the United Nations Charter is *prima facie* evidence of an act of aggression, defined in article 3 to include the invasion by armed forces of another state. Article 3 lists some acts which qualify as acts of aggression, and includes the sending of armed bands to carry out acts of armed force against a state of sufficient gravity to be tantamount to an invasion or attack against the state itself. Finally, article 5 adopts the Nuremberg Principles, which make armed aggression a "crime against peace," and prohibit territorial acquisition by virtue of such aggression.

   b. **Article 41 measures short of armed force:**   This provision authorizes the Security Council to call upon member states to implement measures not involving the use of armed force in order to give effect to its decisions. Such measures may include "complete or partial interruption of economic relations and of rail, sea, air, postal, telegraphic, radio, and other means of communication, and the severance of diplomatic relations."

Example: In 1965, a white minority regime in Southern Rhodesia (now Zimbabwe) declared independence from the United Kingdom and control of the government. In 1966, the Security Council imposed economic sanctions against Southern Rhodesia. The sanctions were terminated in 1979 when majority rule was accepted. Although this was the first time economic sanctions were imposed, they have been imposed in a number of cases, more recently against Yugoslavia and Iraq.

c. **Article 42 use of armed force:** Should the Security Council consider that peaceful measures "would be inadequate or have proved to be inadequate, it may take such action by air, sea or land forces as may be necessary to maintain or restore international peace and security. Such action may include demonstrations, blockade, and other operations by air, sea or land forces of Members of the United Nations." It should be noted that the Security Council is not required to take peaceful measures under article 41 before proceeding under article 42; the Security Council need only find that peaceful measures would be inadequate.

d. **Provision of forces for enforcement:** Article 43 provides that a state is not required to take part in military operations authorized under article 42 unless it has concluded a special agreement with the U.N. At this time, no such agreements have been concluded. However, article 43 generally is not considered to prohibit the Security Council from assembling military forces by other means. The Security Council may not order states to take part in military operations, but it can authorize them to do so.

e. **Specific enforcement actions involving the use of force:** There have been only a few instances in which such enforcement action has been taken, but the breaking up of the Soviet Union has led to a recent upsurge in Security Council enforcement. Some examples follow.

    i. **The Korean conflict:** In 1950, when the Soviet Union walked out of the Security Council over the issue of which government represented China, the Security Council passed resolutions recommending that member states furnish assistance to the Republic of Korea against North Korea, and placing forces there under a unified command to be appointed by the U.S. The legal authority for the Korean forces is unclear. They flew the U.N. flag, were awarded U.N. medals, but the commander took orders from the U.S. and the allied side of the peace conference consisted only of states which had sent troops. The forces may be considered an enforcement action, or an exercise by the states of collective self-defense with Security Council recognition of such right.

   ii. Iraq: In 1990, the Security Council "acting under Chapter VII" gave Iraq until January 15, 1991 to withdraw from Kuwait or be subject to military action. As with the Korean conflict, the question has been raised whether the military action taken against Iraq was enforcement action or Security Council authorization of collective self-defense under article 51.

   iii. Somalia: In 1992, the Security Council acting under Chapters VII and VIII and regional arrangements authorized member states to contribute to a U.S.-led military operation "to establish as soon as possible a secure environment for humanitarian relief operations in Somalia."

   iv. Bosnia: In 1993, the Security Council authorized the NATO allies to enforce a ban on military flights over Bosnia.

f. **General Assembly enforcement action under the Uniting for Peace Resolution:** In 1950, the General Assembly passed the Uniting for Peace Resolution, which provides in part: . . . if the Security Council, because of lack of unanimity of the permanent members, fails to exercise its primary responsibility for the maintenance of international peace and security in any case where there appears to be a threat to the peace, breach of the peace or act of aggression, the General Assembly shall consider the matter immediately with a view to making appropriate recommendations to Members for collective measures, including in the case of a breach of the peace or act of aggression the use of armed force when necessary, to maintain or restore international peace and security.

   Whether the General Assembly can take enforcement action is highly debatable. Article 11, ¶ 2 says that "any . . . question on which action is necessary shall be referred to the Security Council by the General Assembly." In upholding the legality of a peacekeeping force placed in Egypt by the General Assembly with Egypt's consent, the ICJ in the *Certain Expenses* case interpreted "action" to mean "enforcement action."

3. **Enforcement actions by regional organizations under article 53:** Article 53 of the Charter provides that the Security Council can utilize regional arrangements or agencies for enforcement action, but that "no enforcement action shall be taken under

regional arrangements or by regional agencies without the authorization of the Security Council."

4. Actions against former enemy states under articles 53, ¶ 1 and 107: Article 107 of the U.N. Charter provides:

> Nothing in the present Charter shall invalidate or preclude action, in relation to any state which during the Second World War has been an enemy of any signatory to the present Charter, taken or authorized as a result of that war by the Governments having responsibility for such action.

Article 53, ¶ 1 specifically waives the requirement of Security Council authorization for actions taken by regional defense organizations pursuant to article 107. While these provisions have been invoked in the past, the view of most scholars is that article 107 and, less clearly, article 53, ¶ 1 are now obsolete.

D. Non-charter justifications of self-help or necessity for the use of armed force: Assuming that the explicit Charter authorizations for force are not exhaustive and that article 2, ¶ 4 should be given a narrow reading, a number of justifications for force have been advanced under customary international law. All or most of these justifications are forms of self-help, the pre-Charter custom allowing a state to take action against another state for a violation of international law.

1. Humanitarian intervention: Some scholars argue that military actions undertaken for humanitarian purposes in response to ***gross violations of human rights*** (a term itself controversial) are permissible under a narrow reading of article 2, ¶ 4. Although scholars have proposed many criteria for "legitimate" humanitarian intervention, it is generally agreed that the state using force would have to act from humanitarian motives (not against "the territorial integrity or political independence" of the target state), act proportionally, and cease military operations as soon as the humanitarian objective was achieved.

Example: In 1976, Israel staged a raid on the Entebbe airport to free Israelis and other nationals being held hostage on a hijacked plane. However, in *Nicaragua v. United States*, the ICJ stated that the "use of force could not be the appropriate method to . . . ensure . . . respect" for human rights.

2. Protection of nationals and property: Protection of nationals is distinguished from humanitarian intervention based on the nationality of the victims. It is legally distinguishable because advocates of the right have asserted that attacks on a state's nationals triggers a right of self-defense under a broad reading of article 51 or as self-help under customary international law.

3. **Reprisals:**   The term "reprisal" means an ***otherwise illegal act*** committed by one state against a second state, in order ***to remedy a prior violation of international law*** by the second state, ***to protect its interests***, or ***to achieve some other objective***. Often, the illegal act involves the use of force. A state which engages in a reprisal in retaliation for past acts is presumably in violation of international law. Prior to 1945, reprisals were an accepted institution in international law, provided that a state acted within the bounds of necessity and proportionality. Such self-help is now presumably ***prohibited*** under the U.N. Charter. The Geneva Conventions of 1949 also prohibit specific types of reprisals (such as reprisals against wounded or sick combatants) during times of armed conflict. Although it is generally acknowledged that reprisals are prohibited by international law, it has been argued that such actions may be justified in limited situations. Reprisals must be distinguished from retorsion, which is an action taken by a state against another state ***in response to an injury arising from a violation of international law*** by the second state. Retorsions do ***not*** generally involve the use of military force; instead, economic force, such as trade sanctions or boycotts, is frequently employed. Depending upon the measures taken, retorsions may be lawful. The principal issue with the legality of retorsions is whether article 2, ¶ 4's prohibition on the use or threat of force is limited to *armed* force.

II. THE HUMANITARIAN LAW OF ARMED CONFLICT

The humanitarian law of armed conflict attempts to place limitations upon the conduct of warfare in order to prevent unnecessary suffering of civilians and combatants. It applies to international armed conflict and, to a more limited degree, internal conflicts or civil wars.

A. **Sources of the law of armed conflict:**   Customary law and international treaties are the primary sources of armed conflict law. Many treaties, including the Hague and the four Geneva Conventions, reflect or have evolved into customary law. Whether a treaty reflects custom becomes very important when the treaty limits its coverage to certain conflicts or parties to a conflict.

1. **Customary law:**   The humanitarian laws of war were articulated by some of the earliest scholars such as Grotius and Emrich von de

Vattel, among others. Many of the principles laid down by these scholars have entered into customary international law are the foundation of the landmark treaties of the 20th century.

2. **International treaties:** Many international treaties regulate the conduct of warfare. Among the most important of these treaties still in force are:

   a. *The Hague Conventions and Declarations of 1907*, especially the Convention Respecting the Law and Customs of War on Land (Hague Convention IV), with Annex of Regulations (referred to as the Hague regulations);

   b. *The Nuremberg Charter of 1945*, the inter-allies agreement for the prosecution and punishment of Nazi leaders;

   c. *The Geneva Conventions of 1949*, including

      i. Convention for the Amelioration of the Condition of the Wounded and Sick in Armed Forces in the Field;

      ii. Convention for the Amelioration of the Condition of Wounded, Sick and Shipwrecked Members of Armed Forces at Sea;

      iii. Convention Relative to the Treatment of Prisoners of War; and

      iv. Convention Relative to the Protection of Civilian Persons in Time of War;

   d. *The Protocols Additional of 1977*, including

      i. Protocol Additional to the Geneva Conventions of August 12, 1949, and Relating to the Protection of Victims of International Armed Conflicts, and

      ii. Protocol Additional to the Geneva Conventions of August 12, 1949, and Relating to the Protection of Victims of Non-international Armed Conflicts.

B. **Protections provided by the Hague and Geneva Conventions:** Certain protections are provided to specific categories of people and property.

1. **Protection of the individual:** The degree of protection the laws of armed conflict extend to any given individual depends largely upon that individual's characterization under the Hague and Geneva Conventions.

   a. **Protections extended to combatants:** The primary sources of protection to combatants is the Annex to Hague Convention IV of 1907. Under the laws of laws of armed conflict, a combatant is *any individual legally entitled to take part in hostilities*. Combatants include not only members of the armed forces of a state involved in a conflict, but also citizens who rise in a levee en masse and members of organized resistance groups who fulfill the criteria of being commanded by a responsible superior, wearing some type of uniform, carrying arms openly, and obeying the laws and customs of war. Under the laws of armed conflict, a combatant is *subject to attack at any time*. The protections extended to active combatants are minimal; in general, the only protections consist of the limitations on weapons and tactics discussed on p. 156, *infra*. The laws of armed conflict also extend certain additional protections against attack to medical personnel, clergy, and the like.

b. **Protections extended to wounded, sick and shipwrecked combatants:** While an active combatant is accorded minimal protection, a combatant who is wounded, sick, or who has surrendered is *accorded considerable protection* under international law; they may not be subjected to further attack. The primary sources of protection to these individuals are the Hague Convention IV, the Geneva Convention for the Amelioration of the Condition of the Wounded and Sick in Armed Forces in the Field, and the Geneva Convention for the Amelioration of the Condition of Wounded, Sick and Shipwrecked Members of Armed Forces at Sea. An individual who is injured or sick is not only protected from further attack but *must be provided with medical care*. Information about the wounded individuals must be forwarded to the central prisoner of war information agency.

c. **Protections extended to prisoners of war:** Any lawful combatant who falls into the hands of the enemy is entitled to prisoner of war status. These protections are extended whether or not the detaining power recognizes the authority of the organization or group which they represent. The primary source of international law relating to the treatment of POWs is the 1949 Geneva Convention Relative to the Treatment of Prisoners of War. Essentially, the Convention provides for the *humane and decent treatment* of POWs and expressly forbids torture, biological experimentation, and other invasions of personal dignity. POWs may be used as a labor force, but non-commissioned officers may only be employed in supervisory roles and commissioned officers cannot be forced to work at all. If POWs are employed as a labor force, they must be compensated, the tasks may not be unhealthy or unreasonably dangerous, and due regard must be given to their physical capabilities. POWs are subject to the disciplinary regulations of the detaining power, and may be tried, within limits set forth in the Convention, for violations of such regulations. The protecting power may oversee all trials and punishments. During a conflict, POWs must be repatriated if they have suffered substantial mental or physical impairment or if they need medical attention which will last more than one year. Upon the conclusion of active hostilities, all POWs must be released and repatriated without delay.

   d. **Protections extended to civilians:** In the 19th century, the protection of civilians was not a major concern of the laws of war. The Hague Convention provided protection to some civilians and undefended areas. With the advent of the concept of total war, (involvement of both the military and civilian populace in the conflict) in World War II, and developments in military technology, the protection of civilians became a prime concern. This concern is reflected in the fourth Geneva Convention of 1949, the Convention Relative to the Protection of Civilian Persons in Time of War. This Convention protects civilians both during active hostilities and during time of enemy occupation of a state by providing for the creation of various protected zones in which hostilities may not be carried out. An occupying power may take security measures, but torture, murder, corporal punishment, and the like are prohibited, as are collective punishments and hostage-taking. While internment of civilians is permitted, the Convention required that internees be provided treatment which roughly corresponds to that of POWs. Perhaps most importantly, while an occupying power may set up a government, the rights of the people under occupation are delineated.

2. **Protection of property:** As with individuals, the degree of protection extended to any particular piece of property depends largely upon its nature. As a general rule, under both the Hague Conventions of 1907 and the Geneva Conventions of 1949, the destruction or confiscation of enemy property is forbidden except for situations of military necessity. In no event is looting of enemy property permissible, although enemy military equipment may be seized as war trophies.

   a. **Military installations:** All military installations, including industries and facilities which directly contribute to the war effort, are *subject to attack*. Article 26 of the Annex to Hague Convention IV provided that the commander of attacking forces must attempt to notify the enemy before such an attack. While often impracticable, this rule still applies, especially if civilians may be at risk.

b. **The civilian populace:** The 1907 Hague Conventions provided that undefended buildings, towns, and the like were *not to be attacked*. However, with the increasing involvement between civilian personnel and military industries, this provision is becoming increasingly difficult to enforce or obey.

c. **Areas with special protection:** The 1949 Geneva Conventions extended special protections to *medical facilities* (both military and civilian) and provided for the establishment of hospital, neutralized, and safety zones in which attacks are forbidden. *Works of art* are also entitled to special protection from attack under both the Annex to Hague Conventions IV and the 1954 Hague Convention on the Protection of Cultural Property in the Event of an Armed Conflict. Cultural property includes both movable and immovable property having special cultural significance.

C. **Conflicts encompassed by the Geneva Conventions and protocols:** Which provisions of the Geneva Conventions and protocols apply depends upon whether the conflict is an international conflict, civil war or a war of self-determination.

1. **International conflicts:** Under common article 2, the Geneva Conventions in their entirety apply to *international conflicts*. Protocol I of 1977 also applies to international conflicts.

2. **Civil wars:** For "armed conflict not of an international character" only common article 3 of the Geneva Convention applies. The protection it provides is general and *much more limited* than the protection provided in international conflicts. Article 3 requires all parties to the conflict to treat humanely "persons taking no active part in the hostilities, members of armed forces who have laid down their arms and those placed *hors de combat* by sickness, wounds, detention, or any other cause. . . ." Discrimination on the basis of race, color, religion or faith, sex, birth or wealth, or similar criteria is prohibited. Specifically prohibited are:

a. violence to life and person, in particular murder of all kinds, mutilation, cruel treatment and torture;

b. taking of hostages;

c. outrages upon personal dignity, in particular humiliating and degrading treatment;

d. the passing of sentences and the carrying out of executions without previous judgment pronounced by a regularly constituted court affording all the judicial guarantees which are recognized as indispensable by civilized peoples.

Because governments and opposing factions alike had resisted application of common article 3 to civil wars, Protocol II relating to "non-international armed conflict" was adopted in 1977. It contains detailed provisions for humane treatment in conflicts between a state's armed forces and dissident armed forces or other organized armed forces which meet a specified level of control and command. Article 1 states, however, that the protocol supplements article 3 without modifying the existing conditions of application for article 3. Some civil wars which fall under the broad coverage of common article 3 will not qualify for coverage under the more restrictive conditions for coverage in Protocol II. The protocol also does not apply to "internal disturbances and tensions, such as riots, isolated and sporadic acts of violence and other acts of a similar nature. . . ." Under this provision, the issue is at what point hostilities reach an intensity that qualifies for coverage under Protocol II. Many countries as of 1993, including the U.S., have refused to ratify Protocol II.

3. **Wars of self-determination:** Protocol I applies not only to international conflicts, but also to "armed conflicts in which people are fighting against colonial domination and alien occupation and against racist regimes in the exercise of their right of self-determination, as enshrined in the Charter of the United Nations and the Declaration on Principles of International Law concerning Friendly Relations. . . ." Protocol I also makes the four Geneva Conventions applicable to such conflicts. Many countries as of 1993, including the U.S., have refused to ratify Protocol I for this reason.

D. **Applicability of general human rights obligations during armed conflict:** *See* p. 148, *supra* (discussing the humanitarian law of armed conflict).

E. **Sanctions and enforcement:** Several treaties and conventions contain sanctions and enforcement provisions.

1. **The Hague Conventions of 1907:** The Hague Conventions of 1907 provided that a state might be required to pay reparations if it, or any member of its armed forces, violated the Convention. However, the Conventions established no procedural framework through which a nation might press its claims that a violation had occurred. The Hague Conventions by their terms were only binding as between parties to the Conventions, and then only if all of the states involved in a conflict were also parties to the Convention. The International Military Tribunal at Nuremberg concluded that the provisions of the Hague Conventions are *customary international law*.

2. **The Geneva Conventions of 1949:** Parties have a general obligation to ensure respect for the Geneva Conventions in all circumstances. The Conventions provide that once a violation has been established, the parties shall "put an end to it and repress it with the least possible delay." The Geneva Conventions also contain provisions allowing a state to subject any individual, regardless of nationality, to *criminal* prosecution for violations of the Conventions. Unlike the Hague Conventions, the Geneva Conventions are not entirely self-administered; the Conventions provide that the interests of each party to the conflict are to be safeguarded by a neutral "protecting power." *See* p. 149, *supra* (discussing the Geneva Conventions and the additional protocols). By their terms, the Geneva Conventions apply to "all cases of declared war or of any other armed conflict" between contracting states. The parties to the convention are bound to apply its terms between themselves, even if not all of the states involved in the conflict are contracting parties. In addition, if a non-party state accepts and applies the provisions of the Conventions, the contracting parties are required to abide by the Conventions as they pertain to that state. The Geneva Conventions are generally regarded as *custom*. States are liable for grave breaches by its nationals for whom they are responsible. With respect to prosecution and enforcement against individuals, the Conventions provide: The High Contracting Parties undertake to enact any legislation necessary to provide effective penal sanctions for persons committing, or ordering to be committed, any of the grave breaches of the present Convention defined in the following Article. Each High Contracting Party shall be under the obligation to search for persons alleged to have committed, or to have ordered to be committed, such grave breaches, and shall bring such persons, regardless of their nationality, before its own courts. It may also, if it prefers, and in accordance with the provisions of its own legislation, hand such persons over for trial to another High Contracting Party concerned, provided such High Contracting Party has made out a *prima facie* case. Each High Contracting Party shall take measures necessary for the suppression of all acts contrary to the provisions of the present Convention other than the grave breaches defined in the following Article.

Grave breaches which are listed under each Convention are generally recognized as *war crimes* under international law. The Conventions provide for enforcement by the states, although the parties are not precluded from conferring jurisdiction upon an international tribunal over those grave breaches which constitute war crimes under international law.

3. **The protocols additional of 1977:** Protocol II does not establish any methods of implementation or enforcement. Protocol I does establish a fact-finding commission to investigate grave breaches if its jurisdiction to do so is recognized by the parties to the conflict. Protocol I expands upon the substantive rules and procedural mechanisms of the Convention for repression of breaches.

4. **The Nuremberg principles:** The Charter of the International Military Tribunal at Nuremberg, which was later recognized as custom by the General Assembly of the U.N., provided for individual *criminal* responsibility for "crimes against peace," war crimes, or "crimes against humanity":

   a. **Crimes against peace:** Namely, planning, preparation, initiation or waging of a war of aggression, or a war in violation of international treaties, agreements or assurances, or participation in a common plan or conspiracy for the accomplishment of any of the foregoing;

   b. **War crimes:** Namely, violations of the laws or customs of war. Such violations shall include, but not be limited to, murder, ill-treatment or deportation to slave labor or for any purpose of civilian population of or in occupied territory, murder or ill-treatment of prisoners of war or persons on the seas, killing of hostages, plunder of public or private property, wanton destruction of cities, towns or villages, or devastation not justified by military necessity;

   c. **Crimes against humanity:** Namely, murder, extermination, enslavement, deportation, and other inhumane acts committed against any civilian population, before or during the war; or persecutions on political, racial or religious grounds in execution of or in connection with any crime within the jurisdiction of the Tribunal, whether or not in violation of the domestic law of the country where perpetrated.

Leaders, organizers, instigators and accomplices participating in the formulation or execution of a common plan or conspiracy to commit any of the foregoing crimes are responsible for all acts performed by any persons in execution of such plan.

In *Application of Yamashita*, 327 U.S. 1 (1946), General Yamashita of Japan was tried by a special United States military commission applying the international laws of war as incorporated into United States domestic law. Yamashita was charged with war crimes, including the massacre of civilian populations in the Philippines, which also is a crime against humanity under the Nuremberg Principles. The gist of the charge was that Yamashita failed as commander to control the troops in his command and thereby prevent the alleged atrocities. In holding Yamashita responsible for the alleged war crimes, the Court established that an official or commander who, through reports received by him or through other means, learns that troops or other persons subject to his control are about to commit or have committed war crimes, and fails to take the necessary and reasonable steps to ensure compliance with the law of war, is responsible for such crimes.

5. **War crimes tribunals and an international criminal court:** The Nuremberg Tribunal is an example of an international tribunal with jurisdiction conferred by agreement of the parties. More recently, in 1993, the Security Council authorized the establishment of a Balkan War Crimes Tribunal. Despite a number of proposals, there is no international criminal court with jurisdiction over war crimes or other crimes under international law. The fact that an individual before the tribunal acted pursuant to the orders of his government or his superior was not a defense, but might be taken into consideration as a mitigating factor.

F. **Limitations on the methods of warfare:** The limitations on the methods of warfare are complex and detailed. The following summary is intended only to give a general outline of the limitations, primarily for weaponry.

1. **Limitations on weaponry:** As ever more destructive weapons have been developed, there have been many specific treaties and declarations to limit the human suffering caused by these weapons. Use of the following weapons is at least arguably *prohibited by customary law:*

    a. **Explosive projectiles under 400 grams:** The St. Petersburg Treaty of 1868 prohibited the use of explosive projectiles weighing under 400 grams.

    b. **"Dum-dum" bullets:** The Third Hague Declarations of 1899 banned the use of expanding bullets and projectiles.

    c. **Poisons and poisonous weapons:** These weapons were prohibited by Article 23(a) of the Annex to Hague Convention IV of 1907.

    d. **Chemical and bacteriological weapons:** The Geneva Protocol of 1925 prohibits the use of poisonous and asphyxiating gases and the use of bacteriological methods of warfare. In addition, the 1972 Convention on the Prohibition of the Development, Production, and Stockpiling of Bacteriological (Biological) and Toxin Weapons and on Their Destruction not only prohibited the use of such weapons, but also their development and production. In January 1993, the Chemical Weapons Convention was signed by more than 100 countries. The Convention, which bans chemical weapons, prevents states from producing and selling materials or facilities that can be used to manufacture chemical weapons. It is the first treaty intended to eliminate an entire class of weapons.

e. **"Arms, projectiles, or materials calculated to cause unnecessary suffering"**: Weapons which cause needless suffering are prohibited by Article 23(e) of the Annex to Hague Convention IV of 1907.

f. **Nuclear weapons**: Although there have been several U.N. General Assembly declarations that use of nuclear weapons is illegal, there is no treaty which expressly prohibits the use of nuclear weapons. There are widely divergent views on whether their use violates custom. Due to the degree of "unnecessary suffering" these weapons cause, it has been argued that their use violates a customary prohibition on the use of any weapon which causes unnecessary suffering, even if custom does not specifically prohibit the use of nuclear weapons *per se*. It has also been argued that the nuclear arms race itself violates the Charter's prohibitions on the threat of force.

2. **Limitations on tactics**: The Hague Convention (IV) of 1907 makes it illegal to "kill or wound treacherously individuals belonging to the hostile nation or army." Although the Convention provides no definition of treachery, it has been interpreted to mean such tactics as disguising soldiers as civilians and the like. Similarly, the Convention also prohibits the improper use of a flag of truce, the national flag or uniform of the enemy, or such symbols as the Red Cross. Tactics of this nature must be distinguished from "ruses of war," which are expressly permitted by the Convention. Ruses, although enabling an army to gain the advantage of surprise or position, do not involve deceit. Spying is also permitted, but, if not in uniform, a captured spy is not entitled to the protections given a prisoner of war.

3. **Limitations on the region of armed conflict**: The region of war is that area in which the combatant states may prepare and execute military operations. In general, the region of war may not be extended to neutral states or areas under their jurisdiction, demilitarized zones, international neutralized zones, or the waterways, territorial seas, or air space of such areas.

III. CIVIL WARS

A. **Generally:** *International law does not prohibit civil war.* Article 2, ¶ 4 of the U.N. Charter only prohibits force against states. Civil wars may be fought for control of the government of the state, for the creation of a new state through succession, or to gain independence from colonial rule. Throughout this section, the parties seeking control of the government or creation of a new state will be referred to as the *insurgents*, and the opposing parties previously in control as the *governing authorities*.

1. **Categories of conflicts:** Traditionally, internal conflicts are classified into three categories:

   a. **Rebellion:** This is a sporadic, isolated act of violence against the governing authorities, deemed to be a domestic matter subject to the control of the state.

   b. **Insurgency:** An insurgency is more severe than a rebellion, but less intense than a belligerency.

   c. **Belligerency:** This state of affairs refers to a full scale, widespread conflict between the governing authorities and the parties opposing them.

B. **Traditional rule regarding intervention:** Under the traditional rule, states could support the governing authorities *until a belligerency was recognized*, at which point they had to remain neutral, or be prepared to justify under international law their intervention for whichever side they supported. This rule was easily manipulated by states wanting to intervene, and recognition of a belligerency rarely occurred during the civil wars of the 20th century. Therefore, analysis of the legality of intervention in civil wars now focuses on the general norms of nonintervention and self determination, the prohibitions on force, and the limited justifications for force in international law after promulgation of the U.N. Charter.

C. **The concept of nonintervention:** One of the purposes of the post-Charter legal system is promotion of self determination. U.N. Charter, art. 1, ¶ 2; art. 55. There is a customary norm of nonintervention in the domestic affairs of other states generally and in civil wars more specifically, because any foreign intervention in a civil war eschews self determination. This norm of nonintervention is based on the sovereign equality of states in article 2, ¶ 1 of the Charter, several General Assembly resolutions (*e.g.,* Declaration of International Law Concerning Friendly Relations and Cooperation Among States, U.N.G.A. Res. 2625 (xxv), 25 U.N. GAOR, Supp. (No. 28) 121, U.N. Doc. A/8028 (1971), Declaration on the Inadmissibility of Intervention in the

Domestic Affairs of the States, U.N.G.A. Res. 2131 (xx) (1966)), and by implication from the prohibition in Article 2, ¶ 7 on United Nations intervention in the domestic affairs of states. In *Military and Paramilitary Activities in and Against Nicaragua (Nicar. v. U.S.)*, 1984 I.C.J. 392, the ICJ concluded that the ***principle of nonintervention is part of customary international law.***

D. **Acts constituting intervention:** To remain neutral in a conflict, a state must not engage in any acts constituting intervention.

 1. **Clear acts of state intervention:** The following acts by a state are clearly acts of intervention when done to support either side of a civil war:

   a. ***sending armed forces***, military instructors or technicians;

   b. ***drawing up*** or ***training regular or irregular forces***;

   c. ***supplying weapons*** or other war material; and

   d. ***allowing the state's territory to be used*** as bases for operations, supplies, or refuge or for passing of forces or war material.

 2. **Acts of a state's nationals as intervention:** It is unclear whether a state must prohibit its nationals from raising contingents, collecting equipment, or crossing the border as mercenaries or volunteers for either side in a civil war. *See* Resolution on the Principle of Nonintervention in Civil Wars of the Institut de Droit International, art. 2, ¶ 1, 56 Ann. Inst. Dr. Int'l 544 (1975); Resolution on the Definition of Aggression, U.N.G.A. Res. 3314 (xxix) (1974). There are often, however, treaties and domestic legislation which prohibit a state's nationals from supporting the overthrow of the government of another state with which the state is not at war. *See, e.g.,* Neutrality Act of 1914. It is also unclear whether a state must prohibit its nationals from selling or providing weapons of other war material in order to remain neutral.

   Example: In *Military and Paramilitary Activities in and against Nicaragua (Nicar. v. U.S.)*, 1986 I.C.J. 14, the Court held that Nicaragua was not liable for allowing weapons to be transported across its territory to insurgents in El Salvador because Nicaragua was unable to stop the flow of weapons. The Court did not appear to find relevant whether the weapons were being sent by private individuals or by another state.

E. **Acts not constituting intervention:** A state may ***provide humanitarian aid*** for food and medical supplies without violating an obligation of neutrality. Although it has been argued that it is not intervention to provide humanitarian aid to one side only, the decision of the ICJ in *Nicaragua v. United States, supra,* suggests otherwise.

("... [I]f the provision of 'humanitarian assistance' is to escape condemnation as an intervention in the internal affairs of Nicaragua, not only must it be limited to the purposes hallowed in the practice of the Red Cross, namely to 'prevent and alleviate human suffering,' and to 'protect life and health and to ensure respect for the human being,' it must also, and above all, be given without discrimination to all in need in Nicaragua, not merely to the contras and their dependents." 1986 I.C.J. at 115.). It does not constitute intervention for a state to express its support for one side over another, so long as such expressions are not accompanied by acts constituting intervention.

F. **Wars of national liberation as an exception to the norm of non-intervention:** There is one possible exception to the post-Charter norm of nonintervention. Several General Assembly resolutions suggest that insurgents engaged in a war of national liberation not only have a right of self determination to do so, but that outside states may aid the insurgents in overthrowing the governing authorities. *See, e.g.,* Declaration of International Law Concerning Friendly Relations and Co-operation Among States, U.N.G.A. Res. 2625 (xxv), 25 U.N. GAOR, Supp. (No. 28) 121, U.N. Doc A/8028 (1971) ("In their actions against and resistance to such forcible action [depriving peoples of their right to self determination], such peoples are entitled to seek and to receive support in accordance with the purposes and principles of the Charter of the United Nations."). In *Nicaragua v. United States, supra,* the Court noted that it was not addressing the "process of decolonization" in evaluating prohibited intervention; the judge from the United States in his dissent criticized the Court for "appearing to justify foreign intervention in furtherance of 'the process of decolonization.'"

G. **Justifications for intervention in civil war:** There have been several justifications put forward by states for intervention in civil wars, but the legal validity of most is questionable in the post-Charter system of international law.

   1. **Consent of the governing authorities:** States have agreed that aiding the governing authorities is *always legal* or, at the least, legal until a belligerency is recognized (which rarely occurs). Whether seen as independent justification for intervention or simply a restatement of the traditional rule for intervention discussed above, this justification is difficult to reconcile with the post-Charter norm of nonintervention and general prohibition on use of force. It is also impractical in that there are no objective criteria for identifying who qualifies as the government in a full scale civil war.

   2. **Collective and individual self-defense:** The justification of collective self defense may arise in two contexts — when state A is aiding the governing authorities in state B to resist insurgents

allegedly supported by state C, or when state A is aiding insurgents against the governing authorities of state B, because the authorities of state B are aiding insurgents in state D. In the second scenario, state D itself may be aiding the insurgents against the governing authorities of state B on grounds of self-defense. The second scenario is that which the U.S. claimed in *Nicaragua v. United States* (the U.S. was aiding the contras in Nicaragua because Nicaragua was allegedly aiding the rebels in El Salvador). The Court found that Nicaragua was not even responsible for the transport of weapons across Nicaraguan territory to the insurgents in El Salvador, and therefore, the U.S. support of the contras could not be justified as a response to an ***armed attack***. Nevertheless, the ICJ went on to say that self-defense was triggered only by an armed attack, and that the supplying of weapons did not constitute an armed attack. The Court did not address the legality or illegality of El Salvador's aid to the contras based on self-defense. The Court did note that an armed attack was not limited to action by regular armed forces across an international border, but would also include under the Resolution on the Definition of Aggression "the sending by or on behalf of a state of armed bands, groups, irregulars or mercenaries, which carry out acts of armed force against another state of such gravity as to amount to . . . an actual armed attack . . . or its substantial involvement therein." Therefore, in both scenarios above, the legality of state A's intervention on grounds of collective self-defense depends upon whether it is responding to an armed attack and, as always, the force must be proportional.

3. **Anticipatory self-defense:** Although not as often invoked in the context of intervention in civil wars, anticipatory self-defense could arise in the two contexts described above in response to another state's imminent intervention. On the question concerning the doctrine's validity under international law (which is even more questionable after the *Nicaragua* case), *see* p. 142, *supra*.

4. **Counterintervention:** The term is used here to mean intervention by a state in response to another state's illegal intervention in a civil war which falls short of an armed attack. Although the U.S. did not claim counterintervention as a justification for its use of force, the Court stated that no state may justify the use of armed force on grounds of counterintervention even when it is responding to illegal intervention by another state. The Court also rejected any right of counterintervention, with or without force, in support of a particular ideology or political movement.

H. Humanitarian rules of war in civil wars: The Geneva Conventions and protocols govern the humanitarian rules of war in civil conflicts, and are discussed at p. 152, *supra*.

CHAPTER 10
THE LAW OF THE SEA

I. GENERALLY

The law of the sea is *one of the oldest subjects of international law*.

A. Historically: Until the 1950s, the law of the sea was based almost entirely on custom. In 1958, under the auspices of the United Nations, four treaties were promulgated: the Convention on the Territorial Sea and Contiguous Zone, the Convention on the High Seas, the Convention on Fishing and Conservation of the Living Resources of the High Seas, and the Convention on the Continental Shelf. These conventions, widely adopted in subsequent years, codified the customary law of the sea but also introduced some new developments which themselves became custom as more and more accepted the provisions.

B. The Law of the Sea Convention: In 1982, again under the auspices of the United Nations, a comprehensive law of the sea treaty was promulgated. It incorporated much of the 1958 treaties, but also addressed issues unresolved in the earlier treaties — such as breadth of the territorial sea, exclusive economic zones, deep seabed regulation, and preservation of the marine environment. The 1982 LOS Convention did not meet with universal acceptance, in large part because of its controversial deep seabed provisions. As a result, controversies in the law of the sea often turn on determining whether the applicable law is that in the 1982 treaty, the 1958 treaties, or custom which may or may not be consistent with the 1958 or 1982 treaty approaches.

II. NATIONALITY OF VESSELS

Three basic principles fundamental to the law of the sea are: (1) *a ship of any state can navigate the oceans freely*; (2) *the state of the ship's nationality has exclusive jurisdiction over the ship on the high seas*; and (3) *no other state can exercise jurisdiction over that ship absent some affirmative rule authorizing concurrent jurisdiction*.

A. Introduction: The nationality of a ship defines the legal relationship between a state and a ship which is authorized by that state to fly its flag. Other terms used to refer to a ship's legal relationship with its "flag state" include "*registration*" or "*documentation*" of a ship. A ship may only fly the flag of one state. *Convention on the High Seas,*

Apr. 29, 1958, art. 6, ¶ 1, 450 U.N.T.S. 82 [hereinafter *High Seas Convention*]; *United Nations Convention on the Law of the Sea*, Oct. 7, 1982, art. 92, ¶ 1, 21 I.L.M. 1261 (1982) [hereinafter *LOS Convention*]. A ship without nationality may be prevented from engaging in international trade or commerce, or navigation of any sort on the high seas. *LOS Convention*, art. 110, ¶ 1, cl. d. A ship without nationality will not benefit from any treaties that confer rights on ships when entering foreign ports.

B. **The right of states to confer nationality upon a ship:** In order to confer its nationality on a ship, a state usually must register the ship, authorize it to fly the state flag, and issue documents indicating the ship's nationality.

  1. **General principle:** The U.S. Supreme Court has recognized the well established rule that "[e]ach state under international law may determine for itself the conditions on which it will grant its nationality to a merchant ship." *Lauritzen v. Larsen*, 345 U.S. 571, 584 (1953). This principle has been included in many international agreements and treaties.

  2. **Limitations:** The general principle that states are free to set the conditions for nationality is subject to two basic limitations.

     a. **One flag limitation:** A state may *not* grant its nationality to a ship that is already authorized to fly the flag of another state, except if necessary to transfer the ship from one state's registry to another. *High Seas Convention*, art. 6, ¶ 1; *LOS Convention*, art. 6, ¶ 1; *LOS Convention*, art. 92, ¶ 1.

     b. **Genuine link necessary:** A state must have a "*genuine link*" to a ship in order for a state to confer its nationality upon it. *High Seas Convention*, art. 5, ¶ 1; *LOS Convention*, art. 91, ¶ 1. The requirement of a sufficient connection between a flag state and its ships is premised upon a belief that a state can carry out is obligations to exercise effective control over its ships only if such a link exists. *Proof of a genuine link* between a flag state and a ship may be based on one or more of the following: (1) *ownership by nationals*; (2) *national officers*; (3) *national crew*; and (4) *national build*.

        i. **"Flags of convenience":** The requirement of a "genuine link" was in response to the use of "flags of convenience," now known as open registries. After World War II, many shipowners had transferred their ships to the registries of countries such as Panama and Liberia to avoid increasingly restrictive regulation in other states.

ii. **Procedure when genuine link questioned:** A state "which has clear grounds to believe that proper jurisdiction and control with respect to a ship has not been exercised may report the facts to the flag State." The flag state then has an obligation to investigate the matter. *LOS Convention*, art. 94, ¶ 6.

C. **Documentation and registration:** A state that authorizes ships to fly its flag must: (1) maintain a register of ships containing the name and description of each ship so authorized; and (2) issue documents to the registered ships evidencing authorization. *High Seas Convention*, art. 5, ¶ 2; *LOS Convention, art. 91, ¶ 2.* A ship may only change its flag during voyage or while in a port of call when there is a real change in registry. *High Seas Convention*, art. 6, ¶ 1; *LOS Convention*, art. 92, ¶ 1. If a ship's owner fraudulently obtains registration of a ship, the vessel may be liable to seizure and forfeiture by the flag state.

D. **Duties of the flag state:** Under international law, each state has a duty to "effectively exercise its jurisdiction and control in administrative, technical and social matters over ships flying its flag." *High Seas Convention*, art. 5, ¶ 1. Article 94 of the LOS Convention further specifies that each flag state has the obligation to:

1. *Maintain a register of ships authorized to fly its flag*;

2. *Govern the internal affairs* of the ship;

3. *Ensure the safety* at sea with regard to the construction, equipment and seaworthiness of ships, labor conditions and the training of crews, the maintenance of communications, and the prevention of collisions;

4. *Ensure that each ship is surveyed* by a qualified surveyor of ships and has on board appropriate charts, nautical publications, and navigational equipment;

5. *Ensure that each ship is manned* by a qualified master, officers and crew; and

6. *Ensure that the master, officers, and, to the appropriate extent, the crew are fully conversant with and are required to observe applicable international regulations* regarding the safety of life at sea; the prevention of collisions; the prevention, reduction, and control of marine pollution; and the maintenance of radio communications.

III. BASELINE DETERMINATIONS FOR MEASURING COASTAL ZONES

A. **Purpose of the baseline:** The baseline is the *starting point from which a coastal state's coastal zones are measured*. Waters on the landward side of the baseline are considered internal waters of the state. *Convention on the Territorial Sea and Contiguous Zone*, Apr. 29, 1958, art. 5, ¶ 1, 516 U.N.T.S. 205 [hereinafter *Territorial Sea Convention*]; *LOS Convention*, art. 8.

B. **Validity of baselines:** Validity of baseline delineations and maritime jurisdiction is determined by international law. *Fisheries (U.K. v. Nor.)*, 1951 I.C.J. 116 (Dec. 18).

C. **Delineation of the baseline:** The baseline is the *low-water mark along the coast*. *Territorial Sea Convention*, art. 3; *LOS Convention*, art. 5; *see also Fisheries (U.K. v. Nor.)*, 1951 I.C.J. 116 (Dec. 18).

1. **Rivers:** If a river flows directly into the sea, the baseline is drawn straight across the mouth of the river between the low-water points of its lands. *Territorial Sea Convention*, art. 13; *LOS Convention*, art. 9.

2. **Bays:** A bay is considered to be internal waters of a state when the bay's area is as large or larger than that of the semi-circle, for which the diameter is a line drawn across the mouth of the bay. The line between the natural entrance points of the bay may not exceed 24 nautical miles. If it does exceed this limit, a straight baseline of 24 nautical miles can be drawn so as to enclose the maximum area of water possible with a baseline of that length. *Territorial Sea Convention*, art. 7; *LOS Convention*, art. 10.

    a. **Exception for "historic bays":** Historic bays are considered internal waters even if they do not meet the above requirements. *Territorial Sea Convention*, art. 7, ¶ 6; *LOS Convention*, art. 10, ¶ 6. The International Court of Justice has defined "historic waters" as internal waters "which would not have that character were it not for the existence of an historic title." *Fisheries (U.K. v. Nor.)*, 1951 I.C.J. 116, 130 (Dec. 18). Three factors have been suggested for evaluating historic title over coastal waters: (1) whether the state *exercises sovereign authority* over the waters; (2) whether the authority has been exercised regularly for a *considerable time*; and (3) whether *other states have acquiesced* in the exercise of that authority. U.N. Secretariat, *Judicial Regime of Historic Waters, Including Historic Bays*, U.N. Doc.A/CN.4/143 (1962), [1962] 2 Y.B. Int'l L. Comm'n 13.

   b. Gulf of Sidra incident: In 1986, when United States warships engaged Libyan forces in the Gulf of Sidra, the United
   States claimed it was exercising a right of innocent passage for
   its warships in the waters of the Gulf beyond the 12 nautical
   mile limit. Libya claimed that the Gulf of Sidra was an historical
   bay and part of its internal waters. A baseline drawn across the
   mouth of the bay would exceed 24 nautical miles.

3. **Islands:**   An island is "a naturally-formed area of land, surrounded
   by water, which is above water at high tide." *Territorial Sea Convention*, art. 10; *LOS Convention*, art. 121. Every island is entitled
   to claim rights in a territorial sea, contiguous zone, exclusive economic zone, and continental shelf.

4. **Indented coastlines and island fringes:**   "In localities where
   the coastline is off the Mainland deeply indented and cut into, or if
   there is a fringe of islands along the coast in its immediate vicinity,
   the method of straight baselines joining appropriate points may be
   employed in drawing the baseline from which the breadth of the territorial sea is measured." *Territorial Sea Convention*, art. 4, ¶ 1;
   LOS Convention, art. 7, ¶ 1; *see also Fisheries (U.K. v. Nor.)*, 1951
   I.C.J. 116 (Dec. 18). A number of limitations on the use of straight
   baselines have been incorporated into the 1958 Convention on the
   Territorial Sea and the LOS Convention.

   a. Fisheries case: The Court in the Fisheries case imposed limitations on the use of straight baselines: They "must not depart to
   any appreciable extent from the general direction of the coast;"
   the "areas lying within these lines" must be "sufficiently closely
   linked to the land domain to be subject to the regime of internal
   waters;" and account should be taken of "certain economic interests peculiar to a region, the reality and importance of which are
   clearly evidenced by a long usage," in determining the appropri-
   ateness of straight baselines in a particular area. *Fisheries (U.K.
   v. Nor.)*, 1951 I.C.J. 116, 133 (Dec. 18). These limitations have
   been incorporated into the *Territorial Sea Convention*, art. 4, ¶
   2; *LOS Convention*, art. 7, ¶¶ 3, 5.

   b. Low-tide elevations: Straight baselines may not be drawn to
   and from low-tide elevations, unless lighthouses or similar
   installations, which are permanently above sea level, have been
   built on them. *Territorial Sea Convention*; *LOS Convention*, art.
   7, ¶ 4.

   c. Cutting off territorial sea: The system of straight baselines
   may not be applied by a state in such a manner as to cut off the
   territorial sea of another state from the high seas or an exclusive

economic zone. *Territorial Sea Convention*, art. 4, ¶ 5; *LOS Convention*, art. 7, ¶ 6.

    d. Innocent passage: Where the establishment of a straight baseline encloses as internal waters areas which had not previously been considered as such, the coastal state must grant other states a right of innocent passage. *LOS Convention*, art. 8, ¶ 2.

5. Archipelagic states: Straight baselines joining the outermost points of the outermost islands may be drawn. Baselines of archipelagic states may not exceed 100 nautical miles and are subject to other limitations. *LOS Convention*, art. 47, ¶ 2.

6. Low-tide elevations: Low-tide elevations situated wholly or partly within a territorial sea may be used as the baseline. *Territorial Sea Convention*, art. 11; *LOS Convention*, art. 13.

7. Harbors and roadsteads: The outermost permanent harborworks, which form an integral part of the harbor system, are regarded as forming part of the coast for determining the baseline. *Territorial Sea Convention*, art. 8; *LOS Convention*, art. 11. Roadsteads do not influence the baseline from which the areas of coastal jurisdiction are measured. *Territorial Sea Convention*, art. 9; *LOS Convention*, art. 12.

D. Demarcation of baseline with adjacent and opposite states: If the coasts of two states are opposite or adjacent to each other, neither state is entitled to extend its territorial sea beyond the median line, defined as every point of which is equidistant from the nearest points on the baseline from which the breadth of the territorial sea is measured. Historic title or special circumstances may require a different division. *Territorial Sea Convention*, art. 12; *LOS Convention*, art. 15. The delimitation of the continental shelf and economic zone between states shall be determined by agreement. *Convention on the Continental Shelf*, Apr. 29, 1958, art. 6, 499 U.N.T.S. 311 [hereinafter *Continental Shelf Convention*]; *LOS Convention*, arts. 74, 83. In the absence of agreement or special circumstances, the 1958 Convention states the boundary shall be the median line, where opposite states are involved; and an equidistant line, where adjacent states are involved. *Continental Shelf Convention*, art. 6. In 1969, the ICJ refused to find that the "equidistant/special circumstances" rule had become custom in continental delimitation between adjacent states absent agreement. *North Sea Continental Shelf*, 1969 I.C.J. 3. Articles 74 and 83 of the LOS Convention states that "[t]he delimitation of the exclusive economic zone [or continental shelf] between states with opposite or adjacent coasts shall be effected by agreement on the basis of international law, as referred to in article 38 of the Statute of the International Court of Justice, in order to achieve an equitable solution." This formulation fails to mention equidistances and emphasizes equitable considerations in delimitation.

IV. INTERNAL WATERS AND PORTS

A. **General definition:** Internal waters are the waters of lakes, rivers and bays *landward of the baseline* of the territorial sea. *Territorial Sea Convention*, art. 5; *LOS Convention*, art. 8. A "port" is a place for loading or unloading a ship. A coastal state has *full sovereignty* over its internal waters and ports.

B. **Freedom of access to ports:** Freedom of access to ports by foreign merchant vessels is a rule of custom *conditioned on reciprocity*.

 1. **Land-locked nations:** Land-locked nations may not be denied freedom of access to ports solely because of their inability to reciprocate. *High Seas Convention*, art. 3; *LOS Convention*, art. 131.

 2. **Closing of ports:** "[P]orts of every state must be open to foreign vessels and can only be closed when the vital interests of a State so require." *Saudi Arabia v. Arabian American Oil Company (ARAMCO)*, Award of August 23, 1938, 27 Int'l L. Rep. 117, 212 (1963).

 3. **Regulation:** A coastal state may condition a foreign ship's access to port upon compliance with laws and regulations governing the conduct of the business of the port, such as pollution and safety controls. Such laws and regulations may not be discriminatory against or among foreign vessels.

C. **Jurisdiction over foreign vessels:** A foreign merchant ship which enters the ports of a state is subject to the *administrative, civil* and *criminal jurisdiction of that state*. Even warships must comply with laws relating to navigation, safety, health, and post administration.

 1. **Matters internal to a ship:** As a matter of public policy, jurisdiction over a ship's internal matters, which do not involve the "peace or dignity" of the coastal state or "tranquility of the port", are generally left to the flag state. *Wildenhus' Case*, 120 U.S. 1, 11 (1887). *See also Benz v. Compania Naviera Hidalgo, S.A.*, 353 U.S. 138 (1957) (withholding application of jurisdiction absent clear congressional intent).

2. **Seeking refuge:** Foreign vessels are not subject to a coastal state's jurisdiction when the vessel is seeking refuge because of distress or *force majeure.*

D. **Jurisdiction of flag state:** If the coastal state does not assert jurisdiction over an offense in its ports or internal waters, "it is the duty of the courts of the [flag state] ... to apply its own statutes." *United States v. Flores,* 289 U.S. 137, 158-9 (1933).

E. **Enlarged port state jurisdiction under the LOS Convention:** A port state may investigate and institute proceedings in respect of any discharge from a ship "voluntarily within a port or at an offshore terminal" in violation of international standards, even if the discharge occurred outside the internal waters, territorial sea and exclusive economic zone of the state. If the discharge occurred in the waters of another state, proceedings may only be instituted by the port state or request of that state, the flag state, or the state damages or threatened by the discharge. *LOS Convention,* art. 218, ¶¶ 1-4, art. 220, ¶ 1, art. 228.

V. THE TERRITORIAL SEA AND CONTIGUOUS ZONE

A. **Coastal state sovereignty over the territorial sea:** A state has the *same sovereignty over its territorial sea, air space, seabed, and subsoil thereof* as it has with respect to its land. *Territorial Sea Convention,* arts. 1-2; *LOS Convention,* art. 2.

B. **Breadth of the territorial sea:** For many years under the so-called "cannon-shot" rule, a three mile territorial sea was recognized as customary international law. After World War II, many states made claims to a more extensive territorial sea, in some cases of up to 200 miles. As a result, no agreement could be reached in the 1958 Convention on the Territorial Sea and Contiguous Zone on the breadth of the territorial sea, although a 12 mile contiguous zone was incorporated. According to the LOS Convention, every state has the right to establish the breadth of its territorial sea *up to 12 nautical miles* as measured from the baseline. *LOS Convention,* art. 3. The United States still adheres to a three-mile territorial sea for domestic law purposes. For international relations, however, the United States has extended its territorial sea to 12 nautical miles to be consistent with the LOS Convention. *Proclamation No. 5928,* 54 Fed. Reg. 777 (1988).

C. **The right of innocent passage:** The right of ships of all states to innocent passage through the territorial sea of any coastal state is an exception to the sovereignty of a state over its territorial sea. *Territorial Sea Convention*, art. 14; *LOS Convention*, art. 17.

1. **General definition of passage:** Passage means navigation through the territorial sea for the purpose of either traversing that sea without entering internal waters, or proceeding to or from internal waters. Passage must be continuous, but a ship may anchor if this is incidental, or necessary to assist persons in distress. *Territorial Sea Convention*, art. 14, ¶ 3; *LOS Convention*, art. 18, ¶ 2.

2. **Meaning of innocent passage:** Innocent passage *must not be prejudicial to the peace, good order, or security* of the coastal state. *Territorial Sea Convention*, art. 14, ¶ 4; *LOS Convention*, art. 19, ¶ 1. The LOS Convention specifies which do *not* qualify as "innocent passage," including: (1) threat or use of *force*; (2) exercise or practice with *weapons*; (3) collecting *information that prejudices the defense or security* of the coastal state; (4) *propaganda affecting the defense or security* of the coastal state; (5) *aircraft* activity; (6) any activity involving a *military device*; (7) loading or unloading of any commodity, currency or person *in violation of the coastal state's customs, fiscal, immigration, or sanitary laws and regulations*; (8) wilful and serious *pollution* in contravention of international law; (9) *fishing*; (10) *research* or surveying; (11) *interfering with communications* of the coastal state. *LOS Convention*, art. 19, ¶ 2.

3. **Coastal state's rights:** Within the territorial sea, the coastal state may not interfere with innocent passage, subject to very limited exceptions.

   a. **Verification:** The coastal state has the unilateral right to verify the innocent character of passage, and it may take the necessary steps in its territorial sea to prevent passage which it determines to be not innocent. *Territorial Sea Convention*, art. 16, ¶ 2; *LOS Convention*, art. 25, ¶ 2.

   b. **Suspension of right of innocent passage:** The coastal state may temporarily suspend the right to innocent passage if essential for protection of the state's security. Suspension may take effect only after due publication. *Territorial Sea Convention*, art. 16, ¶ 3; *LOS Convention*, art. 25, ¶ 3.

   c. **Regulation of right of innocent passage:** Under the LOS Convention, the coastal state may also adopt regulations relating to innocent passage with regard to: (1) safety of navigation and the regulation of maritime traffic; (2) the protection of navigational aids and facilities and other facilities and installations; (3) the protection of cables and pipelines; (4) the conservation of living resources; (5) the preservation of the environment of the coastal state and the prevention, reduction and control of pollution thereof; (6) marine scientific research; and (7) the enforcement of fishing, customs, fiscal, immigration and sanitary regulations. *LOS Convention*, art. 21, ¶ 1. Any regulation of design, construction, manning or equipment must be in conformity with generally accepted international rules and standards. Art. 21, ¶ 2. The coastal state may also establish sea lanes and traffic separation schemes for passage through its territorial sea, where they are necessary to ensure the safety of navigation. Art. 22. Included in the above regulations is the right of the coastal state to require high risk ships, such as large tankers, nuclear-powered ships, and ships carrying inherently dangerous substances, to confine their passage to identified sea lanes. Art. 22, ¶ 2.

d. **Exercising criminal jurisdiction:** A coastal state may exercise criminal jurisdiction on board a foreign ship passing through the territorial sea for the purpose of arresting a person or conducting an investigation only in the following circumstances: (1) the consequences of the crime extend to the coastal state; (2) the crime is of a kind to disturb the peace of the country or the good order of the territorial sea; (3) the assistance of the local authorities has been requested by the master of the ship or by a diplomatic agent of the flag state; or (4) such measures are necessary for the suppression of illicit traffic in narcotic drugs. *Territorial Sea Convention*, art. 19, ¶ 1. *LOS Convention*, art. 27, ¶ 1. The coastal state may not take any steps on board a ship in connection with any crime committed before the ship entered the territorial sea, if the ship is only passing through the territorial sea without entering internal waters. *LOS Convention*, art. 27, ¶ 5.

e. **Exercising civil jurisdiction:** The coastal state may not exercise civil jurisdiction over foreign ships passing through the territorial sea, except for obligations assumed in the course of, or for the purpose of, the ships' voyage through the waters of the coastal state. However, a coastal state may levy execution against or arrest for civil proceedings a foreign ship lying in the territorial sea or passing through the territorial sea after leaving internal waters. *Territorial Sea Convention*, art. 20; *LOS Convention*, art. 28.

4. **Warships:** The LOS Convention does not require prior notification or authorization for innocent passage of a warship through territorial sea. The United States takes the position that no prior notifica-

tion is required. A warship which does not comply with the laws of the coastal state and disregards any request for compliance may be required to leave the territorial sea immediately. *LOS Convention*, art. 30. Submarines must navigate on the surface and show their flag. *Territorial Sea Convention*, art. 14, ¶ 6; *LOS Convention*, art. 20.

D. Transit passage: Transit passage is navigation or overflight for the purpose of ***continuous and expeditious transit***. *LOS Convention*, art. 38, ¶ 2. Under the 1958 Convention on the Territorial Sea, straits which are used for international navigation between one part of the high seas and another part of the high seas or the territorial sea of a foreign state. *Territorial Sea Convention*, art. 16, ¶ 4. The LOS Convention grants the right between two areas of the high seas on two exclusive economic zones. *LOS Convention*, art. 38, ¶ 2. The right does not exist where a strait is broad enough to allow navigation through a high seas route in its middle. *LOS Convention*, art. 36; *contra Corfu Channel*, (*U.K. v. Alb.*), 1949 I.C.J. 4 (Corfu Channel was an international strait even though not a necessary route between two areas of the high seas).

    1. Distinguished from innocent passage: The LOS Convention established a regime governing transit passage through straits which is separate from innocent passage through territorial seas. *LOS Convention*, arts. 34-35. Unlike innocent passage, transit passage ***extends to aircraft and submarines***. Also, states may not unilaterally suspend transit passage. art. 42, ¶ 5. The fields in which a state bordering a strait may regulate transit passage are more limited than those for innocent passage. A state may regulate for pollution control, fishing, and enact customs, fiscal, immigration and sanitary regulations. Art. 42. These laws may not discriminate against foreign ships or in any way act to impede transit passage. Art. 42.

    2. Archipelagic sea lanes passage: Under the LOS Convention, all ships also have a right of archipelagic sea lanes passage. *LOS Convention*, art. 53.

E. Contiguous zone: The coastal state may exercise the control necessary to prevent infringement of its customs, fiscal, immigration or sanitary laws and regulations in a zone contiguous to its territorial sea. *Territorial Sea Convention*, art. 24, ¶ 1; *LOS Convention*, art. 33, ¶ 1. Under the 1958 Convention, the contiguous zone may not exceed 12 nautical miles. Under the LOS Convention, the contiguous zone may not extend beyond 24 nautical miles from the baseline. *LOS Convention*, art. 33, ¶ 2.

VI. EXCLUSIVE ECONOMIC ZONE

A. **High seas to fishery zones to exclusive economic zone:** No state had jurisdiction over waters beyond the territorial sea and contiguous of the state until the middle of this century. The Exclusive Economic Zones (EEZ) established in the LOS Convention give states exclusive economic rights in expanded zones contiguous to their coasts.

1. **Early coastal management:** In the 1940s, increased exploitation of fisheries in waters contiguous to coastal states led many states to enter into conservation and management agreements for fisheries. In 1945, the United States asserted the right to claim jurisdiction over the natural resources contained in the subsoil and seabed of its continental shelf. *See* p. 178, *infra.* Additionally, the United States proclaimed sole fishery conservation and management authority in areas where its nationals historically had fished. Following the United States assertion of sole jurisdiction of its coastal waters, a number of South American states asserted exclusive fishing rights over their own coastal waters. The South American proclamations established zones which extended up to 200 nautical miles. The United States and 33 other nations signed the 1958 Fishing on the High Seas Convention. The Convention granted coastal states special rights to conserve, manage and exploit fisheries in areas contiguous with their coasts without specifying any zone within which such rights might apply. The International Court of Justice subsequently recognized that a coastal state has preferential rights to exploit fisheries around its coasts, but the coastal state must consider the fishing rights of those states which have traditionally fished in the same waters. Both parties must negotiate in good faith to find an equitable solution to their differences. *Fisheries Jurisdiction (U.K. v. Ice.),* 1974 I.C.J. 3 (July 25).

2. **The 200-mile Exclusive Economic Zone:** The 200-mile exclusive economic zone was adopted at the Third United Nations Conference on the Law of the Sea in 1982. The LOS Convention established *exclusive rights* for coastal states to explore, exploit, conserve, and manage *all living and nonliving resources within the zone.* The Convention also allows coastal states to exercise limited jurisdiction in establishing and using artificial islands, installations and structures. *LOS Convention,* arts. 55-75. Aside from the coastal state's exclusive right to exploit the zone's resources, the waters are otherwise treated like the high seas. All states are free to operate ships and aircraft and to lay submarine cables and pipelines within an EEZ. They may also engage in other internationally lawful uses of the sea which are part of high seas freedoms. In exercising these freedoms, all states must give due

regard to the rights and duties of the coastal state and obey all lawful regulations of the coastal state. Reciprocally, the coastal state must give the same due regard to the rights and duties of the other states operating lawfully in the EEZ. The United States, in 1983, adopted the 200-mile EEZ set forth in the LOS Convention. The United States and other major maritime states agree that the EEZ continues to be part of the high seas, although subject to the special rights of exploitation of coastal states. Other states insist that the EEZ is a special zone of the coastal state subject only to the freedoms of navigation and overflight. Conflicts are to be resolved based upon equity in light of all relevant circumstances, taking into account the respective importance of the interests of the states involved as well as the interests of the entire international community. *LOS Convention*, art. 59.

B. Management and conservation of the living resources within the EEZ: The coastal state has several responsibilities in the management of the resources within the EEZ.

1. Duty of the coastal state to prevent over-exploitation of living resources in the EEZ: Coastal states must maintain levels of fishing which produce a "maximum sustainable yield", a level at which the maximum amount of fish can be harvested without depleting the stock. *LOS Convention*, art. 61, ¶¶ 2-3. Maximum sustainable yield is calculated based upon scientific data, but the coastal state must also consider the economic needs of its coastal fishing communities and those of developing states in the region.

2. Duty of coastal state to promote optimum utilization of the living resources within its EEZ: "Optimum utilization" is a flexible concept by which a coastal state determines the allowable catch of the living resources within its EEZ and its own capacity to harvest the allowable catch. Although a coastal state may not set an allowable catch which would cause over-exploitation of living resources, the state may set the allowable catch at the same level as its own capacity to harvest. This prevents foreign states from harvesting the surplus which the coastal state cannot harvest. However, if the allowable catch exceeds the capacity of the coastal state to harvest, the coastal state must grant access to other states to harvest the surplus taking into account "all relevant factors." *LOS Convention*, art. 62, ¶ 2.

C. Right of geographically disadvantaged states and land-locked states in the EEZ: Geographically disadvantaged states are coastal states which can claim no EEZ of their own or whose geographic locations make them dependent upon exploitation of the EEZ of other coastal states in the region. *LOS Convention*, art. 70, ¶ 2. Landlocked states do not border coastal waters.

1. **Rights:** Land-locked and geographically disadvantaged states have the right to participate, on an equitable basis, in the exploitation of any fishery surplus in the EEZs of coastal states in the region. These equitable rights take into account the relevant economic and geographic circumstances of all states concerned. *LOS Convention*, arts. 69, ¶ 1, 70, ¶ 1. This includes the need to minimize detrimental effects on states whose citizens have habitually fished in the EEZ.

2. **Terms of participation:** In establishing terms of participation, the states involved must consider the following factors: (1) the need to avoid detriment to fishing communities or industries of the coastal state; (2) the extent to which the disadvantaged state participates in the exploitation of other states' EEZs; (3) avoidance of a particular burden on any single coastal state; and (4) the nutritional needs of the populations concerned. *LOS Convention*, arts. 69, ¶ 2, 70, ¶ 2. When a coastal state raises its capacity to harvest to the point where it could harvest its entire allowable catch, the coastal state must establish equitable arrangements to allow developing geographically disadvantaged states in the region to exploit living resources in the EEZ.

3. **Special access of developing states to limited surplus:**
   When a coastal state is near a point of being able to harvest the entire allowable catch, it must cooperate with *developing* land-locked and geographically disadvantaged states in the region to establish equitable arrangements for participation. *LOS Convention*, arts. 69, ¶ 3, 70, ¶ 4.

D. **Species subject to special rules:** Several species have been singled out for special treatment within EEZs.

1. **Species extending beyond a single EEZ:** Coastal states must cooperate to enact conservation and management measures for the same stock of species which occur within the EEZs of more than one coastal state, or "straddling stocks." This obligation also applies when the species stock is in an EEZ adjacent to an area of high seas frequented by foreign fishermen, *LOS Convention*, art. 63, and for highly migratory species such as tuna. Art. 64.

2. **Marine mammals:** Exploitation of marine mammals may be more strictly regulated by the coastal state than fish stocks. *LOS Convention*, art. 65. *See also* the Marine Mammal Protection Act of 1972, 16 U.S.C. § 1361-1362, 1371-1384, 1401-1407 (1972).

3. **River stocks:** Anadromous and catadromous species are the primary responsibility of the states in whose rivers the species originate or spend the greater part of their life cycles. The coastal state must cooperate with other states outside its EEZ in whose waters the river species migrate. Coastal states must also cooperate with other states when their nationals fish the anadromous or catadromous stocks outside their EEZ. *LOS Convention,* arts. 66, 67.

4. **Sedentary species:** Sedentary species exploitation is not governed by the LOS Convention. Sedentary species are immobile or under the seabed at their harvesting stage. They are considered part of the natural resources of the continental shelf. *See* p. 180, *infra.*

E. Enforcement of conservation and management measures:
Enforcement of conservation and management measures of the EEZ depends upon whether the violation occurred within the EEZ or beyond it. A coastal state has more enforcement rights within the EEZ.

1. **Within the EEZ:** A coastal state has the right to *enforce all laws enacted* to conserve and manage living resources. The coastal state authorities may board and inspect a ship, impound the ship and arrest its crew, and institute judicial action against them. Punishment for violators may not include imprisonment or corporal punishment under the LOS Convention. Upon arrest, the enforcing coastal state must notify the flag state of the seized vessel.

2. **Outside the EEZ:** Enforcement of regulation of anadromous species, highly migratory stocks, and straddling stocks beyond the EEZ is allowed if all states concerned agree. Arrest for violations which occur in the EEZ may occur outside the EEZ in cases of "hot pursuit." *See* p. 185 *infra.*

F. U.S. legislation relating to conservation and exploitation of the living resources in the EEZ: In the 1976 Fishery Conservation and Management Act, the U.S. established a 200-mile fishery conservation zone to counteract over-exploitation of certain fishery stocks. The Act places regulatory planning authority in regional fishery management councils. The plans must prevent over-exploitation of the fisheries while promoting the harvest of an "optimum yield" from each area. 16 U.S.C. § 1851-1855 (1976). The Act defines "optimum yield" as a yield which provides the maximum overall benefit to the U.S. The Act also allows control of foreign access to the fishery zones. Foreign fishing is authorized only if an existing treaty requires access or if the foreign state entered into a fishery agreement with the U.S. which acknowledged U.S. fishery conservation and management jurisdiction in the zone. 16 U.S.C. § 1821(a)-(b) (1977). If there is no surplus, no foreign fishermen may harvest. Amendments in 1980 set a new method for determining the allowable level of foreign fishing which may result in the U.S. phasing out foreign fishing. Until phase out occurs, "market access" gives preferential allocation of fishery surpluses to nations that give preferential access to their surpluses to the U.S. Highly migratory species regulation is left to international agreement but anadromous species regulation is allowed.

G. **Non-living resources of the EEZ:** A coastal state may also exploit non-living resources in its EEZ, such as production of energy from water, currents or winds.

H. **Marine scientific research:** Coastal states may regulate, authorize, and conduct marine scientific research within its EEZ. Other states must obtain consent to conduct marine scientific research in the EEZ of another coastal state. If the proposed scientific research is for peaceful purposes for the scientific benefit of all mankind, the coastal state must consent. A coastal state may refuse consent, however, if the research: directly involves exploration and exploitation of natural resources; involves drilling or the use of explosives and other dangerous materials; involves the construction of artificial islands; contains inaccurate information; or if the applicant has outstanding obligations to the coastal state. *LOS Convention*, art. 246. The coastal state has a right to be informed of the nature and progress of the research project.

I. **Artificial islands and installations:** The coastal state has the exclusive right to construct and regulate construction, operation and use of any artificial islands, and of installations and structures built for economic purposes in its EEZ. The coastal state also has exclusive jurisdiction over such artificial islands, installations and structures. *LOS Convention*, art. 60, ¶¶ 1, 2, 7.

VII. CONTINENTAL SHELF

A. **Early claims:** In 1945, the U.S. proclaimed its control over the natural resources of the seabed and subsoil on the continental shelf surrounding the U.S. This proclamation, however, recognized the freedoms of the high seas in the seas above the continental shelf. Other states soon asserted various claims to the shelf and the superadjacent waters. The 1958 Convention on the Continental Shelf recognized the principle of sovereign rights of exploration and exploitation for coastal states over the natural resources of their continental shelves. *Continental Shelf Convention*, art. 2. The rights do not affect the freedoms of the high seas in the waters above the continental shelf. These basic principles were elaborated on in the LOS Convention in 1982.

B. **Definition and delimitation:** Geologically, the continental shelf *begins at the shore and ends where the continental slope to the deep seabed begins.*

1. **The 1958 Convention on the Continental Shelf:** The 1958 Convention on the Continental Shelf defines continental shelf as the seabed and subsoil of submarine areas adjacent to the coast but outside the limits of the territorial sea to a depth of 200 meters or to where the water depth allows exploitation of natural resources. The first criteria came to be considered as too arbitrary and the second as too vague. The concept of an economic zone also necessitated revision of the delimitation in the LOS Convention.

2. **The LOS Convention:** The LOS Convention establishes two alternative measures for continental shelves. The first is the geological definition, which recognizes the continental shelf as running to the edge of the continental margin. The second delineation allows a coastal state to claim a continental shelf 200 nautical miles from the baseline. If the continental margin extends beyond 200 nautical miles, the outer limit of the shelf may not exceed 350 nautical miles from the baseline, or 100 nautical miles from the point at which the depth reaches 2500 meters. *LOS Convention,* art. 76.

C. **Rights and duties of the coastal state over the continental shelf:** The coastal state has *limited obligations* in managing the continental shelf and has *extensive rights* in the resources of the shelf.

1. **Extent of sovereign rights:** The coastal state has *exclusive sovereignty* over its continental shelf for the purpose of exploring and exploiting "natural resources." Natural resources are minerals and other non-living resources of the seabed and subsoil, as well as sedentary living plant and animal species. *Continental Shelf Convention,* art. 2, ¶ 4; *LOS Convention,* art. 77, ¶ 4. Shipwrecks and lost cargo on the shelf are not natural resources. If a coastal state does not exercise its rights to explore and exploit, no one else may do so without the express consent of the coastal state. *LOS Convention,* arts. 77, 81. The coastal state's rights over the continental shelf do not extend to the superadjacent waters and airspace. Thus, the coastal state may not unjustifiably interfere with the high seas freedoms of navigation, overflight, fishing, laying of submarine cables and pipelines, and the right to conduct scientific research. *LOS Convention,* arts. 78, 87. However, the course of submarine cables or pipelines is subject to the coastal state's consent.

2. **Duties:** When a coastal state exploits non-living resources on its continental shelf beyond the 200-mile limit, the coastal state must

pay a fee to the deep seabed mining Authority established under the LOS Convention. *LOS Convention*, art. 82.

D. **Sedentary fisheries:** The coastal state has sovereign rights over all sedentary fisheries on its continental shelf. Unlike fishery zones, sedentary fisheries are not subject to "optimum yield" regulations. Therefore, the coastal state need not grant access to any portion of its sedentary fisheries to other states.

E. **Marine scientific research on the continental shelf:** The same rules apply to research in the continental shelf as apply to the EEZ. *See* p. 178, *supra*. For research on a shelf more than 200 nautical miles from the baseline, a coastal state may not withhold consent to a research project if it will be conducted in an area where the coastal state has not or will not begin exploitation or exploration activities within a reasonable time. *LOS Convention*, art. 246.

F. **United States practice and legislation relating to the continental shelf:** In the United States, control over the continental shelf area is divided between the federal government and its coastal states.

1. **Federal sovereignty:** The United States government has "paramount rights in, and full dominion and power over, the lands, minerals and other things" beyond the low water mark. *United States v. California*, 332 U.S. 19 (1947).

2. **The Outer Continental Shelf Lands Act (OCSLA):** This Act establishes a federal regulatory system for the resources of the outer continental shelf (generally the area more than three miles from the baseline). The Submerged Lands Act granted states full jurisdiction and rights over the inner continental shelf area. 43 U.S.C. § 1331. The U.S. reserved its powers to regulate commerce, navigation, defense, and international affairs within the inner shelf. 43 U.S.C. § 1214.

VIII. EXPLOITING THE MINERAL RESOURCES OF THE DEEP SEABED

International law pertaining to exploitation of mineral resources of the deep seabed, despite its uncertainty, will continue to grow in importance as resources become scarce and technology improves. Potential conflicts may arise over conflicting claims to mineral resources until there is more widespread agreement on the legal principles governing exploitation of the deep seabed.

A. **Current status of the legal regime of the deep seabed:** There is no universally agreed upon legal regime governing exploitation of the mineral resources of the deep seabed. Ever since scientists in the 1960s discovered vast resources in the form of manganese nodules on the deep ocean floors, the legal status of the deep seabed has been highly disputed. Three views have developed regarding the legal status of the deep seabed.

1. **"Common heritage of mankind" view:** The "common heritage of mankind" view is that the mineral resources of the deep seabed may be exploited only by or under the auspices of an *international authority acting on behalf of all countries* to assure equitable division. No state or person may claim, explore, or exploit these resources until the establishment of such an authority. This view is adhered to mostly by developing states and is premised on the theory that the seabed belongs to every member of the international community in common (*res communis*). It differs from the pure *res communis* view, which is that what belongs to everyone can be exploited by no one.

   a. **"Declaration of Principles Governing the Sea-Bed... Beyond the Limits of the National Jurisdiction":** In 1970, the United Nations General Assembly adopted this measure by a unanimous vote. The Declaration states in part that the deep seabed and its natural resources "are the common heritage of mankind," and that all shall benefit from its exploitation. The Declaration envisions an international treaty that shall set up a regime to govern the resources of the deep seabed, but did not prohibit exploitation of resources before the establishment of a "generally agreed upon" international regime. The earlier, so-called "Moratorium Resolution" which prohibited exploitation until such time was voted against by the United States and other developed countries.

   b. **The LOS Convention:** In 1982, the LOS Convention established a deep seabed mining regime. Whether regime of the Convention will become customary international law, binding upon non-parties, is troublesome given the opposition of most developed countries, including the United States, to the regime. The principal objections to the regime focused on the methods of distributions profits from exploitation to the international community and of sharing technology. The Convention regime would be clearly established as custom only if a majority of all regional groups, of both developed and developing states, accepts it and conforms mining practices to it.

2. **Freedom of the high seas view:** The freedom of the high seas view is that the right to explore and exploit the mineral resources of the deep seabed is a *freedom of the high seas*. A state may autho-

rize or engage in the exploration and exploitation of deep seabed mineral resources, provided that such activities are conducted with reasonable regard for the rights of other states to do similar activities. *No state may claim or acquire exclusive rights* over any part of the deep seabed or its mineral resources. This view, at least pending an agreed upon regime, is asserted by the United States and most other developed nations.

3. *Res nullius* view: The *res nullius* view is that the seabed belongs to no one (*res nullius*), and that the seabed, as well as its mineral resources, may be explored and exploited to the exclusion of all others by the first state which claims it. This view has been adopted by some legal scholars but has not gained widespread acceptance.

B. **Seabed mining under the LOS Convention:**   No state may claim, exercise sovereign rights over or appropriate any part of the deep seabed or its resources because the mineral resources of the seabed are the common heritage of mankind. *LOS Convention*, arts. 136, 137, ¶ 1.

1. **The Authority:**   The Convention establishes an Authority, which shall act on behalf of mankind in governing the deep seabed. *LOS Convention*, arts. 137, ¶ 2, 153, 156-157. The Authority consists of an Assembly, a Council and a Secretariat. The Authority's membership consists of all states which are parties to the LOS Convention. Arts. 156, ¶ 2, 158.

2. **The Assembly:**   The Assembly is the "supreme organ" of the Authority and establishes its policies. The Assembly's membership consists of one representative from each member of the Authority. *LOS Convention*, arts. 159, ¶ 1, 160, ¶ 1.

3. **The Council:**   The Council is the "executive organ" of the Authority and establishes "specific policies" and approves "plans of work" for each mining project. The Council's membership consists of 36 members of the Authority, chosen to represent the following interests: (1) consumers of minerals to be produced by deep seabed mining; (2) investors in deep seabed mining activities; (3) terrestrial producers of the same minerals; (4) developing states; and (5) a geographic distribution of the members. *LOS Convention*, arts. 160, 161.

4. **The Enterprise:**   The Enterprise is the separate legal entity which will carry out mining activities on behalf of the Authority. *LOS Convention*, art. 170.

5. **Regulation of mining:**   Annex III provides the basic guidelines for exploring and exploiting the deep seabed. Applicants who apply for a license to explore or exploit the deep sea bed must be either a citizen or be controlled by a state party to the LOS Convention. *LOS*

Convention, art. 153. Each applicant must submit a "plan of work" with the following conditions: (1) payment of $500,000 application processing fee; (2) description of the activity; (3) two sites of estimated equal commercial value, one for the Enterprise (which may turn it over to a developing country) and the other for the applicant's use; and (4) full disclosure to the Authority of equipment, non-proprietary technology, and methodology to be used. *LOS Convention*, Annex III, arts. 13, ¶ 2, 8, 9, 5, ¶ 1. If the permit is granted, the contractor must pay an annual fixed fee of $1 million until the date of commencement of commercial production. *LOS Convention*, Annex III, art. 13, ¶ 3. Thereafter, the contractor shall pay the greater of $1 million or the "production charge" — calculated either as 5 percent of the market value of the processed metals during the first ten years of commercial production and at a 12 percent market value thereafter, or calculated as a fixed fee of 2 percent of the market value of the processed metals during the first period of commercial production, rising to 4 percent in the second period of production. *LOS Convention*, Annex III, art. 13, ¶¶ 3-6. After the contractor has recovered its developments costs, it shall pay a share of its net proceeds to the Authority on a graduated scale of 35 to 70 percent. *LOS Convention*, Annex III, art. 13, ¶ 6, cl. c. The Enterprise's exploration activities are in part financed by assessments against state parties to the Convention, and a Seabed Disputes Chamber is established for resolution of disputes under the regime.

C. **United States legislation:** The 1980 Deep Seabed Hard Mineral Resources Act (hereinafter "the Act") establishes an interim program to regulate United States citizen exploration for and commercial recovery of hard mineral resources of the deep seabed pending establishment of an international regime. 30 U.S.C. § 1401 (1980). Applicants must obtain a license for initial exploration activities and a permit for commercial recovery of resources.

IX. FREEDOM OF THE HIGH SEAS

A. **General Principles:** From the 17th century, it has been recognized that all states, whether coastal or landlocked, may exercise certain freedoms of the seas. Under the 1958 Convention and the LOS Convention, these freedoms include, but are not limited to: (1) *freedom of navigation*; (2) *freedom of overflight*; (3) *freedom of fishing*; and (4) *freedom to lay submarine cables and pipelines*. The LOS Convention also lists freedom to construct artificial islands, installations and structures, and freedom of scientific research. These freedoms must be exercised with due regard for the interests of other states. All states are bound to refrain from acts which unreasonably interfere with the high seas freedoms of other states. *LOS Convention*, art. 87. No state may exercise its jurisdiction over any part of the high seas.

B. **Reservation of the high seas for peaceful purposes:** The high seas must be used for *peaceful purposes*. Naval forces may use the high seas, but use or threat of force violates the LOS Convention and article 2, ¶ 4 of the United Nations Charter absent other justification of international law (*e.g.*, self-defense).

C. **Freedom of navigation:** Every state has the right to sail ships on the high seas bearing its national flag. *LOS Convention*, art. 90. With this right comes the obligation to give due consideration to the interests of others. This includes: (1) observing rules relating to safety of navigation; (2) protecting life at sea; and (3) preventing and reducing pollution. Absent a state of war, warships and state-owned ships have complete immunity from jurisdiction of any other state than the flag state, when on the high seas. Arts. 95, 96. The flag state of merchant ships has exclusive jurisdiction in terms of arrest or any other physical interference over a merchant ship on the high seas. There are, however, a number of exceptions to this exclusive jurisdiction by which a warship may interfere with another state's merchant ship.

1. **Treaty exception:** A flag state may expressly provide by international agreement to allow another state to exercise jurisdiction over its ships on the high seas. *High Seas Convention*, art. 6, ¶ 1; *LOS Convention*, art. 92, ¶ 1. A government ship of a foreign state may board, search and, in some instances, seize a ship on the high seas if a treaty so provides or a flag state has consented. Specifically, the LOS Convention provides that a state which has reasonable grounds to believe a ship flying its flag is engaged in illegal drug traffic may request the cooperation of other states to suppress such traffic. *LOS Convention*, art. 108.

2. **Collision cases:** When conduct on the flag state's ship on the high seas has effects on a foreign ship or foreign territory, the foreign state has concurrent jurisdiction based on the territoriality principle. *See The S.S. Lotus (Fr. v. Turk.)*, P.C.I.J. Ser. A, No. 10 (1927), discussed on p. 66, *supra*. In collision cases, jurisdiction is now limited to the flag state of the vessel alleged to be responsible and to the state of nationality of the accused. *High Seas Convention*, art. 11; *LOS Convention*.

3. **Right of visit:** A warship is entitled to board another ship when there is reasonable grounds for suspecting that the ship is engaged in piracy, slave trade or (under the LOS Convention) unauthorized broadcasting. *High Seas Convention*, art. 22, ¶ 1; *LOS Convention*, art. 110. Piracy is defined in both Conventions as:

   a. Any illegal acts of violence, detention or any act of depredation, committed for private ends by the crew or the passengers of a private ship or a private aircraft, and directed:

      i. On the high seas, against another ship or aircraft, or against persons or property on board such ship or aircraft;

      ii. Against a ship, aircraft, persons or property in a place outside the jurisdiction of any State;

   b. Any act of voluntary participation in the operation of a ship or of an aircraft with knowledge of facts making it a pirate ship or aircraft;

   c. Any act of inciting or of intentionally facilitating an act described in sub-paragraph [a] or sub-paragraph [b] of this article.

High Seas Convention, art. 15; *LOS Convention*, art. 101. A government ship may also board a ship when it has reason to suspect that, though flying a foreign flag, the ship has the same nationality as the government ship. *High Seas Convention*, art. 22, ¶ 1, cl. e; *LOS Convention*, art. 110, ¶ 1, cl. e. A stateless ship or a ship flying the flag of more than one state has ***no protection*** against boarding and search on the high seas. *High Seas Convention*, art. 6, ¶ 1; *LOS Convention*, art. 92, ¶ 2. Depending upon the nature of the violation suspected, search and arrest may follow.

4. **"Hot pursuit":** The "right of hot pursuit" allows a warship to engage in pursuit of a foreign ship continuing into the high seas if the state has good reason to believe the ship has violated its laws. The right of hot pursuit ceases as soon as the ship pursued enters the territorial waters of another state. The pursuit must begin in the internal waters, territorial sea, contiguous zone, exclusive economic zone, or continental shelf of the pursuing state. For pursuit convening in or beyond the contiguous zone, the pursuit must be for a violation of the coastal state's rights in that zone.

5. **Necessity:** The LOS Convention provides that nothing in the section on preservation of the marine environment prejudices the right of states pursuant to custom and treaty law to take proportional measures to protect their coasts and related waters from pollution or the threat of pollution from a maritime casualty which may reasonably be expected to result in major harmful consequences. *LOS Convention*, art. 221.

Example: In 1967, when a Liberian oil tanker, the Torrey Canyon, ran aground on a reef in the English Channel, the United Kingdom bombed the tanker to minimize the pollution of its coasts.

6. **Self-defense:** The rules governing the threat or use of force in self-defense are governed by the U.N. Charter, and are discussed at p. 142, *supra*.

7. **Action authorized by the United Nations:** The role of the United Nations is discussed at pp. 88-96, *supra*.

D. **Freedom of overflight:** All civilian and military aircraft have the right to fly over the high seas.

E. **Freedom of fishing and conservation measures:** All states have the right to fish the high seas. This right is limited by treaties and by the rights of coastal states to regulate their continental shelves. The LOS Convention includes a section on conservation and management of the living resources of the high seas which requires states to cooperate in the conservation and management of resources. *LOS Convention*, art. 118. Coastal states acting in cooperation and international organizations may also regulate to protect marine mammals. Art. 120.

F. **Freedom to lay submarine cables and pipelines:** The route of cable and pipeline is subject to coastal state regulations on the continental shelf. *LOS Convention*, arts. 79, 112.

G. **Freedom to construct artificial islands:** Construction and operation of artificial islands, installations and structures is subject to coastal state regulations involving such activities on the continental shelf or in the EEZ.

H. **Freedom of scientific research:** All states and competent international organizations have the right to conduct scientific marine research outside EEZs. *LOS Convention*, art. 257.

X. PRESERVATION OF THE MARINE ENVIRONMENT

Prior to the 1960s there was very little protective regulation of the marine environment. The limited provisions of the 1958 Convention on the High Seas contemplated future action. In the 1970s, general rules for the preservation of the global environment imposed a few limitations on pollution of the seas. Growing concern with marine pollution led to inclusion of extensive provisos in the LOS Convention for protection and preservation of the marine environment. A crucial issue is whether these provisions can be said to reflect customary international law or whether they are only binding on parties to the Convention.

A. **The 1958 Conventions:** The only provisions of the 1958 Convention specifically addressed to preservation of the marine environment are articles 24 and 25 of the Convention on the High Seas. Article 24 requires states to regulate to prevent pollution of the seas by oil discharge from ships, pipelines, or deep seabed activities. Article 25 calls on states to take measures to prevent pollution of the seas from radioactive materials.

B. **The Stockholm Declaration and general obligation to preserve the environment:** In 1972, the Stockholm Declaration was adopted at the United Nations Conference on the Human Environment. Principle 7 of the Declaration requires states to take "all possible steps" to ***prevent pollution*** of the seas. Principle 21 provides that states must ensure, in exercising their sovereign rights to exploit their resources, "that activities within their jurisdiction or control do not cause damage to the environment or other states or of areas beyond the limit of national jurisdiction." Principle 21 expanded upon the international law principle that no state could use or permit its territory to be used in a manner injurious to another state's territory. *See, e.g., The Trail Smelter Case (U.S. v. Can.),* 3 R.I.A.A. 1905 (1941). Principle 22 further requires states to cooperate to develop international law for liability and compensation for damage caused by states to areas beyond their jurisdiction.

C. **Third United Nations Conference on the Law of the Sea:** Article 192 of the LOS Convention outlines the general obligations of states to ***protect and preserve the marine environment***. States are required to meet this obligation by taking all measures necessary to prevent pollution of the marine environment from any source. *LOS Convention,* art. 194, ¶ 1. All sources of pollution of the marine environment must be considered, such as: (1) the release of toxic, harmful or noxious substances from land-based sources, from or through the atmosphere, or by dumping; (2) pollution from vessels; (3) pollution from installations and devices used in the exploration or exploitation of the natural resources of the seabed and subsoil; and (4) pollution from other installations operating in the marine environment. Art. 194, ¶ 3. The provisions apply to commercial ships; states have only to ensure that warships, as far as practicable, act consistently with international rules and standards. Art. 236.

1. **Regional standards adopted:** States are required to harmonize their policies on a regional level with regard to pollution from land-based sources and from seabed activities within zones of national jurisdiction. *LOS Convention,* arts. 207, ¶ 3, 208, ¶ 4.

2. **Global standards adopted:** States are requested to harmonize their policies on a global level with regard to pollution from land-based sources, seabed activities subject to national jurisdiction, pollution from dumping, and pollution of the marine environment through or from the atmosphere. *LOS Convention*, arts. 207, ¶ 4, 208, ¶ 5, 210, ¶ 4, 212, ¶ 3.

D. **Vessel source pollution:** States are required to establish international guidelines governing vessel-source pollution through international organizations, such as the International Maritime Organization or through general diplomatic conference. *LOS Convention*, art. 211.

1. **Flag state jurisdiction:** Flag states are required to adopt laws and regulations for the prevention of pollution of the marine environment from ships flying their flag or of their registry. Areas of regulation include: (1) the design, construction, equipment, operation and manning of vessels; (2) accident prevention; (3) emergency procedures; (4) operations of sea safety standards; and (5) prevention of intentional and unintentional discharges. *LOS Convention*, arts. 194, ¶ 3, cl. b, 211.

2. **Coastal state regulation in ports, in internal waters and in the territorial sea:** Coastal states may adopt laws and regulations for the prevention, reduction and control of marine pollution from foreign vessels within their territorial sea but may not hamper innocent passage. States may set standards for pollution prevention as a condition for entrance into their ports or for internal waters. *LOS Convention*, art. 211, ¶¶ 3-4.

3. **Coastal state jurisdiction in the EEZ:** States may regulate vessel-source pollution in the EEZ in accordance with generally accepted rules and standards through a competent international organization or diplomatic conference. Coastal states may request a competent international organization to authorize the states to adopt additional regulations if the reviewing organization finds that the international rules and standards are inadequate to protect an area of their exclusive economic zones. *LOS Convention*, art. 21, ¶ 6.

E. **Pollution from land-based sources:** All states must adopt laws or regulations to prevent pollution of the marine environment from land-based sources. *LOS Convention*, art. 207.

F. **Ocean dumping:** States are required to adopt laws and regulations to prevent pollution of the marine environment by the dumping of sewage, sludge, and other waste materials into the ocean. *LOS Convention*, art. 210. These laws must be no less stringent than global standards. Dumping in the territorial sea, exclusive economic zone, or continental shelf of a state, requires permission from the proper state authorities.

The 1972 Convention on the Dumping of Wastes at Sea sets forth regulations regarding three categories of waste. The Convention prohibits the dumping of materials listed in Annex I: (1) high level radioactive wastes; (2) materials produced for biological and chemical warfare; and (3) non-biodegradable synthetic materials. Dumping of wastes in the second category, which includes low-level radioactive wastes, requires a special permit. The third category of waste materials requires only a general prior permit. Annex III to the Convention specifies terms and conditions upon which general and special permits are issued.

G. **Pollution from seabed activities subject to national jurisdiction:** States are required to adopt all laws and regulations necessary to prevent pollution of the marine environment arising from or in connection with their exploration and exploitation of the seabed and subsoil, or from artificial islands, installations and structures under their jurisdictions, taking into account any internationally agreed upon standards. *LOS Convention*, art. 194, ¶ 3, cl. e, art. 208.

H. **Pollution from deep seabed mining:** Part XI of the LOS Convention authorizes the Authority to adopt appropriate rules and regulations to prevent pollution of the marine environment from deep seabed activities. *See* p. 182, *supra.*

I. **Pollution from or through the atmosphere:** All states are required to adopt laws and regulations to prevent pollution of the marine environment from or through the atmosphere, taking into account internationally agreed upon rules. All vessels flying a state's flag or aircraft under the state's registry must abide by the regulations. *LOS Convention*, art. 212.

J. **Protection of fragile ecosystems:** States are obligated specifically to take measures necessary to protect and preserve rare or fragile ecosystems as well as the habitat of depleted, threatened or endangered species and other forms of marine life. *LOS Convention*, art. 194, ¶ 5, 211. A Coastal state also may adopt and enforce non-discriminatory laws and regulations for the prevention, reduction, and control of marine pollution from vessels in ice-covered areas within its exclusive economic zone, where severe climatic conditions and the presence of ice for most of the year create obstructions or exceptional hazards to navigation. Art. 234.

K. **Liability:** A state which fails to fulfill its obligations to protect and preserve the marine environment is liable in accordance with international law. States must ensure recourse is available for prompt and adequate relief for damage caused by pollution. States must cooperate to be developed to assure prompt and adequate compensation for damage caused by pollution of the marine environment, such as compulsory insurance or compensation funds. *LOS Convention*, art. 235.

1. **Liability for nuclear accidents:** Article 2 of the 1962 Nuclear Ships Convention provides that the operator of a nuclear ship "shall be absolutely liable for any nuclear damage upon proof that such damage has been caused by a nuclear incident involving the nuclear fuel of, or radioactive products or waste produced in, such ship." The licensing state is obligated to insure payments are made for the claims for compensation for injuries resulting from a nuclear accident.

2. **Liability for oil pollution:** The 1969 Convention on Civil Liability for Oil Pollution Damage governs injuries caused by oil pollution in a state party's territory or territorial sea. Because this Convention did not provide full compensation for victims of oil pollution injuries, the 1971 Convention concerning an International Fund for Compensation for Oil Pollution Damage was promulgated.

L. **Enforcement:** Flag states, coastal states and port states may enforce rules and regulation relating to the marine environments. The extent of their enforcement powers varies, depending on the source of pollution, the location of the violation, and the degree of harm to the environment.

1. **Flag state enforcement:** Flag states are obligated to ensure that all ships flying their flags or registry comply with international rules and standards established by the competent international organization or diplomatic conference, and state laws adopted in accordance with the Convention. *LOS Convention*, art. 217, ¶ 1. Flag states must inspect ships to issue and periodically verify certificates of compliance with the laws of the state. Other states must accept these certificates as evidence of the condition of the ship. Art. 217, ¶¶ 2-3. Flag states must establish penalties harsh enough to discourage violations by their ships. Art. 217, ¶ 8. In the event a ship violates international rules and standards, the flag state must investigate immediately and institute proceedings if appropriate. Art. 217, ¶ 4.

2. **Coastal state enforcement:** When a ship is in port, a coastal state may institute proceedings against it for violation of its laws adopted under the Convention or any international standards if the violation occurred on its territorial sea or exclusive economic zone. When a ship is in the territorial sea of a state, the state may undertake physical inspection if it has clear grounds for suspecting a violation and institute proceedings if the violation occurred during its passage through the territorial sea. When a ship is in the exclusive

economic zone or territorial sea, the coastal zone may require it to provide relevant information if it has clear grounds for believing the ship committed a violation in the exclusive economic zone. Whether the coastal state may take further steps for violations in the EEZ depends upon the extent of damage caused or threatened by the violation. *LOS Convention*, art. 220.

3. **Port state enforcement:** If a ship in a foreign port is responsible for a discharge beyond the port state's EEZ in violation of international standards, the port state may investigate and, if warranted, institute enforcement proceedings. If the discharge occurred within the EEZ, territorial sea, or internal waters of another state, the port state cannot institute proceedings unless so requested by that state, the flag state of the ship, or another state damaged by the discharge, unless the waters of the port state itself have been or are likely to be polluted by the discharge. As far as practicable, the port state is obligated to investigate or institute proceedings if so requested by the flag state of the ship, any state whose coastal waters are damaged by the discharge, or any state within whose waters the discharge occurred. *LOS Convention*, art. 218.

4. **Liability for wrongful enforcement:** A state is obligated to compensate the flag state for any injury or loss attributable to unlawful or excessive measures taken against a foreign ship. The legal systems in all states must provide for private actions in respect to such injury or loss. *LOS Convention*, art. 232. Also, under the 1973 Convention for the Prevention of Pollution from Ships (MARPOL), a ship "shall be entitled to compensation for any loss or damage suffered" from a state's measures that cause the ship to be unduly delayed or detained. International Convention for the Prevention of Pollution from Ships, art. 7, ¶ 2, 12 I.L.M. 1319 (1973).

M. **Notification and cooperative action:** As soon as a state is aware that injury to the marine environment has occurred or is imminent, it must *notify* immediately the appropriate global or regional international organizations and all states likely to be affected. *LOS Convention*, art. 198. In order to eliminate or minimize the effect of an accident causing marine pollution, neighboring states have a duty to develop contingency plans to respond to pollution. Art. 199.

N. **Government noncommercial ships:** Ships that are used by governments for noncommercial purposes are not subject to the international rules, standards, and enforcement procedures discussed above. Each state must adopt measures to insure that such ships follow the international rules and standards as far as practical. *LOS Convention*, art. 236.

CHAPTER 11
AIR AND SPACE LAW

I. DEFINING STATE SOVEREIGNTY OVER AIRSPACE

A. **Common law view:** Common law doctrine held that a state's control over airspace *extended to the end of the universe*.

B. **Balancing free airspace with states' self-preservation:** Early attempts to define states' sovereignty over airspace balanced the inherent nature of airspace as free from sovereign control against the need of the sovereign to provide for self-preservation and the defense of its citizens.

C. **Exclusive control:** With the increased use of aircraft during World War I came the need to reach an international agreement regarding states' control of airspace. In 1919, the international community resolved at the Paris Convention to establish each state's *exclusive control over its superincumbent airspace*.

1. **Territory limited by territorial waters:** States retained this exclusive control of the airspace above only the territory of the state itself and above its territorial waters.

2. **No control over high seas:** Airspace above the high seas has long been considered *free from state control* and remained so under the Paris Convention.

D. **The Five Freedoms and accommodation of international air travel:** During World War II, the international community witnessed a dramatic rise in international air traffic. The need arose to establish some general principles to govern international air travel.

1. **The Five Freedoms:** At this time in the development of the law of international aviation free airspace had been broken down into five components. These so-called *"five freedoms"* became the basis of the international agreements of this era. The five freedoms are as follows:

a. **Overflight:** The privilege to fly across a state's territory without landing.

b. **Non-traffic landing:** The privilege to land for non-traffic purposes.

c. **Putting down traffic:** The privilege to put down passengers, mail and cargo in the state whose nationality the aircraft possesses.

d. **Picking up traffic:** The privilege to take on passengers, mail and cargo destined for the state whose nationality the aircraft possesses.

e. **International traffic:** The privilege to take on or put down passengers, mail and cargo destined for or coming from any contracting state.

2. **The Chicago Convention:** The most important of the World War II-era agreements was the Chicago Convention. The Chicago Convention took place in 1944 and created the International Civil Aviation Organization and the International Air Services Transit Agreement. The Chicago Convention extends all five freedoms to non-scheduled international air service.

   a. **Aircraft must follow prescribed safe routes:** For safety reasons, states reserved the right to prescribe routes that aircraft must follow when flying over regions which are inaccessible or without adequate navigation facilities.

   b. **Right to refuse intra-state traffic:** States also reserved the right to refuse to allow aircraft from other states to take on traffic in its territory that is destined for a another point within its territory.

   c. **Applies only to civil aircraft:** The Chicago Convention governs only civil aircraft and does not apply to state aircraft, including military aircraft.

   d. **Discrimination based on nationality prohibited:** States may promulgate regulations regarding air travel within the states' airspace but such regulations must be applied identically to all aircraft without regard to nationality. A state or entity in that state may promulgate rules that when applied evenly impact adversely on some states but not others. A court will not view such an impact as a violation of applicable international anti-discrimination standards.

   Example: The Port Authority of New York had established a set of noise regulations for Kennedy Airport. France and Great Britain wished to begin supersonic transport (SST) service to Kennedy but the Port Authority placed an ad hoc ban on SSTs at the site even though the SSTs complied with the existing noise regulations. The Port Authority claimed the ban was necessary to study further the environmental effects of the SSTs' unique low frequency sound. Great Britain and France sued the Port Authority claiming discrimination. The court held that the disparate impact of the ban on Great Britain and France did not render it discriminatory or unlawful. Anti-discrimination principles do not require the Port Authority to "blind itself to significant differences in the noise characteristics of aircraft, merely because they are operated by foreign carriers." *British Airways v. Port Authority of New York*, 558 F.2d 75 (2d Cir. 1977).

3. **International Air Services Transit Agreement extends limited freedoms to scheduled air service:** Only the first two freedoms, *i.e.*, overflights and non-traffic landings, are generally available under the International Air Services Transit Agreement for scheduled air service.

   a. **No general agrement on remaining three freedoms:** The International Air Transport Agreement extended the final three freedoms to scheduled international air service. However, very few states have signed this agreement. Due to this, the United States withdrew from the agreement in 1947.

   b. **Scheduled air service governed by bilateral agreement:** Because no single agreement has satisfied the needs of the international aviation community with regard to scheduled air service, states have entered into a complex web of bilateral arrangements to govern international air traffic.

4. **Definition of "scheduled international air service":** Because the rules governing scheduled and non-scheduled international air service differ, the International Civil Aviation Organization promulgated the following definition. A "scheduled international air service" is a series of flights that possesses all of the following characteristics:

   a. **Overflies more than one state:** It passes through the airspace of more than one state;

   b. **Open to public:** It is performed for the transport of passengers, mail or cargo for remuneration, in such a manner that each flight is open to members of the public; and

   c. **Regular service:** It serves traffic between the same two or more points, either

      i. according to a published timetable; or

      ii. with flights so regular or frequent that they constitute a recognizable, systematic series.

5. **Prescriptive jurisdiction for international air travel:** When an aircraft engages in international air travel, it will at all times be traveling either in airspace governed by a state's domestic regula-

tions or in airspace above the high seas. Regulations regarding air travel differ by jurisdiction.

a. Domestic regulation applies over subjacent state: When the aircraft is in airspace above a state or its territorial water, the regulations of that state apply. In airspace other than over the high seas, ICAO rules apply but only to the extent they do not conflict with rules published by the subjacent state in Annex 2 of the Chicago Convention.

b. ICAO regulation applies over high seas: When the aircraft is in airspace above the high seas, rules promulgated by the ICAO under article 12 of the Chicago Convention apply.

   i. Flight Information Regions: The global airspace is divided into Flight Information Regions (FIRs). The ICAO allocates responsibility for administering navigational duties and dispensing weather information in each FIR to local states.

   ii. Air Defense Identification Zones: Some states maintain Air Defense Identification Zones (ADIZs) in global airspace. An ADIZ is a region of airspace where ready identification, location information and control of a civil aircraft are required to further national security.

   Example: The United States requires that aircraft operating in its ADIZs (1) file a flight plan with the appropriate aeronautical facility and (2) cannot enter the United States from the ADIZ unless it gives its position when it is between one and two hours cruising distance from the United States.

   (1) Legal under the Chicago Convention: The Chicago Convention is silent on the subject of ADIZs. Thus, states are not precluded from maintaining ADIZs.

   (2) No effect on entry: When an aircraft complies with the requirements of the ADIZ, the ADIZ does not preclude any aircraft from entering the airspace of the state.

6. Aircraft has nationality of state of registration: Article 17 of the Chicago Convention defines the nationality of any aircraft as the state in which it is registered.

II. LIABILITY OF AIR CARRIERS

A. Limitations on liability needed to foster airline industry: The original purpose for placing limits on the recovery from airlines for damages was to assist the growth of the fledgling airline industry. For example, in 1929, the Warsaw Convention limited liability for death or personal injury to approximately $8,300. In 1965, the limitation was increased by the Montreal Convention to $75,000.

1. **Need to attract capital:** The airline industry needed capital to assist its growth and it was hoped that a limitation on costs for damages would further that cause.

2. **Need to obtain insurance:** The limitations also served to make the airlines more attractive to insurance carriers that would otherwise not extend policies to the airlines because of the prospect of a catastrophic accident causing heavy losses.

3. **Limitations narrowly construed:** Many United States courts construe the limitation of liability provisions very strictly against air carriers on the theory that the original purpose behind the provisions is no longer valid.

B. **Standard of liability:** In exchange for the limitation on liability, the Warsaw Convention provided a stricter standard of liability for the airlines. Carriers shall be liable for death or personal injury unless it can prove that it or its agents have taken ***all necessary measures to avoid the damage*** or that it was ***impossible for the carrier to take such measures***. This creates a presumption that the carrier must rebut in order to escape liability. In cases where a plaintiff can prove willful misconduct on the part of the carrier, the carrier cannot take advantage of the liability cap.

1. **Requirement of delivery of ticket:** Under the Warsaw Convention, if the carrier accepts a passenger without a passenger ticket having been delivered the carrier cannot avail itself of the liability limitation. Courts in the United States are split as to how strictly to interpret this provision.

   a. **Liberal interpretation:** Because courts in the United States dislike the liability limitation, they have often construed the delivery requirement very liberally to allow full recovery. These courts require that delivery of the ticket must be made in such a manner as to provide adequate notice to the passenger of the limitations in order to allow the passenger the opportunity to obtain further protection for herself against injury or death.

   b. **Strict interpretation:** Other courts have held that the delivery requirement merely demands that the passenger physically possess a ticket before boarding. These courts do not read the Warsaw Convention or the Montreal Agreement as requiring adequate notice.

Example: The plaintiffs sued the airline for damages caused when the airline's plane was destroyed in flight. The plaintiffs argued that delivery of the ticket was invalid because the limitation was printed in 8-point size type, which is smaller than the 10-point size required by the Montreal Agreement. The court held that neither the Warsaw Convention nor the Montreal Agreement require that the limitation be held invalid because the type size is smaller than that specified in the Montreal Agreement. *In re Korean Air Lines Disaster of September 1, 1983*, 829 F.2d 1171 (D.C. Cir. 1987), *aff'd sub nom. Chan v. Korean Air Lines*, 490 U.S. 122 (1989).

2. **Limitation not applicable to certain flights:** The limitation on liability only applies to two types of international travel. The limitation applies to travel that *initiates and terminates in different states, both of which are parties to the Convention*. The limitation also applies to travel that *initiates and terminates in a single state that is a party to the Convention* even if the travel involves stops abroad.

C. **Jurisdiction:** The Warsaw Convention specifies when a state has jurisdiction for actions brought under its terms. Under article 28, there is jurisdiction in the state of:

1. the carrier's *domicile*;

2. the carrier's *principle place of business*;

3. the *location at which the ticket was purchased*; and

4. the passenger's *place of destination*.

III. VIOLATIONS OF AIRSPACE

A. **Violation of airspace:** Under the various international conventions and bilateral agreements governing international aviation, an aircraft normally needs authorization to enter a state's airspace and is required to follow certain procedures while operating in that airspace.

Example: In the well known *Powers Case*, Powers, a citizen of the United States, violated the airspace of the Soviet Union in a U2 plane equipped for espionage. Soviet military shot down Powers' aircraft. The Soviet government tried and convicted Powers for espionage and he was sentenced to confinement for ten years in the Soviet Union. *Powers Case*, 30 Int'l L. Rep. 69 (1966). Note that Powers was not tried for violation of airspace under international law but was found guilty of a crime under the laws of the Soviet Union.

B. Use of force to terminate a trespass: By analogy to the law of the sea, states may use only "necessary and reasonable force" in response to intruding aircraft. *See The I'm Alone*, 3 R.I.A.A. 1609 (1935). The ICAO has taken the position that force should never be used against civilian aircraft.

Example: In 1983, the Soviet Union shot down a Korean Air Lines passenger jet that had violated Soviet airspace, killing everyone on board. The Secretary General of the United Nations concluded that the magnitude of the deviation into Soviet territory was difficult to explain but found no evidence that the pilots were aware of the deviation or intentionally flew off-course. In contrast, the Soviet Union attempted to use evidence that the flight passed directly over sensitive military installations to support its contention that the aircraft was on a spy mission and was mistaken for a military aircraft. The ICAO condemned the Soviet Union's use of armed force.

IV. OFFENSES COMMITTED ABOARD AIRCRAFT

A. Jurisdiction generally: Article 17 of the Chicago Convention provides that an aircraft takes on the nationality of the flag state, thus *giving the flag state jurisdiction* over offenses committed on board the aircraft. In addition, the *subjacent state over which the aircraft flies may assert concurrent jurisdiction* based on territoriality. Other states may also assert jurisdiction for offenses committed based on other aircraft principles, such as the nationality of the defendant, universality, or the nationality of the victim. *See* p. 67-69, *supra*.

B. Hijacking and sabotage: Hijacking involves the use or threat of the use of force to exercise control over an aircraft. Sabotage generally addresses efforts to place the safety of the aircraft in jeopardy. The international community has established conventions to govern both of these offenses. The Convention for the Suppression of Unlawful Seizure of Aircraft ("Hague Convention") governs hijacking and the Convention for the Suppression of Unlawful Acts Against the Safety of Civil Aviation ("Montreal Convention") deals with sabotage. Many of the articles of the two conventions are identical.

    1. Duty to extradite or prosecute: Both conventions place upon the state in which the alleged offender is found the duty to either prosecute or extradite the alleged offender.

    2. Jurisdiction: The Hague and Montreal Conventions (as well as the International Convention for the Taking of Hostages) recognize hijacking and sabotage as universal crimes. *See* Hague Convention art. 4, § 2; Montreal Convention art. 5, § 2; art. 7 in both.

V. OUTER SPACE

A. Definition of "outer space": Two fundamental issues arise in the context of delimiting the border of outer space. First, is a definition even necessary? Second, if a definition is necessary, how shall that definition be derived?

1. Necessity of a definition debatable: States disagree on whether a definition is even necessary.

　　a. Definition not necessary: The United States, among other states, takes the position that there is no need to define where outer space begins.

　　　　i. No complaints: Throughout the history of space exploration, no state has ever complained that another state has violated their airspace during the launch or landing of a space vehicle.

　　　　ii. Definition would be arbitrary: Science is not yet able to define exactly where outer space begins so any attempt to set a definition would be arbitrary.

　　　　iii. Definition of practical importance: The minimum height at which satellites can remain in orbit is far beyond the maximum height at which aircraft can fly.

　　b. Definition is necessary: Other countries assert that a definition should exist for the following reasons:

　　　　i. Future applications of international law: A definition is necessary for applying the international law of air and space as technology develops.

　　　　ii. Secure state sovereignty: Lack of a definition invites states to violate the sovereignty of other states.

　　　　iii. Basis for domestic law: A definition serves as the basis for enacting domestic law to provide for a state's defense and for the full exercise of state sovereignty.

2. Scientific versus contrived definition: A definition can be based on scientific principles or be based on the needs of the international community.

　　a. Scientific definition: Some states that argue for a definition of outer space contend that a scientific determination of the line between air and outer space is possible.

　　b. Contrived definition: Scholars note that the "indivisibility principle" supports the notion that air and outer space are merely different degrees of one another. Thus, if a definition is necessary, it should be arrived at through traditional decision-making processes that take into account social, cultural, economic, historical and political needs.

3. **Possible definitions:** At least seven possible definitions have been supported over the years:

   a. the *limit of the atmosphere*;

   b. the *limit of air flight*;

   c. the *point at which the atmosphere will no longer sustain human life*;

   d. the *lowest point at which a satellite can orbit*;

   e. the *point at which centrifugal forces replace aerodynamic forces*;

   f. the *limit of a state's effective control over its airspace*; and

   g. the *current orbital minimum* (approximately 100-110 km).

B. **Control of outer space:** The widely adopted Treaty of Principles Governing the Activities of States in the Exploration and Use of Outer Space, Including the Moon and Celestial Bodies ("Outer Space Treaty") generally provides for *free access to outer space and celestial bodies by all nations*. The Outer Space Treaty prohibits states from appropriating by claim of sovereignty any part of the outer space, the moon or any other celestial body by any means. A state's activities must be conducted in accordance with international law and must not interfere with the activities of other states in outer space.

C. **Liability for damage caused by space objects:** Under the Outer Space Treaty and the more detailed Convention on International Liability for Damage Caused by Space Objects ("Liability Convention"), a state which launches or authorizes launching of an object, or from whose territory an object is launched, can be held liable for damages caused by the object.

   1. **Standards of Liability:** The standard of liability varies depending upon where and how the damage occurs.

      a. **Strict liability:** A state will be held strictly liable for damage caused by its space object on the surface of the earth or to aircraft in flight.

      b. **Fault-based liability:** If a state's space object causes damage to another state's space object which is not on the surface of the earth, the former state will be held liable only if the damage is due to its fault or the fault of persons for whom it is responsible.

c. **Joint and several liability:** States will be jointly and severally liable in two situations.

   i. **Previous damage:** States A and B will be jointly and severally liable to state C when, elsewhere than on the surface of the earth, a space object of state A causes damage to a space object or the persons or property on board a space object of state B and damage is thereby caused to state C or its natural or juridical persons.

   ii. **Joint mission:** When two or more states jointly launch a space object, they will be held jointly and severally liable for any damages. A state from whose territory a space object is launched is considered a participant in a joint mission.

2. **Measure of damages:** Damages are determined in the Liability Convention by the amount needed to return the injured party, whether that party is a person, state or international organization, "to the condition which would have existed if the damage had not occurred."

3. **Defenses:** Only one affirmative defense is available under the Liability Convention. An otherwise liable state is not liable if the damage at least partially results from "gross negligence or from an act or omission done with intent to cause damage on the part of the claimant."

4. **Obligation to consider rendering assistance:** In cases in which the damage caused "presents a large scale danger to human life or seriously interferes with the living conditions of the population or the functioning of vital center," the responsible state shall examine the possibility of rendering assistance to the damaged state.

5. **Responsibility for activities in outer space:** Under the Outer Space Treaty, states bear international responsibility for national activities in outer space regardless of whether the activity is carried out by governmental or non-governmental entities. For activities in outer space conducted by an international organization, the international organization bears responsibility.

6. **State retains jurisdiction over objects it launches into space:** States retain jurisdiction over objects launched into space which are registered to it. This applies to component parts and objects landed or constructed on a celestial body. Objects registered to a state that are found outside the territory of that state are to be returned to the state of registration.

D. Military applications in outer space: The Outer Space Treaty bans military use of outer space and celestial bodies but permits some military use of orbiting space craft.

   1. **Ban on weapons of mass destruction:** The Treaty prohibits nations from placing nuclear weapons or other weapons of mass destruction *in orbit*, *on celestial bodies*, or *in outer space* in any other manner. Other military uses of spacecraft orbiting the earth are implicitly permitted.

   2. **Ban on nonpeaceful use of celestial bodies:** In contrast to the rules for orbiting spacecraft, the moon and other celestial bodies can only be used for *peaceful purposes*. The Treaty specifically prohibits states from erecting military fortifications, bases or installations or undertaking military maneuvers on celestial bodies. The Treaty does not, however, prohibit the use of military personnel in the conduct of research or for other peaceful purposes.

E. Geostationary orbits: A satellite in a geostationary orbit remains over the *same position* on earth. Such orbits occur only over the equator.

   1. **Valuable resource:** Geostationary orbits are valuable because satellites occupying these orbits are always within reception range and require little tracking. Furthermore, because satellites must be spaced apart to avoid interference, the available orbital lots are limited in number, enhancing their value.

   2. **Not controlled by any particular state or states:** Although some states along the equator claim special rights to geostationary orbits, the prevalent view is that such orbits are properly considered "outer space" and therefore are under no state's control.

      Example: In 1976, eight equatorial nations signed the Bogota Declaration which declared their sovereignty over the superjacent segments of the geostationary orbit. The Declaration did not receive widespread acceptance and regulation of the geostationary orbits have been generally recognized as the province of the International Telecommunications Union (ITU) of the United Nations.

   3. **Regulated use of geostationary orbits:** Because geostationary orbits are so valuable and are limited in number, the international community has sought agreement on their use.

      a. **Squatter's rights rule:** Formerly, a practice of squatter's rights applied to geostationary orbits, that is, any country that had the technology to launch such a satellite could pick any available orbital slot. Developing states objected to this practice because they would not have the means to place a satellite in a geostationary orbit until after the orbit was saturated.

    b. ITU approach: The participants at the World Administrative Radio Conference of the ITU in 1989 agreed to guarantee all states at least one satellite position and an associated block of frequencies.

F. Remote sensing: Remote sensing occurs when one state obtains, for example, through satellite photography, information about another state from a remote location, such as a satellite in outer space. Some states object to being observed without their consent. The United Nations General Assembly has adopted a set of principles that govern remote sensing. Principle 12 requires that a sensed state shall have immediate access on a non-discriminatory basis and at reasonable costs to all primary, processed and analyzed data concerning territory under its jurisdiction.

VI.   CELESTIAL BODIES

A. Territory not subject to state control: Under the Outer Space Treaty *no state may exercise any claim of right to the moon or any other celestial body*. The moon and other celestial bodies may be used only for peaceful purposes.

B. Control of resources on the moon and other celestial bodies: Only a few states (not including the United States) have signed the Agreement Governing the Activities of States on the Moon and other Celestial Bodies which addresses exploitation of the moon's resources. The Agreement provides, *inter alia*:

    1. Development of a governing regime: Parties to the Agreement shall develop a regime to govern the exploitation of the moon's resources. The regime shall address the following activities:

        a. Development of resources: The orderly and safe development of the natural resources of the moon;

        b. Management of resources: The rational management of those resources;

        c. Expansion of opportunity: The expansion of opportunities in the use of those resources; and

        d. Equitable sharing of benefits: The equitable sharing of those resources, giving special consideration to the interests and needs of developing states.

2. **Common heritage:** The treaty also provides that the moon and its resources are the common heritage of mankind. Lack of United States support for the treaty has been attributed to this provision.

CHAPTER 12

INTERNATIONAL ENVIRONMENTAL LAW

I. EMERGENCE OF INTERNATIONAL ENVIRONMENTAL LAW

Several international organizations, including the United Nations, have played a fundamental role in developing general principles of international environmental law. The modern development of international environmental law is marked by the 1972 Stockholm Conference and recently culminated in the 1992 "Earth Summit" in Rio.

A. Stockholm Conference: In 1972, the United Nations sponsored the first global conference on the environment in Stockholm. The 113 parties to the Stockholm Conference adopted the Stockholm Declaration on the Human Environment, and an Action Plan for the Human Environment.

1. Stockholm Declaration on the Human Environment: In this Declaration, the Stockholm Conference parties set forth 26 principles which addressed the major environmental themes of the time, and established a global approach to the problem of environmental protection.

a. Principle 1: Principle 1 recognizes a "fundamental right to freedom, equality and adequate conditions of life, in an environment of a quality that permits a life of dignity and well-being . . . ."

b. Principle 21: This principle provides that although states have the *right to exploit their own resources*, states must ensure that "activities within their jurisdiction or control do not cause damage to the environment of other states or of areas beyond the limits of national jurisdiction."

c. Principle 22: This principle affirms that states should cooperate in developing international law regarding liability and compensation *for victims of pollution and other environmental damage* produced outside boundaries.

2. Action Plan for the Human Environment: In this Plan, the parties to the Conference adopted 109 resolutions which addressed the following items: a global environmental assessment program, environmental management activities, and supporting measures.

B. United Nations Environment Program (UNEP): Partly as a result of the Stockholm Conference, the United Nations General Assembly created UNEP in 1973, a specialized subsidiary organ of the United Nations which coordinates environmental protection activities for the United Nations as a whole.

1. **Structure of UNEP:** UNEP has a Governing Council of 58 members; a Secretariat based in Kenya; and an Environment Fund.

2. **Functions of UNEP:** These functions include gathering information on environmental problems and existing efforts to solve them, recommending and initiating environmental protection programs, and funding chosen environmental protection programs through utilization of UNEP's Environment Fund.

3. **UNEP's Legal Activities:** UNEP plays a lead role in the formulation of international environmental law, and sponsored major international environmental agreements including, *inter alia*, the Vienna Convention for the Protection of the Ozone Layer, the Montreal Protocol on Substances that Deplete the Ozone Layer, and the Convention on Biological Diversity.

C. World Charter for Nature: Drafted by the World Conservation Union (IUCN) in 1982, the World Charter sets forth global environmental principles. The Charter contains a preamble and 24 articles divided into three sections: general principles, functions, and implementation.

1. **General principles:** These principles state that ***nature shall be respected*** (Principle 1), and that unique areas of the globe should receive special protection (Principle 3).

2. **Functions:** These principles stress the importance of integrating nature conservation into social and economic development planning (Principle 7), and the necessity of avoiding destruction of natural resources through either waste, pollution, natural disaster, or other adverse processes (Principles 10-11).

3. **Implementation:** These principles focus on the importance of incorporating the U.N. Charter principles into the law and practice of each state. Of particular importance, Principle 21 provides that states and other entities shall . . .

   a. Cooperate through common activities, such as information exchanges, to conserve nature,

   b. Establish standards for products and manufacturing processes with adverse effects on nature,

   c. Implement international legal provisions for nature conservation and environmental protection,

    d. Ensure that their own activities do not harm the natural systems of other jurisdictions or those areas beyond national jurisdiction, and

    e. Safeguard and conserve natural areas beyond national jurisdiction.

D. Draft Articles on State Responsibility: The International Law Commission (ILC) has drafted various articles focusing on state responsibility and liability for ***transboundary pollution*** and other environmental damage. Since 1978, it has separately addressed state responsibility for activities not otherwise prohibited by international law.

1. **Article 1:** Article 1 of the Draft Articles states that "every internationally wrongful act of a State entails the international responsibility of that state."

2. **Article 3:** Article 3 states that an intentionally wrongful act occurs when (1) conduct is an act or omission "attributable to the state under international law," and (2) "that conduct constitutes a breach of an international obligation of the state."

3. **Article 19(3)(d):** In this Article, the ILC listed among international crimes "a serious breach of an international obligation of essential importance for the safeguarding and preservation of the human environment, such as those prohibiting massive pollution of the atmosphere or of the seas."

4. **Articles 29, 30 and 31:** These articles describe three circumstances that preclude a state's liability for an otherwise wrongful act under international law: 1. the affected state has consented to the act, 2. the act was a response to an internationally wrongful act of the other state, and 3. the act was due to "an irresistible force or to an unforeseen external event beyond its control." An act consented to by the affected state that is not in conformity with an existing obligation to that state is not wrongful "to the extent that the act remains within the limits of that consent." This defense, however, "does not apply if the obligation arises out of a peremptory norm of general international law." An act done in response to a wrongful act of another state is not wrongful only if the act also "constitutes a measure legitimate under international law against that other state, in consequence of . . . [the] wrongful act of the other state." Finally, the "***force majeure*** and fortuitous event" defense requires that the extraordinary event made it "materially impossible" for the state to act in conformity with its international obligations, and that the state in question "has [not] contributed to . . . the situation of material impossibility."

E. Restatement (Third) on Foreign Relations Law in the United States: The American Law Institute has also addressed state responsibility for environmental damage in the Restatement on Foreign Relations Law. Section 601 provides:

(1) A State is obligated to take such measures as may be necessary, to the extent practicable under the circumstances, to ensure that activities within its jurisdiction or control

  (a) conform to generally accepted international rules and standards for the prevention, reduction and control of injury to the environment of another state or of areas beyond the limits of national jurisdiction; and

  (b) are conducted so as not to cause significant injury to the environment of another state or of areas beyond the limits of national jurisdiction.

(2) A state is responsible to all other states

  (a) for any violation of its obligations under Subsection (1)(a), and

  (b) for any significant injury, resulting from such violation, to the environment of areas beyond the limits of national jurisdiction.

(3) A state is responsible for any significant injury, resulting from a violation of its obligations under Subsection (1), to the environment of another state or its property, or to persons or property within that state's territory or under its jurisdiction or control.

F. The 1992 Rio Earth Summit: On the twentieth anniversary of the Stockholm Conference, the United Nations sponsored in Rio de Janeiro, Brazil the U.N. Conference on Environment and Development (UNCED), the largest global conference on the environment, also known as the "Earth Summit."

  1. **Summit Documents:** The Earth Summit produced five major documents: the Convention on Biological Diversity, the Climate Change Convention, the Declaration of Principles on Forest Conservation, the Rio Declaration, and Agenda 21.

  2. **The Rio Declaration:** The modern equivalent of the 1972 Stockholm Declaration, the Rio Declaration is a non-binding declaration of 27 principles adopted by the Conference and endorsed by the U.N. General Assembly. It is a result of compromise between the developed and developing nations, and reflects a balance of the goals of each, including the "right to development" insisted upon by the developing countries. Important principles include:

a. **Principle 2:** This principle is a revision of Principle 21 of the Stockholm Declaration with greater emphasis on ***states' right to develop their own resources***. It provides:

> States have, in accordance with the Charter of the United Nations and the principles of international law, the sovereign right to exploit their own resources pursuant to their own environmental and developmental policies, and the responsibility to ensure that activities within their jurisdiction or control do not cause damage to the environment of other States or of areas beyond the limits of national jurisdiction.

b. **New elements:** New concepts not encompassed in the Stockholm Declaration include the precautionary approach to environmental management (Principle 15), the right to development (Principle 2), and an obligation to undertake environmental impact assessments of proposed activities likely to have a significant adverse impact on the environment (Principle 17).

c. **Other Key Environmental Principles:** A number of other concepts address problems associated with transboundary pollution: notification of environmental emergencies or disasters (Principle 18), notification and consultation with states regarding transboundary effects of proposed activities (Principle 19), liability and compensation for pollution victims (Principle 13), and warfare (Principle 24).

3. **Agenda 21:** Agenda 21 is an 800-page comprehensive program of action for sustainable development and environmental preservation. It includes a set of priority actions and means for accomplishing the priority actions. There are six priorities:

a. ***achieving sustainable growth***, through integrating environment and development in decision-making;

b. ***fostering an equitable world***, by combating poverty and protecting human health;

c. ***making the world habitable*** by addressing issues of urban water supply, solid waste management, and urban pollution;

d. ***encouraging efficient resource use***, a category which includes management of energy resources, care and use of fresh water, forest development, management of fragile ecosystems, conservation of biological diversity, and management of land resources;

e. ***protecting global and regional resources***, including the atmosphere, oceans and seas, and living marine resources; and

f. *managing chemicals and hazardous and nuclear wastes*.

A Commission for Sustainable Development, which reports to UNESCO, is established to monitor and review implementation of Agenda 21.

II. TRANSBOUNDARY POLLUTION

A. **General rule:** As indicated in several of the sources above, no state may use or permit the use of its territory in a manner that is injurious to another state, or that other state's persons or property.

1. **Trail Smelter Case:** The ***Trail Smelter Case*** (*United States v. Canada*), 3 R.I.A.A. 1911 (1949) established two fundamental principles of liability for transboundary pollution under international law: (1) a state must show material damage and causation to be entitled to legal relief, not merely that emissions or releases from one state have crossed into the territory of another state, and (2) a state has a duty to prevent, and may be held responsible for pollution by private parties within its jurisdiction if such pollution results in demonstrable injury to another state.

    In *Trail Smelter*, a smelter near Trail, Canada emitted 300-350 tons of sulphur dioxide daily. The United States contended that these emissions were harming forests vital to Washington State's lumber industry. The United States and Canada submitted the dispute for arbitration. An arbitration tribunal found that fumes from the smelter had already caused $78,000 damage to the forests, and would continue to cause damage there in the future. The Tribunal held that Canada was legally responsible for the actions of the smelter, ordered Canada to pay damages, and required the smelter to refrain from causing further damage to the United States.

2. **Corfu Channel Case:** The ***Corfu Channel Case***, (*U.K. v. Alb.*), 1949 I.C.J. 4, established the principles that every state has an obligation not to knowingly allow its territory to be used for acts contrary to the rights of other states, and every state has a duty to notify states of any imminent danger that might harm another state.

    In *Corfu Channel*, the United Kingdom sued Albania in the International Court of Justice (ICJ) for physical damage and loss of life sustained by two British warships which ran into moored contact mines in the Straits of Corfu. The ICJ determined that the laying of the minefield could not have been done without Albania's knowledge, and that Albania did not notify the United Kingdom of the minefield's existence or warn the approaching warships. The ICJ recognized that permitting extraterritorial damage from intrastate activity which is in and of itself lawful may, nevertheless, render a state responsible for the damage inflicted, and held Albania responsible for the damages caused to the United Kingdom.

3. **Lake Lanoux Arbitration:** The *Lake Lanoux Arbitration* (*France v. Spain*), 12 R.I.A.A. 281 (1957), held that downstream states do not have a right of veto over an upstream state's use of water, but the panel also stated that an upstream state must consider the counterproposals of a downstream state offered to it.

4. **Nuclear Test Cases:** The *Nuclear Test Cases* (*Australia v. France*), 1973 I.C.J. 99 and (New Zealand v. France), 1973 I.C.J. 135, left the legality of atmospheric nuclear testing unresolved on the merits, although the International Court of Justice did preliminarily enjoin France from testing while it heard the dispute.

In the *Nuclear Test Cases*, Australia and New Zealand claimed that atmospheric nuclear testing by France was causing them to incur risks and damages. The I.C.J. enjoined France from further testing until final judgment. The merits of the case were never reached, however, because the French government unilaterally decided to halt its testing, thus rendering the case moot according to the I.C.J.

B. **Possible theories of liability for transboundary pollution under international law:** Such theories include: (1) an absolute duty to protect against harm from ultrahazardous activities which, if violated, results in a state being held strictly liable; (2) responsibility for negligent or intentional acts ("abuse of rights"); and (3) liability for a state which permits transboundary pollution to exceed that which its neighbors can reasonably be expected to endure ("good neighborliness"). Of these theories, the least clearly established in customary international law is strict liability for ultrahazardous activities.

1. **Specific treaties focusing on transboundary pollution:** Treaties in this area take a variety of approaches, such as agreeing to try to reach agreement ("framework conventions"), establishing substantive standards, "freezing" pollution at current levels, providing for notification and consultation, and authorizing an international organization to establish applicable rules.

a. **Acid rain treaties:** Various treaties and agreements have been negotiated in response to the growing problem of acid rain. Acid rain is caused by gases, such as sulfur oxides and nitrogen oxides, dissolving into water carried in the air. These gases form acids in the atmosphere, and the acids descend to land through precipitation.

i. **Convention on Long-Range Transboundary Air Pollution 1979:** This Convention was adopted in Geneva and went into force March 16, 1983. As of December 1991, 33 states including the United States were parties to the Convention. The purpose is to "limit, and as far as possible, gradually reduce and prevent air pollution including long-range transboundary air pollution." The Convention provides for enforcement through research, exchange of information, and an Interim Executive Body (IEB). The IEB was established to carry out a cooperative program for monitoring pollution in Europe. The Convention also includes notice and consultation requirements. The Convention's weakness is the lack of ceilings and timetables to achieve reduction in acid rain.

(1) **Sulphur Emissions Protocol:** This Protocol went into force in 1987. Using 1980 levels as a basis, the Protocol requires the reduction of sulphur emissions or their transboundary fluxes by 30 percent by 1993. The Protocol also requires annual reporting of sulphur emissions. Several major sulphur producers — including the United States and the United Kingdom — did not ratify this Protocol.

(2) **Nitrogen Oxides Protocol:** This Protocol requires the stabilization of nitrogen dioxide emissions or their transboundary fluxes at 1987 levels by 1994. The Protocol covers major stationary sources and vehicle emissions. The Protocol also requires use of the best available technology for national emissions standards, and eventual negotiation of internationally accepted "critical loads."

III. OZONE DEPLETION AND GLOBAL WARMING

A. **Protection of the ozone layer:** Several treaties address the problem of the depletion of the ozone layer. The ozone layer in the atmosphere filters out harmful ultraviolet radiation from the sun. Chlorofluorocarbons (CFCs) are primarily responsible for the depletion of the ozone layer. CFCs are used in air conditioning, aerosols, styrofoam, and refrigerators. As more radiation reaches the earth due to the depletion of the ozone layer, the incidence of cancer, smog, and eye disease increases.

1. **Vienna Convention for the Protection of the Ozone Layer 1985:** This framework convention primarily focuses on information exchange and cooperation among states in research and scientific assessments on the depletion of the ozone layer. The Convention's goal is to develop appropriate measures to protect human health and the environment against adverse effects resulting from or likely to result from activities which modify or are likely to modify the ozone layer. The Convention also allows the parties to the Convention to adopt protocols to implement the goals of the Convention.

2. **Montreal Protocol on Substances that Deplete the Ozone Layer:** This Protocol to the Vienna Convention was originally adopted in 1987 and was amended in 1990.

   a. **1987 Protocol:** This Protocol was in force in 1989. The Protocol sets forth a timetable for the reduction in use of CFCs — 50% by 1999. The Protocol also bans CFC imports of non-parties unless the non-parties meet the reductions of the Protocol. The Protocol freezes halons at 1986 levels.

   b. **1990 amendments:** These amendments place a total ban on CFCs by the year 2000 (by the year 2010 for developing countries). The amendments provide for graduated reduction in CFCs: 20% by 1993, 50% by 1995, and 85% by 1997 (based on 1986 levels). The amendments also establish a fourteen-member executive committee, and a $240 million fund to assist developing countries in the transition to technology free of CFCs.

B. **Protection of the Climate:** Another serious environmental problem is climate change due to the ***greenhouse effect***. The greenhouse effect results when gases in the air, such as carbon dioxide, methane, CFCs, and nitrogen dioxide, trap infrared radiation near the surface of the earth, preventing the radiation from escaping into the atmosphere and thus elevating global temperatures.

1. **United Nations resolutions on climate change:** Two resolutions passed in 1989 recognize climate change as a common concern of mankind and a topic to be given high priority by United Nations organizations and programs. These resolutions emphasize the need for governmental and intergovernmental efforts to prevent detrimental effects on the climate. The resolutions also review possible elements that may be included in an international convention on climate change.

2. **The United Nations Framework Convention on Climate Change:** This Convention was signed at the Earth Summit held in Rio de Janeiro during June 1992. The Convention emphasizes the concern over changes in the Earth's climate, especially those

changes caused by greenhouse gases, and has as its objective the stabilization of greenhouse gas concentrations in the atmosphere. No specific controls or deadlines are set, although the Convention has an implicit goal of returning to 1990 levels of emissions by the year 2000.

a. **Commitments of the parties:** The parties to the Convention commit themselves to the following goals: periodic national inventories of antropogenic emissions and removal by sinks of greenhouse gases; mitigation programs on a national and regional level; the development of technology to control emissions; the consideration of climate change in various decision-making processes; and cooperation in the exchange of information, education and public awareness. In addition, developed countries commit to the adoption of national policies and mitigation measures; the use of the best available scientific technology for calculation; and the financing of developing countries to help them meet their obligations under the Convention.

b. **Structure of the Convention:** The Convention establishes a Conference of the Parties to review implementation of the Convention and to adopt protocols, amendments, and annexes as needed. A Secretariat is also established to arrange for sessions of the Conference and to prepare reports on climate change. The Convention also provides for two subsidiary bodies, one for implementation and another for scientific and technological advice. A financial mechanism is included in the Convention to enable developing countries to meet the demands of the Convention.

IV. WILDLIFE PRESERVATION

A. **Provisions under the Stockholm Declaration and the World Charter of Nature:** Both the Stockholm Declaration and the World Charter for Nature contain provisions focusing on the preservation of wildlife.

1. **Stockholm Declaration:** In Principle 4, the Declaration states that the plants and animals of the earth are a world heritage, and that man has a special responsibility to safeguard nature. Principle 4 also states that nature conservation should receive a place of importance in economic development planning.

2. **World Charter for Nature:** In Principle 2, the World Charter stresses the need to safeguard necessary habitats so that the genetic viability of the earth is not compromised, and the necessity

of maintaining population levels of all life forms sufficient for survival. In Principle 3, the World Charter states that all areas of the earth are subject to conservation, and that special protection should be provided for unique areas.

B. International Convention for the Regulation of Whaling: The International Whaling Commission was established by the International Convention for the Regulation of Whaling of 1946. The original intent of the Convention's framers was to negotiate a fishing treaty to regulate the whaling industry. Implementation of the Convention has increasingly been directed to conservation of whales.

1. Structure of the Commission: The Commission has one member from each contracting government. The Commission holds annual sessions to analyze information about the whaling industry and adopt recommendations for regulation. Three standing committees are the technical, scientific, and finance and administration committees.

2. Functioning of the Convention: A schedule with whaling regulations is published annually. The Commission has the power to modify the schedule. The Convention also contains an opt-out provision — any member may exempt itself from compliance with any regulation by objecting. The Commission adopted a three-year moratorium on commercial whaling in 1982 and extended that moratorium in 1990 for ten more years.

C. Convention on International Trade in Endangered Species of Wild Fauna and Flora (CITES): With over 100 parties, this Convention sets up a complex system of import and export permits and regulations to safeguard endangered species from over exploitation.

1. Structure of the Convention: The Convention establishes a Secretariat operated under UNEP which prepares scientific and technical studies. The Secretariat also coordinates the national record keeping and reporting required by the Convention. The Convention establishes a Conference of State Parties which meets every two years to adapt the Convention to evolving conditions.

2. Functioning of the permit system: The import and export permits required under the Convention are nationally administered and are keyed to categories of endangered species. Exemptions from the permits system exist, and states are permitted to take stricter measures if they wish. The categories of endangered species are contained in the appendices to the Conventions. Appendix I contains all species threatened with extinction which are or may be affected by trade; Appendix II contains those species which are not currently threatened but which may become so; and Appendix III contains species states designate as "locally endangered." No permit may be issued for commercial use of an Appendix I species or a recognizable part or derivative of such a species.

D. **United Nations Convention on Biological Diversity:** This Convention was signed at the Earth Summit held in Rio de Janeiro in June 1992. The objectives of the Convention include conserving biological diversity and the sustainable use of its components, and the equitable sharing of benefits of utilizing genetic resources.

1. **Commitments of the parties:** The parties of the Convention obligate themselves to the following: developing national strategies for the conservation of biological diversity; integrating conservation into sectoral or cross-sectoral plans; developing identification and monitoring schemes; establishing a system of protected areas, adopting incentive measures; cooperating in the establishment of research and training programs; public education and awareness programs; and impact assessment procedures.

2. **Structure of the Convention:** The Convention establishes a Conference of the Parties to review implementation, and to adopt protocols, amendments, and annexes. A Secretariat is also established to arrange meetings of the Conference and prepare reports on biological diversity. The Convention sets up a subsidiary body to provide scientific, technical, and technological advice to the Conference. The Convention also contains an arbitration mechanism and the opportunity for a conciliation commission.

V. HAZARDOUS WASTE, RADIOACTIVE POLLUTION, AND ENVIRONMENTAL EMERGENCIES

A. **Early conventions on civil liability for nuclear damage:** These conventions include the Paris Convention of Third Party Liability in the Field of Nuclear Energy of 1960, the Brussels Convention Supplementary to the Paris Convention, the Vienna Convention on Civil Liability for Nuclear Damage of 1963, and the Joint Protocol Relating to the Application of the Vienna Convention and the Paris Convention of 1988.

1. **Vienna Convention on Civil Liability for Nuclear Damage 1963:** Based on the Paris Convention and its Brussels Supplementary Convention, this Convention gives jurisdiction to the courts of the state in whose territory the damage occurred. The operator of a nuclear installation is absolutely liable for nuclear damage, but exemptions exist. A victim of nuclear damage must present a claim within ten years from the date of the accident or the claim is barred

by the Convention. The Convention also requires the installation state to insure payment of the claim against the operator. Few states are parties to the Convention, and none of the parties are major nuclear powers.

2. **Joint Protocol Relating to the Application of the Vienna Convention and the Paris Convention 1988:** This Protocol was negotiated by the International Atomic Energy Agency (IAEA) in cooperation with the Nuclear Energy Agency (NEA) of the Organization for Economic Cooperation and Development (OECD). The purposes of the Protocol are to eliminate conflicts of law when both conventions apply, and to require the parties of each convention to grant each other a right of compensation under each instrument.

B. **The Chernobyl Accident and resulting Conventions:** On April 26, 1986, an explosion occurred in a reactor at the Chernobyl nuclear power plant in the Soviet Union. The accident raised questions about the inadequacy of international law in compensating victims of nuclear accidents, in utilizing international law to prevent such accidents in the future and in informing states when such accidents occur. As a result of the accident, two conventions were negotiated.

1. **The Convention on Early Notification of a Nuclear Accident:** This Convention was signed by 58 states on September 26, 1986. The Convention provides for notification "forthwith" and information regarding nuclear accidents "which has resulted or may result in a international transboundary release that could be of radiological safety significance for another state." States are also required to notify the IAEA of the authority responsible for the accident.

2. **Convention on Assistance in the Case of a Nuclear Accident or Radiological Emergency 1986:** Also signed on September 26, 1986, this Convention provides that parties should cooperate in coordinating emergency response and assistance in the event of a nuclear accident that could involve transboundary radiological release. Under this treaty, any exposed state can claim assistance. The Convention focuses on efforts prior to and after nuclear accidents. Prior to accidents, the Convention requires the identification of experts, equipment and materials available; financial assistance; and elaboration of emergency plans. After accidents, states which require assistance are required to indicate the scope and type of assistance needed. The IAEA has a central role under the Convention in facilitating cooperation among the parties, receiving and dispersing information about accidents, and coordinating emergency response to nuclear accidents.

C. **Basel Convention on the Control of Transboundary Movements of Hazardous Wastes and their Disposal:** This Convention seeks to limit and regulate international traffic in hazardous waste products.

1. **Obligations of the parties:** General obligations include prohibiting the export of hazardous waste without prior approval of the importing country, and proof that the importing country has adequate facilities to dispose of the waste; prohibiting trade with non-parties; minimizing the generation of hazardous waste; managing exported waste in an environmentally sound manner; labeling and packaging shipments of waste in accordance with generally accepted international rules and standards; and cooperating in training of technicians, the exchange of information, and the transfer technology.

2. **Structure of the Convention:** The Convention establishes a Conference of the Parties to review implementation, and to adopt protocols, amendments, and annexes. The Convention also establishes a Secretariat to arrange meetings of the Conference and to prepare reports.

VI. ANTARCTICA

Antarctica comprises about ten percent of the earth's land and water mass, and is the ***only continent that has not been economically exploited***. The principal mechanisms for protection of the Antarctic environment are described below.

A. **Antarctic Treaty of 1959:** The Antarctic Treaty was the first international agreement governing the use of Antarctica. Its goal was to assure continued scientific research while suspending the right of states to claim "sectors" of the continent.

1. **Antarctic Treaty Consultative Parties ("ATCPs"):** The ATCPs include thirty-eight states: the twelve original signatories (the Antarctic Directorate) and twenty-six other states who have since signed the treaty and have conducted substantial scientific research activity there. Other signatories are referred to as non-consultative parties.

2. **Environmental provisions:** Two provisions are environmentally important: Article 5 prohibits nuclear explosions and disposal of radioactive waste material; and Article 9(1) requires the original signatories meet regularly to exchange information, consult on matters of common interest, and, if necessary, formulate measures to further the objectives of the Treaty which may concern preservation and conservation of living resources in Antarctica. State representa-

tives have adopted several measures designed to protect living organisms on the continent, including the establishment of a "special conservation zone" within the boundaries of the treaty, and "Specially Protected Areas" within that zone.

B. Convention for the Conservation of Antarctic Seals: This Convention, signed in 1972, recognizes the necessity to protect Antarctic seals, which had almost disappeared because of excessive hunting. The Treaty does not ban hunting, but instead establishes a regulatory system to prevent over-exploitation. Some species are totally protected by the Treaty.

C. Convention on the Conservation of Antarctic Marine Living Resources: This Convention, signed in 1980, covers conservation of Antarctic marine resources within the entire Antarctic marine ecosystem. This zone, called the Antarctic Convergence, extends beyond the original Antarctic Treaty area to the physical boundaries of the Antarctic Ocean. Its objectives, described in Article II(3), reflect its ecological perspective: maintenance of the levels of population sufficient to ensure their viability, protecting ecological relations, and prevention of changes that could have irreversible effects. The "rational use" of resources is permitted within this context. The Convention has created two organs to implement the Treaty, the Commission for the Conservation of Antarctic Marine Living Resources, which must meet at least once a year, and a Scientific Committee to assist the Commission.

D. Agreed Measures for the Conservation of Antarctic Fauna and Flora: The ATCPs adopted these measures in 1964. The most significant provision is the declaration of the Antarctic Treaty Area as a "Special Conservation Area." It establishes a regulatory permit system for the killing or harming of mammals or birds and requires states to take steps to minimize habitat interference and water pollution. Areas of outstanding scientific interest are designated as "Specially Protected Areas" subject to special regulatory protections.

E. The 1991 Madrid Protocol: The Madrid protocol provides the *first comprehensive protection of the Antarctic environment*.

1. **Specific Protection:** Article 3 establishes the basic environmental principle underlying the Protocol, with paragraph 1 stating that protection of the Antarctic environment "shall be the fundamental consideration in the planning and conduct of all activities in the Antarctic Treaty Area." In furtherance of this principle, paragraph 2 of Article 3 provides for the first time a basis for a uniform standard to assess all human activity on Antarctica. It states that all activities "shall be planned and conducted so as to limit adverse impacts on the Antarctic environment ... [and] on the basis of

information sufficient to allow prior assessments of . . . their possible impacts on the Antarctic environment." Subparagraph (d) of Article 3(2) provides for "regular and effective monitoring . . . to allow assessment of impacts . . . including the verification of predicted impacts." Article 11 establishes a Committee for Environmental Protection, an independent body meant to oversee compliance with the Protocol. Under Article 9 of the Protocol, the Annexes constitute an integral part of the agreement. They include: Annex 1 (establishing procedures for environmental impact assessment, including a provision for public notice and comment), Annex II (conservation of wild flora and fauna), Annex III (procedures on waste disposal and management that aim to reduce and remove waste "to the maximum extent possible"), Annex IV (prevention of marine pollution), and Annex V (area protection and management). The most controversial aspect of the Protocol is that it effectively bans mining on Antarctica for at least 50 years. Article 7 expressly prohibits "any activity relating to mineral resources other than scientific research."

2. **Amending the Protocol:** Although Article 12 contains amendment and modification procedures which may be invoked at any time, amendments to ban requires unanimity of the consultative parties. In the year 2041, the Protocol will be open for review by the parties, who will have an opportunity to amend the agreement. An amendment requires adoption by a majority of the parties, including three-fourths of the states which are consultative parties at the time of adoption of the Protocol. However, no amendment takes effect until ratification by three-fourths of the consultative parties, including all of the states which were consultative parties at the time of adoption of the Protocol. Under Article 25, a party may opt-out from Article 7, effective two years after giving notice, if an amendment to the Article has been successfully adopted but fails to be entered into force within three years of its adoption.

VII. DEFORESTATION

Deforestation involves the ***unsustainable use of forests and their genetic resources***. Of primary concern today is the destruction of tropical rainforests.

A. **Consequences:** Although states have not agreed on a definition of the problem, a ***fundamental cause is thought to be poverty***. Local impacts include floods and droughts, siltation of rivers, destruction of breeding areas, and the threat to the survival of over 140 million forest dwellers worldwide. Globally, deforestation is thought to be the primary cause of loss of biodiversity, including medicinal plants, and a major contributor to the greenhouse effect due to the release of carbon dioxide from forest burning and the loss of tropical forests as consumers of carbon dioxide.

B. The 1984 International Tropical Timber Agreement: This agreement, administered by the International Tropical Timber Organization (ITTO), is the only international agreement regulating tropical timber. It includes twenty-two producing states and twenty-four consuming states and accounts for over 95 percent of the international trade in tropical timber. Although any trade restrictions on tropical timber would likely require action by the ITTO, the Timber Agreement is based on the principle of free trade, and is unlikely to be changed for environmental reasons alone.

C. The Rio Forest Principles: The United States proposed a binding deforestation agreement during a preparatory meeting for UNCED, but was met with considerable opposition from developing countries concerned about threats to sovereignty over their natural resources. The result was an agreement adopted by the Conference called the Non-Legally Binding Authoritative Statement of Principles for a Global Consensus on the Management, Conservation and Sustainable Development of All Types of Forests — or Rio Forest Principles. In the Rio Forest Principles, the parties agree to promote international cooperation on forestry, but do not commit to any specific actions or deadlines.

D. Debt-for-nature swaps: Debt-for-nature swaps, first introduced in 1987 by non-governmental organizations ("NGOs"), involve the purchase of foreign debts of debtor countries in exchange for the creation of domestic forest reserves or other environmental projects. Countries such as Bolivia, Ecuador, and Costa Rica have already participated in such swaps, and many other countries are currently considering similar plans.

   1. Public vs. private debt-for-nature swaps: The first generation of debt-for-nature swaps were "private," meaning at least one of the parties involved was private. A "second generation" of swaps has recently emerged, called "public" swaps. These occur between sovereign states and, to date, have provided a greater amount of debt reduction than private swaps.

   2. New types of public debt-for-nature swaps: Three types of public swaps have emerged, each with different enforcement mechanisms:

      a. Government debt purchases: Similar to private debt exchanges, this swap involves the government of one country agreeing to buy private debt of another in exchange for reforestation or conservation projects. Enforcement mechanisms are determined by the nature of the agreement between the parties. To date, these agreements have lacked traditional enforcement provisions, and instead rely on the friendly relations between the parties.

b. **Government grants to environmental groups:** The United States Agency for International Development has statutory authority to make grants to NGOs, which in turn may support reforestation efforts in countries that have "the capacity, commitment and record of environmental concern to oversee the long-term viability of ... the project." Although legal agreements are required prior to a grant, specific terms and enforcement provisions have not been mandated.

c. **Debt forgiveness:** The largest debt-for-nature exchange is contained in the Enterprise for Americas Initiative ("EAI") proposed by the United States. Within the EAI, the United States has structured a number of environmental framework agreements with countries such as Chile, Bolivia, and Jamaica that are designed to replace old debt with new, and funnel funds directly to environmental projects. By statute, enforcement provisions of these agreements must be "reasonable." One example is a strong mechanism for dispute resolution: the host country can cut off all future funds to a country if a dispute cannot be solved. Other exchanges proposed in Europe focus on environmental cleanup efforts rather than conservation.

VIII. DESERTIFICATION/LAND DEGRADATION

Desertification is identified in Agenda 21 as one of the key global environmental problems that not only affects the quality of the environment but also is critically linked to the goal of achieving sustainable development in all countries. Desertification affects about one sixth of the population and one quarter of the total land area of the world. While some degraded lands can be reclaimed with a reasonable amount of effort and resources, severely or totally degraded land may be permanently lost.

A. **Definition:** Desertification is defined by the U.N. as land degradation in arid, semi-arid and dry sub-humid areas (including irrigated cropland) resulting mainly from adverse human impact (improper land use). A number of factors are involved, including demographics, overgrazing, deforestation, sources of energy, water resources and irrigation, and erosion.

B. The Lome IV Convention: Signed in 1989 between the EEC and the African, Caribbean and Pacific States (ACP), this agreement specifically addresses the problem of desertification in Title I, which calls for specific actions on national, regional, and international levels to preserve resources and protect ecosystems against desertification and drought.

C. Past U.N. efforts to combat desertification: The U.N. Conference on Desertification (UNCOD), held at UNEP in Nairobi in 1977, was the first world conference to set out a Plan of Action for initiating and sustaining a cooperative effort to combat desertification. Focusing on technical and economic reforms, the Plan attempted to reinforce and integrate national, regional, and global actions within and outside of the U.N. The status of the Plan of Action was reviewed in 1992, when it was found that little progress had been made.

D. Current U.N. efforts: Chapter 12 of Agenda 21 includes six program areas countries agree to focus on:

1. Strengthening the knowledge base and developing information and monitoring systems for regions prone to desertification and drought;

2. Combating land degradation through, *inter alia*, intensified soil conservation and reforestation activities;

3. Creating integrated development programs for the eradication of poverty and promotion of alternative livelihood systems in areas prone to desertification;

4. Developing comprehensive anti-desertification programs and integrating them into national development plans and national environmental planning;

5. Developing drought preparedness and relief schemes and programs to cope with environmental refugees; and

6. Promoting environmental education about desertification and drought.

E. Treaty envisioned: Paragraph 12.40 of Agenda 21 requires the U.N. General Assembly to establish a committee to oversee the creation of an international convention to combat land degradation and drought. The committee, established in 1992, is currently formulating an agreement.

IX. MARINE ENVIRONMENT

A. Generally: The preservation of the marine environment is discussed at pp. 186-191, *supra*.

X. INTERNATIONAL TRADE AND ENVIRONMENT

There is growing recognition that trade and environment are inextricably linked, and trade implications of environmental policy, and environmental implications of the world trade system, are emerging as issues of international concern.

A. The GATT: Most of the rules governing international trade are codified in the General Agreement on Tariffs and Trade, which was first established in 1948 and is periodically negotiated by the parties. The rules are based primarily on the ideology of free trade, with a view that is skeptical of regulations that inhibit trade. Thus, many proponents of free trade see environmental regulations as a type of non-tariff barrier to be forbidden under GATT.

1. **Lack of environmental protection under GATT:** There is no mention in GATT of environmental protection as a justification for limiting trade; however, states may legitimately restrain trade under Article XX if "necessary to protect human, animal or plant life or health" and impose measures "relating to the conservation of natural resources."

2. **The Uruguay Round:** The Uruguay Round of GATT talks, begun in 1985 and concluded in 1994, was the first round to link international trade and the environment in the contexts of agricultural subsidies, harmonization of certain environmental standards, prohibition of export controls, and the liberalization of import restrictions. Although these issues were not resolved, the participants signed an agreement pledging to undertake a dialogue on the "interlinkages between environmental and trade policies."

   Despite opposition from environmental and consumer groups as well as some local governments, implementing legislation for the Uruguay Round of the General Agreement on Tariffs and Trade was approved by Congress at the end of 1994. Environmentalists expressed concern that GATT and the GATT implementing legislation, unlike the case with NAFTA, contain no environmental provisions and therefore leave U.S. conservation laws open to attack as unfair trade barriers. Also, under the prior GATT procedures, a nation could veto a GATT panel ruling with which it did not agree. Under the new procedures, trade disputes heard by the newly established World Trade Organization cannot be vetoed. Failure to comply with a WTO ruling can lead to imposition of trade sanctions by other GATT parties.

   a. **Environmental impact statement rejected:** A suit filed by public interest groups to require the Office of the U.S. Trade Representative to prepare an environmental impact statement for the Uruguay Round of the GATT was dismissed by the District of Columbia federal district court. *Public Citizen v. Kantor*, 864 F.Supp. (D.D.C. 1994). The court relied on *Public Citizen v. U.S. Trade Representative*, 5 F.3d 549 (1993), *cert. denied*, 114 S. Ct. 685 (1994), in which a federal appeals court had dismissed a similar challenge to NAFTA because there was no "final agency action" to trigger judicial review under the Administrative Procedure Act.

3. **GATT Group on Environment Measures and Trade:** First established in 1971, the Group on Environment Measures and Trade was dormant until first activated in 1991 following a GATT debate on environment and trade. The Group's initial agenda includes: (1) trade provisions in existing multilateral environmental agreements, (2) national environmental regulations likely to have an international effect, and (3) trade effects of packaging and labeling requirements aimed at protecting the environment.

B. **Conflicting views of traditional free trade theorists and environmentally oriented economists:** GATT negotiators have a difficult time coming to an agreement about issues concerning trade and environment because economists' theories in this area conflict. According to environmentally oriented economists, when the prices of goods that enter the international market do not reflect the environmental costs of production, the producers are receiving an effective subsidy equal to the resources used in the process. Thus, they claim that these goods distort the trade process, giving an unfair advantage to producers who degrade the environment, termed "ecological dumping." However, under the GATT, no such explicit environmental subsidy is recognized. Instead, these goods are viewed as having only an "implicit subsidy," one that is unforbidden.

C. **The Tuna/Dolphin Decision:** In February of 1991, Mexico filed a formal complaint against the United States claiming a U.S. embargo on Mexican yellowfin tuna was protectionist in nature, and a violation of GATT. The U.S. had imposed the embargo pursuant to the Marine Mammal Protection Act as a trade sanction to compel Mexico (and other states) to bring its kill rate of dolphin in the harvesting of yellowfin tuna in the Eastern Tropical Pacific in line with U.S. standards. The U.S. argued that the measure was justified under Article III of GATT, which requires only that imported products be accorded no less favorable treatment than products of national origin, or under the exemptions in Article XX for protection of natural resources and animals. The panel concluded that the U.S. import ban violated GATT. Dispute Settlement Panel Report on United States Restrictions on Imports of Tuna, Aug. 16, 1991, *reprinted at* 30 I.L.M. 1594. According to the panel, Article III only allows for regulation of a product based on the qualities of the product itself, not on the process by which it is made. The Article XX exemptions can only be used to protect living or natural resources under the jurisdiction of the party invoking the exemptions. In May, 1994, a second panel upheld the European Community's claim that GATT is also violated by the U.S. embargo on intermediary nations that import and then export yellowfin tuna harvested in violation of U.S. standards. The GATT panel concluded that the secondary embargo by the U.S. on imports of tuna from intermediary nations was inconsistent with its GATT obligations because the ban was too attenuated to preservation of dolphins to be "necessary" to protect the life or health of dolphins, or to be "related to" conserving dolphins.

D. The CAFE standards decision: In 1994, a GATT dispute settlement panel rejected a European Union claim that U.S. fuel conservation and tax measures were discriminatory against European auto imports. The EU had challenged the United States corporate average fuel economy standards, the "gas guzzler" tax, and the luxury tax on cars over $30,000. The decision upheld these taxes and the 19-year-old corporate average fuel economy (CAFE) standards, but the panel agreed with the EU that the CAFE accounting rules which establish separate domestic and import fleets for determining overall fuel economy were discriminatory. The panel apparently rejected the EU's claim that the U.S. had to take the least restrictive trade measures to serve environmental goals.

E. The Global Environment Facility (GEF): The Global Environment Facility was established by the World Bank in 1991 as a pilot program under which grants or loans will be provided to developing countries to help them implement programs addressing problems of global environmental significance. These include: protection of the ozone layer, limiting emissions of greenhouse gases, protection of biodiversity, and protection of international waters. GEF is currently considering the inclusion of desertification programs. A number of global environmental treaties that address these problems contain funding mechanisms provided by GEF, including the 1992 biodiversity treaty and the Montreal Protocol. Multilateral contributions to the GEF are currently made by participant states on a voluntary basis. Programs funded under GEF are implemented through a "tripartite arrangement" by the World Bank, UNEP and UNDP.

F. North American Free Trade Agreement (NAFTA): NAFTA is a unique trade agreement for its incorporation of environmental protections. The preamble states that trade must be consistent with environmental protection and conservation. The agreement calls for "harmonization of the parties domestic standards with international environmental standards, while preserving in certain circumstances each country's ability to maintain domestic environmental standards which exceed prevailing international standards. Disputes over environmental standards may be resolved by an arbitral panel, with the burden under NAFTA on the party challenging the environmental measure. Although NAFTA by its terms is generally to be given priority over conflicting international agreements, exceptions are made for several major international environmental treaties. A separately negotiated environmental agreement focuses on cleanup of the Mexico/U.S. border area and establishment of a Commission on Environmental Cooperation to ensure enforcement of environmental standards by the parties.

In *Public Citizen v. U.S. Trade Representative*, 5 F.3d 549 (D.C. Cir. 1993), the D.C. Circuit Court of Appeals held that an environmental impact statement did not have to be prepared for NAFTA because it was not "final agency action" under the Administrative Procedure Act and NEPA itself does not create a private right of action.

XI. MILITARY ACTIVITIES AND THE ENVIRONMENT

The international community is increasingly willing to condemn military acts that harm the environment, and may impose legal liability on an aggressor. Liability for environmental harm that results from military activities may arise from a number of international agreements.

A. Protocol I to the 1949 Geneva Conventions Relating to the Protection of Victims of International Armed Conflicts: Article 35 prohibits methods of warfare which "are intended, or may be expected, to cause widespread, long-term and severe damage to the natural environment." Article 55 of Protocol I of the Geneva Conventions states that "care shall be taken in warfare to protect the natural environment against widespread, long-term and severe damage .... Attacks against the natural environment by way of reprisals are prohibited." The status of the Protocol as customary international law is controversial.

B. Environmental Modification Convention of 1977 (ENMOD): This Convention was drafted during the Vietnam War in response to concern over the use of "deliberate manipulation of natural processes" that change the "dynamics, composition or structure of the earth . . . ." ENMOD prohibits member states from engaging in environmental modification techniques that have "widespread, long-lasting, or severe" effects as a means to harm another state.

C. General customary laws of war: The customary laws of war impose a requirement of proportionality and necessity on all methods of warfare. It has also been argued that the body of law restricting use of certain weapons gives rise to a more general prohibition of any method of warfare that causes unnecessary suffering. Finally, it is unclear whether or not the general norms of international environmental law are suspended in the context of armed conflict.

ESSAY EXAM
QUESTIONS AND ANSWERS

Following are some sample essay exam questions dealing with various doctrines of Public International Law. They will be useful for testing your knowledge and for practicing exam-taking. You should write out your answers fully in essay form and then check them against the sample answers. Note that while the sample answers demonstrate a good way to approach the questions, they are not the only good way nor do they address all possible issues raised by the questions.

QUESTIONS

QUESTION 1: Assume the following story appears in the press:

Malta, April 30, 1993 — About 50 passengers aboard a hijacked civilian Maltese jetliner were killed here Sunday night when Egyptian special forces stormed the plane and the hijackers retaliated by tossing three grenades at the passengers.

The grenades set off an inferno, filling the Boeing 737 airliner with flame and thick smoke as Egyptian troops blasted their way into the plane through its baggage hold and poured gunfire down the cramped cabin, where passengers had been held in terror for nearly 24 hours.

Joel Levy, deputy chief of the United States Embassy in Malta, said that three Americans were aboard the jetliner and that one was killed. He did not name the American who was killed.

He said that at least two bodies, including that of an American, were thrown off the plane before the assault. Several wounded passengers, including the two other Americans, were also thrown off the plane. Eleven women were allowed to leave before the commando charge, he said.

The plane was hijacked Saturday night, shortly after it took off from the Athens airport on its way to Cairo. The Egyptian troops stormed the plane at 8:15 Sunday night (2:15 P.M. Sunday, Eastern standard time). The operation lasted no more than 10 minutes, the Maltese government said.

The Maltese government said the four or five hijackers on the plane — their exact number had not been established — had "most probably" all been killed.

Evaluate fully under international law the legality of **Egypt's** actions as described in the above news article.

QUESTION 2: Terria and Rantya have experienced steadily worsening diplomatic relations between the two states for the past five years. Terria, a "super power" in world politics, was one of the first states to develop and possess nuclear bombs shortly after World War II. Terria has **not** placed its nuclear facilities under the International Atomic Energy Agency (IAEA) safety standards, which are mandatory only by agreement between the IAEA and a state. Rantya, on the other hand, is not known to have any military nuclear capability, but does have a nuclear power facility which it has subjected to the IAEA safety standards.

Shortly after several disagreements between Terria and Rantya over trade relations and boundary disputes, Terria staged a military exercise 250 miles off the Rantyan coast. As part of the exercise, Terria exploded a nuclear bomb planted in the deep seabed in an area where, as a result, radioactive debris was confined to the high seas falling just short of Rantya's claimed 200 mile exclusive economic zone and its continental shelf.

Disturbed by the worsening of relations and intensification of the arms race between Terria and Rantya, a Terrian nuclear freeze group known as the Nuclear Liberation Front (NLF) decided to utilize information from several of its members that Terria had virtually no established security systems for its scientific and military installations. By breaking into the Terrian Satellite control System Building, the NLF members successfully interfered with the flight plan of a nuclear-powered weather satellite belonging to Terria in orbit around the earth, causing it to explode and several weeks later to shower several states with low level radioactive debris. The NLF members fled to Rantya, where they were greeted as heroes by the government and applauded for their attack on the satellite control system.

Terria filed charges of criminal destruction of government property (punishable by three years imprisonment) against the members of the NLF, who were tried, convicted, and sentenced to three months imprisonment by a criminal court without their being present at the trial or sentencing. Terria is now seeking extradition. Assume that the treaties governing extradition between Terria and Rantya contain standard extradition provisions. Rantya has signed and ratified the 1982 Convention on the Law of the Sea. Terria has signed and ratified the 1958 Geneva Conventions on the High Seas, the Continental Shelf, the Territorial Sea and Contiguous Zone, and the Convention on Fishing and Conservation of Living Resources of the High Seas.

PART A. Discuss all arguments for and against extradition by Rantya of the NLF members to Terria.

PART B. Discuss and evaluate all questions of Terria's liability under international law raised by: (1) Terria's military exercise and nuclear bomb test off the coast of Rantya and (2) the NLF's destruction of the nuclear-powered satellite and the resultant showers of law level radioactive debris.

PART C. Assume that Rantya has asked the United Nations Security Council to consider a resolution calling for Terria to place its nuclear facilities under the IAEA safety standards and to agree to safety inspections by the IAEA of all its nuclear facilities, civilian and military. The resolution goes on to provide that should Terria fail to agree within two months to imposition of the safety standards and inspections, it will be subjected to economic sanctions, including an expansive trade embargo, and "such other measures as may be necessary to restore international peace and security." Evaluate the legality of such a resolution under the United Nations Charter.

QUESTION 3: On February 23, 1993, a lawsuit was filed in a federal district court against the Bosnian Serbian leader, Radovan Karadzic. The suit is a multimillion-dollar civil class action lawsuit filed by three human rights organizations, charging Karadzic with responsibility for systematic rape, forced pregnancies, murder, and torture allegedly carried out by Serbian forces under his command in Bosnia-Herzegovina primarily against Serbian Moslems. The class action was filed on behalf of two anonymous female plaintiffs — a 16-year-old raped and beaten by Serbian soldiers, and an 18-year-old raped by Serbian soldiers who also killed her mother. The suit is a class action on behalf of all "women and men who suffered rape, summary execution, other torture or other cruel, inhuman and degrading treatment inflicted by Bosnian Serb military forces under the command and control of the defendant."

Assume that you are a law clerk for the federal district court judge who will decide the case. The judge has asked you to do a memo addressing the jurisdiction of the court over the suit, its justiciability, and the decision on the merits (she wants you to evaluate the merits even if you conclude the court does not have jurisdiction).

ANSWERS

SAMPLE ANSWER 1:

The armed intervention of Egypt into the territory of Malta may be viewed as a violation of a number of U.N. Charter provisions which state that countries must refrain from resorting to the use of force to settle international disputes.

Egypt could assert consent, necessity or self-help, self-defense, protection of property or nationals, and humanitarian intervention as grounds for its intervention aboard the Egyptian jetliner.

Article 2(4) of the U.N. Charter prohibits the use of force against "the territorial integrity or political independence of any state, or in any manner inconsistent with the purposes" of the U.N. Moreover, states may only resort to force when necessary after resorting to peaceful means has failed under article 2(3). One of the few exceptions to the prohibition on force is Article 51 which preserves the right of self-defense against an "armed attack."

Self-defense. Self-defense is ordinarily triggered when there is an attack on a state or state vessels and aircraft by another state. In this problem, the attack is by individuals who may or may not be state-sponsored against nationals of a state on a privately owned aircraft in another state. Attacks against a state's nationals may not qualify as self-defense under Article 51, and are usually justified on some other grounds such as protection of nationals. The legality of Egypt's actions will be dependent upon whether these justifications outside of Article 51 are still part of custom. Although the hijacking is clearly a violation of international law, there is nothing in the facts to suggest that Malta has in any way supported or protected the hijackers.

Consent. Valid consent of the Maltese government would legitimize the actions of Egypt. With the consent of the Maltese government, Egypt's actions would not be a violation of Malta's sovereignty. No facts presented indicate whether Malta consented to Egypt's intervention. If Malta did not consent, Egypt presumably violated Malta's sovereignty by intervening upon Malta's territorial jurisdiction.

Necessity or self-help. Egypt may assert necessity or self-help generally as justification for its actions because it acted in order to protect an essential state interest threatened by imminent danger. Many publicists, however, contend that 2(3) and 2(4) negate the concept of self-help.

Egypt will argue that 2(3) and 2(4) have been eroded by state practice, thus permitting resort to self-help measures. Egypt will also maintain that its actions had no effect on the territorial integrity or political independence of Malta and are therefore not a violation of 2(4).

In the *Corfu Channel* case, however, the International Court of Justice rejected the customary right of self-help despite pre-Charter recognition of the right. The adoption by the General Assembly of the Declaration of Principles on Friendly Relations in 1970 reinforced the broad scope of 2(4) and its prohibition on the use of force.

Protection of Nationals. Egypt may argue that an attack on its nationals is equivalent to an attack on the state because population is an essential interest of the state. Egypt would therefore assert self-defense based on protection of nationals as grounds for its actions or protections of nationals as a justification independent of self-defense.

Prior to the establishment of the United Nations, countries assumed the right to use force to protect nationals abroad when their lives and property were in imminent danger. Much debate exists as to whether the U.N. Charter incorporated the custom of protection of nationals into Article 51.

Egypt may submit the 1976 Israeli Entebbe raid as precedent that states maintain the customary right to use force abroad in the protection of nationals, or in humanitarian intervention.

Humanitarian Intervention. Egypt may claim that it intervened for humanitarian purposes because there existed a gross deprivation of basic human rights. The terrorists deprived the passengers of their liberty and bodily security. Egypt may assert that its intervention was confined solely to humanitarian protection and did not affect the territorial integrity of Malta.

According to a broad reading of 2(4), however, humanitarian intervention may not be accomplished through military means. Pacific means of settlement were available and apparently not even attempted by Egypt. Although preservation of human rights is one of the purposes of the Charter, another aim of the U.N. Charter is to restrict the unilateral right of states to use force as far as possible. Egypt's immediate resort to force in response to the hijacking is explicitly contrary to the tenets of the Charter. International law should not be enforced at the expense of international peace. Even though the hijacking was a universal violation of international law, Egypt should have pursued pacific settlement rather than matching violence with violence.

Proportionality. Assuming Egypt properly intervened, Egypt's response must be limited to that which was necessary and proportional to the threat posed by the hijacking. Some type of immediate action was necessary in order to prevent further loss of life. Arguably, however, the actions of Egypt were not proportional. Egypt's raid endangered the lives that Egypt purported to protect. The storming of the plane resulted in 50 deaths, compared to the few deaths prior to the raid. Egypt apparently did not first pursue peaceful means of settlement because Egypt stormed the plane less than 24 hours after the hijacking. Egypt's use of force was premature. Before the raid, the hijackers allowed eleven women to deplane which indicated a possible willingness to negotiate. Egypt will argue that its actions were not excessive. The terrorists showed blatant disregard for human life, and drastic measures were its only recourse.

Protection of Property. Egypt cannot rely exclusively on the defense of protection of property. Protection of property has not been recognized under customary international law as a sole justification for use of force.

SAMPLE ANSWER 2:

Part A: Extradition by Rantya of the NLF members to Terria

No duty to extradite exists in the absence of an applicable treaty. To require extradition by Rantya of the NLF members, Terria must meet the requirements outlined in a standard extradition treaty. Terria seeks extradition of the NLF members for the carrying out of a sentence. Extradition is available for conduct which is a crime in both the requesting state and the asylum state (double criminality principle). Presumably, destruction of government property is a punishable offense in Rantya as well as Terria. If Rantya does not recognize the conduct as a punishable offense, Rantya is not obligated to return the NLF members to Terria. Alternatively, the treaty may have a list of extraditable offenses.

An extraditable offense must be punishable by a maximum period, usually at least one year, or the punishment awarded must be for a specified period, usually at least several months. The Terrian criminal court sentenced the NLF members to three months imprisonment.

Terria may assert territorial jurisdiction because the crime charged to the NLF members was committed within Terrian territory. None of the accused appear to be Rantyan nationals, and there appears to be probable cause for the charge.

Political Offense Exception. Relying on the political offense exception, Rantya may refuse to extradite the NLF members even if the conduct of the NLF members is otherwise considered an extraditable offense. Rantya has great discretion to decide whether the conduct of the NLF members constituted a political offense. Terria will maintain that the destruction of the weather satellite is not a political offense because the act was not done with the purpose of overthrowing Terria's political regime, but was an ordinary criminal offense.

The destruction of the weather satellite is not a "pure" political offense. Only such crimes as treason, sedition and espionage are considered "pure" political offenses.

Rantya, however, may find NLF's crime to be a "relative" political offense according to one of the three customary approaches: the "political incidence" test, the "political objective" test, or the "predominant motive" test.

Under the "political incidence" test, the criminal offense must be committed in the course of a dispute between the government and the party with political aims. The purpose of the crime must be to further the aims of the party. Rantya may find that the NLF members acted in response to Terria's refusal to effect a nuclear freeze. The NLF members acted to change the nuclear policies of Terria. Terria will argue that the NLF members did not act in the course of a dispute with the Terrian government. Terria will also argue that NLF actions cannot constitute political offenses because the NLF is an environmental group with no aim of attaining political power.

The "political objective" approach requires that the means used must relate to the political objective and a degree of proportionality exist between the political objective and the crime. Terria will challenge the nexus between the NLF's goal of a nuclear freeze and their destruction of a nuclear-powered weather satellite. Destruction of a weather satellite has little connection to the goal of increased security at Terria's nuclear facilities or eradication of nuclear arms. The risk created by the NLF's actions is in fact counter to the goals of the NLF. Terria may also argue that the destruction of the satellite and resultant damage are not proportional to the objective of modification of governmental policy. The NLF members may contend that their purpose was not to destroy the satellite but rather to inconvenience the government so it would take notice of NLF's proposals. The analysis under the "political motive" would be similar but Rantya will have to show a direct link between the crime and the political act.

Rantya may also refuse to honor Terria's extradition request if Rantya believes that the purpose of the extradition request is to prosecute or punish the NLF members for their political opinions. Rantya may argue that the *in absentia* trial by Terria is evidence of Terria's prejudice and indifference to the rights of the NLF members. Terria will argue that its purpose is not persecution of the NLF members, evidenced by the light sentence given to the NLF members.

Acts of Terrorism. According to many extradition provisions for the suppression of terrorism, an act which creates a collective danger for civilians is not regarded as a political offense for extradition purposes. Terria will argue that NLF's offense should not be covered by the political offense for extradition purposes. Terria will argue that NLF's offense would not be covered by the political offense exception as an act of terrorism because the NLF's destruction of the satellite created a serious danger by the resultant shower of radioactive debris on several states. The political offense exception is based on the theory that political crimes do not threaten international public order. Although the NLF members may have directed their actions at domestic public policy, their actions clearly caused damage of an international nature.

Part B: Terria's Liability for the Nuclear Bomb Test

Terria's nuclear bomb test may itself be a violation of customary international law. Terria may also be liable for the injurious consequences of its bomb test.

Threat of Force. Terria's nuclear bomb test may constitute a violation of Article 2(4), which specifically prohibits the threat or use of force against the territorial integrity of another state. Because of the worsening diplomatic relations between Terria and Rantya, the explosion as well as the otherwise lawful military exercise on the high seas may be seen as a threat of force within 50 miles of Rantya's EEZ. It has also been agreed that the nuclear arms race itself violates Article 2(4). Terria will respond that neither was intended as a threat of force, but that such military exercises and weapons testing are a necessary adjunct to a state's right to use force in certain situations, including self-defense.

General Prohibitions on Nuclear Weapons. The U.N. General Assembly has adopted several resolutions which proscribe the use of nuclear arms. Terria will argue that the U.N. Resolutions are merely aspirational in nature and have no binding effect. Although there are treaties restricting testing and limiting proliferation, the world community has not enacted a treaty prohibiting the use of nuclear arms.

Terria's bomb test may be found to violate international customary law regarding use of the high seas and the deep seabed. The convention on the High Seas and the LOS Convention require all states to show reasonable regard to the interests of other states in their exercise of the freedom of the high seas. It may be argued that Terria's explosion of a nuclear bomb on the high seas demonstrates a disregard for the interests and safety of the vessels of other nations. On the other hand, military exercises have long been considered part of the freedom of the high seas. If the Partial Test Ban Treaty is recognized as custom, however, testing on the high seas is clearly prohibited. Even more troublesome for Terria is its use of the deep seabed for military purposes. The General Assembly has passed a number of resolutions reserving the seabed for peaceful purposes, as reaffirmed in the LOS convention. Taken together, it appears that custom prohibits military use of the deep seabed. Moreover, the fallout in the high seas may also violate custom. Provisions in the Stockholm Declaration, the Partial Test Ban Treaty, and the LOS Convention for preservation of the marine environment are evidence of such custom.

Terria's Liability for Destruction of Satellite and Resultant Radioac-

tive Showers. The first issue is whether Terria may be held responsible for the acts of the NLF. A state is not ordinarily liable for the acts of private individuals. States have been, however, considered responsible for injuries to aliens by failing to provide reasonable protection. Under Chorzow Factory, a state injuring the rights or property of another state in violation of its international obligations incurs international responsibility. The Trail Smelter case, the Stockholm Declaration, and the Restatement indicate that a state may be held responsible for activities within its jurisdiction or control that cause material injury to the environment of another state. It is not clear what element of fault on the part of Terria must be demonstrated. It has been argued by scholars that strict liability for ultrahazardous activities should be extended to international law. Terria's maintenance of nuclear facilities falls in the ultrahazardous category, and Terria would be responsible for all harm caused by the destruction of the nuclear-powered satellite. It is very debatable, however, whether liability without fault is recognized in a custom or general principles of law. The Trail Smelter case established the "good neighborliness" principle by which a state is liable if it permits transboundary pollution from within its territory to exceed that which its neighbors may be reasonably expected to endure. The affected States will argue that a shower of radioactive debris exceeds reasonable expectations. Even if it must be demonstrated that Terria acted in abuse of its rights as a state, the lack of sufficient safeguards and security at the nuclear facility may constitute negligence on Terria's part.

Terria may assert as a defense *force majeure* so that it should not be held liable for the illegal acts of private individuals. The defense, however, is not available to a state which contributes to the event, and it may be asserted by Rantya that the criminal activities of groups such as the NLF are foreseeable and that Terria had failed to exercise any control or take necessary precautions against such vandalism. Terria could have foreseen the possibility of trespass onto the facility in the absence of reasonable security precautions. The lack of security at the nuclear facilities was a matter of public knowledge because it came to the attention of the NLF.

International law requires proof of material damage as a precondition of the polluting state's responsibility to the affected state. International law does not recognize the violation of sovereignty as a compensable harm.

PART C: *Legality of U.N. Resolution Proposed by Rantya*

Chapter VII Intervention. Article 2(7) prohibits U.N. interference in matters which are essentially within the domestic jurisdiction of any state unless the Security Council finds a threat to peace, breach of peace or an act of aggression. The Security Council has broad authority to determine whether the situation in Terria constitutes a threat to peace, breach of peace, or act of aggression under Chapter VII. The Security Council might take the position that Terria's unguarded nuclear installations produce a threat to peace. The evidence of the NLF's ability to gain access to the installation and the resultant shower of radioactive debris supports the finding of a threat to peace.

U.N. intervention to regulate an environmental hazard from nuclear facilities would be unprecedented in U.N. practice. Compliance with IAEA safety standards is voluntary, and Terria has not agreed to abide by the standards.

To support its position, the Security Council may argue that Terria's military exercise constituted a threat to peace in light of the worsening diplomatic relations between Rantya and Terria.

If the Security Council finds the requisite threat to peace, Article 41 authorizes the Security Council to institute "interruption of economic relations." If the Security Council finds the Article 41 measures to be inadequate, the Security Council may "take such actions as may be necessary to maintain or restore international peace and security." Article 42. The overriding limitation on the Security Council's enforcement actions is that it must act consistently with the purposes of the Charter.

SAMPLE ANSWER 3:

Federal Court Jurisdiction. The jurisdictional mechanisms for bringing this lawsuit in federal court are the Alien Tort Statute and the Torture Victim Protection Act.

Alien Tort Statute. The federal district court may claim jurisdiction based on the Alien Tort Statute, which grants original jurisdiction to U.S. federal courts of any civil action by an alien for tort committed in violation of the law of nations. Interpretations of the prerequisites for jurisdiction under the statute are controversial, as exemplified by the *Filartiga* and *Tel-Oren* decisions.

Under the narrow interpretation of the statute espoused in Bork's *Tel-Oren* opinion, the federal court would not assert jurisdiction based on the statute. The Bork approach limits the scope of the statute to a narrow class of cases for which an individual cause of action for the violations is recognized in international law.

The broader view of the Alien Tort Statute found in the *Filartiga* case and Edward's opinion in *Tel-Oren* supports a finding of jurisdiction in this case. *Filartiga* held that "deliberate torture perpetrated under color of official authority violated universally accepted norms of the international law of human rights . . . ." Thus, whenever an alien is within U.S. borders, the Alien Tort Statute provides federal jurisdiction. The acts charged to Karadzic may be deemed "torture perpetrated under color of official authority." As for any other violations alleged, the court would have jurisdiction so long as the violation is one prohibited by customary international law.

Torture Victim Protection Act. The district court may assert jurisdiction based on the Torture Act, which supplements the Alien Tort Statute. The Act provides alien victims of torture with a private right of action in U.S. courts. The acts charged to Karadzic constitute torture as defined in the Act. Under the Act, Karadzic may be held liable "in a civil action for damages to the individual" victims of torture.

Genocide Convention Implementation Act of 1987. The federal district court may not claim jurisdiction based on the Genocide Act. Karadzic is not a U.S. national and the acts charged to Karadzic did not occur within U.S. territory. The Act applies only to criminal charges and would not cover the civil suit filed against Karadzic.

Justiciability and Immunity. The federal district court may dismiss the case even if the court could claim jurisdiction under the two statutes.

Political Question. The federal district court may find that the case is non-justifiable because of the politically volatile nature of the case and its bearing on U.S. foreign policy. In *Tel-Oren*, Judge Robb dismissed as a political question a tort action based on a terrorist attack in Israel. Judge Bork's opinion in *Tel-Oren* also supports the argument that adjudication of plaintiffs' claims would require the analysis of international legal principles that are not clearly defined. The counterargument is that the issues presented primarily involve interpretation of a number of treaties, which is the quintessential job of the courts. The doctrine does not require that all questions involving foreign affairs be considered political questions. No separation of power issues were raised, as in a clash between branches of government or with judicial usurpation of a role confined to another branch.

Sovereign Immunity. Karadzic may argue sovereign immunity as a state actor. Under modern international law, specifically the Nuremberg Charter, the Geneva Conventions, and the Genocide Convention, however, state actors may be held personally liable for international crimes such as war crimes, genocide, and torture. This principle of nonimmunity is both by treaty and custom and, as such, is part of U.S. domestic law. Also, provisions of the Foreign Sovereign Immunities Act arguably deny immunity for violations of obligations imposed by international agreement.

Act of State Doctrine. In *Sabbatino,* the Supreme Court indicated that the greater the degree of consensus concerning an area of international law, the more appropriate it is for judicial resolution despite the act-of-state doctrine. The defendant would argue that the doctrine precludes review because of the highly politicized and controversial nature of the human rights violations alleged. The counterargument would be that the central ideas of the complaint — allegations of war crimes, torture, and genocide — are well-established fundamentals of international law, whatever difficulties might be raised in their application to the case at hand.

Merits of the Case. The Torture Act provides a remedy for any alien who is a victim of torture. The plaintiff under the Alien Tort Stature must demonstrate a tort in violation of the "law of nations" or "a treaty of the United States." There is a strong consensus that custom prohibits genocide, torture, and war crimes, among other violent acts. The U.S. is also a party to the Geneva and Genocide Conventions, and the Senate has ratified the Torture Convention. Severe pain and suffering, both mental and physical, intentionally inflicted on the Serbian Moslems would meet the definition of torture under the Torture Convention and the Torture Act. Systematic rapes could also be deemed serious bodily injury or mental harm under both. The torture and rapes allegedly carried out by the Serbian forces under Karadzic's command, primarily against Serbian Moslems, have also resulted in death, serious bodily injury, and mental harm to the members of an identifiable religious and ethnic groups. Such acts, if coupled with intent to destroy the group as such, constitute genocide. The crucial issue will be whether it can be demonstrated that the acts were done with the purpose of destroying the group. Complicity in genocide or torture is also a violation of international law. Under the *Yamash-*

ita case, an official or commander who, through reports received by him or through other means, knows that troops or other persons subject to his control are about to commit or have committed war crimes, and fails to take the necessary and reasonable steps to ensure compliance with the law of war, is responsible for such crimes. Regardless of whether the conflict is deemed a civil war or international war, the serious offenses against civilians alleged would violate the humanitarian laws of war.

TABLE OF CASES

TABLE OF CONVENTIONS ON THE LAW OF THE SEA

TABLE OF U.N. CHARTER REFERENCES

TABLE OF ADVISORY OPINIONS, REPORTS, AND DECLARATIONS

TABLE OF STATUTES AND RESTATEMENT PROVISIONS

INDEX OF INTERNATIONAL AGREEMENTS

SUBJECT MATTER INDEX

NOTE: For International Agreements,
please refer to the separate Tables and the Index of International Agreements

C

Products for 1996-97 Academic Year

emanuel®

Emanuel Law Outlines

Steve Emanuel's Outlines have been the most popular in the country for years. Twenty years of graduates swear by them. In the 1995–96 school year, law students bought an average of 3.0 Emanuels each–that's 130,000 Emanuels.

Civil Procedure, *rev.* '96–97 Ed. ◆	$18.95
Constitutional Law, *rev.* '96–97 Ed.	23.95
Contracts, '93–94 Ed. ◆	17.95
Corporations, '92–93 Ed.	18.95
Criminal Law, '92–93 Ed. ◆	14.95
Criminal Procedure, *rev.* '96–97 Ed.	14.95
Evidence, '95–96 Ed.	17.95
Property, '93–94 Ed. ◆	17.95
Secured Transactions, '88–89 Ed.	12.95
Torts (General Ed.), '94–95 Ed. ◆	17.95
Torts (Casebook Ed.), '94–95 Ed.	17.95
Keyed to '94 Ed. Prosser, Wade & Schwartz	
Also, Steve Emanuel's First Year Q&A's (see opposite page)	$18.95

◆ *Special Offer...*First Year Set

All outlines marked ◆ *plus* Steve Emanuel's First Year Q & A's *plus* Strategies & Tactics for First Year Law. Everything you need to make it through your first year.

Complete Set	*$97.50*

Emanuel Law Tapes - Constitutional Law
Includes mnemonics, skits, a special night-before-the-exam review tape, and a printed supplement.

11 Cassette Set, '92-93 Ed.	*$32.95*

Smith's Review

All titles in this series are written by leading law professors. They follow the Emanuel style and format. They have big, easy-to-read type, extensive citations and notes, and clear, crisp writing. Most have capsule summaries and sample exam Q & A's.

Agency & Partnership, '88–89 Ed.	$12.95
Bankruptcy, *new* '96 Title	15.95
Commercial Paper, '95–96 Ed.	13.95
Family Law, '93–94 Ed.	15.95
Fed. Income Taxation, '94–95 Ed.	14.95
Intellectual Property, *rev.* '96–97 Ed.	15.95
International Law, '95 Ed.	15.95
Labor Law, '88–89 Ed.	12.95
Products Liability, *rev.* '96–97 Ed.	12.95
Torts, '91–92 Ed.	13.95
Wills & Trusts, '93–94 Ed.	15.95

Emanuel Electronic Format Software (Windows® only)

Complete Satisfaction Guaranteed or Your Money Back

Our band-new software, consisting of 10 unabridged Emanuel outlines on one CD-ROM, is based on Folio infobase technology and was developed in conjunction with LEXIS®-NEXIS®. Features: full searchability; easy insertion of your own notes and comments; complete hyperlinking; and printing of all or any part of the outline.

Pick the CD-ROM up free at your local bookstore or get it from your LEXIS®-NEXIS® representative. Or, if you wish, call 1-800-EMANUEL. Click on any Emanuel outline and review the introductory demo material. If you decide you want to utilize the full outline, just "unlock" it by means of your modem or by telephone. You will be charged $19.95 per outline via your Mastercard or Visa.

If, within 30 days after your order, you are dissatisfied with the outline FOR ANY REASON, phone us and we will arrange a full credit via your credit card...no questions asked.

Unlocking Price per Title:

Civil Procedure	$19.95
Constitutional Law	19.95
Contracts	19.95
Corporations	19.95
Criminal Law	19.95
Criminal Procedure	19.95
Evidence	19.95
Property	19.95
Secured Transactions	19.95
Torts (General Ed.)	19.95

For any titles not available at your local bookstore, call us at 1-800-EMANUEL. Mastercard and Visa accepted.

Law In A Flash Flashcards

Flashcards

Civil Procedure 1 ◆	$16.95
Civil Procedure 2 ◆	16.95
Constitutional Law, *rev.* '95-96 Ed. ▲	16.95
Contracts ◆▲	16.95
Corporations	16.95
Criminal Law ◆▲	16.95
Criminal Procedure ▲	16.95
Evidence, *rev.* '95-96 Ed. ▲	16.95
Future Interests ▲	16.95
Professional Responsibility (840 cards)	32.95
Real Property ◆▲	16.95
Sales (UCC Art.2) ▲	16.95
Torts, *rev.* '95-96 Ed. ◆▲	16.95
Wills & Trusts, *new* '96–97 Title	16.95

Flashcard Sets

First Year Law Set	95.00

(includes all sets marked ◆ *plus* the book
Strategies & Tactics for First Year Law.)

Multistate Bar Review Set	165.00

(includes all sets marked ▲ *plus* the book
Strategies & Tactics for MBE)

Professional Responsibility Set	45.00

(includes the *Professional Responsibility* flashcards
plus the book Strategies & Tactics for the MPRE Exam.)

Law In A Flash Software

Brand-new for 1996, our software (for Windows® only)
contains the following features:

- Complete text of the corresponding *Law In A Flash* title
- Side-by-side comparison of your own answer to the answer on the card
- Fully customizable sessions: pick which cards to review and in what order
- Mark cards for further review or printing
- Score your answers, to help you spot those topics in which you need further review

Individual titles	$19.95
Professional Responsibility (covers 840 cards)	34.95
First Year Law Set*	115.00
Multistate Bar Review Set*	195.00
Professional Responsibility/MPRE Set*	49.95

* These software sets contain the same text as printed card sets *plus*
corresponding Strategies & Tactics books.

Strategies & Tactics Books

◆ S & T for First Year Law	$12.95
● S & T for the MPRE	19.95
(Multistate Professional Responsibility Exam)	
▲ S & T for the MBE (Multistate Bar Exam)	34.95

Over 500 actual questions and answers from past
Multistate Bar Exams, *plus* an actual 200-question
practice MBE with correct answers and explanations.

Question & Answer Collections

Siegel's Essay & Multiple–Choice Q & A's

Each book contains 20–25 essay questions with model
answers, plus 90–110 Multistate format Q & A's. The objective is to acquaint the student with the techniques needed to
handle law school exams successfully. Titles are:

Civil Procedure, *rev.* '96 Ed.	Criminal Procedure
Constitutional Law	Evidence, *rev.* '96 Ed.
Contracts	Real Property, *rev.* '96 Ed.
Corporations, *new* '96 Title	Torts
Criminal Law	Wills & Trusts

Each title   *$15.95*

Steve Finz's Multistate Method

967 MBE (Multistate Bar Exam)–style multiple choice questions and answers for all six Multistate subjects – *Plus* a
complete 200 question practice exam modeled on the
MBE – perfect for law school and BAR EXAM review.

'92–93 edition   *$33.95*

Steve Emanuel's First Year Q&A's

1,144 Objective–style questions & answers in first year subjects. A single volume covers Contracts, Torts, Civil
Procedure, Property, Criminal Law & Criminal Procedure.

'95–96 edition   *$18.95*

We'd like to know . . . .
Smith's Review on International Law

We value your opinions on our study aids. After all, we design them for *your* use, and if you think we could do something better, we want to know about it. Please take a moment to fill out this survey and feedback form and return it to us.

We'll enter you in our monthly drawing where 5 people will win the study aid of their choice! If you don't want to identify yourself, that's OK, but you'll be ineligible for the drawing.

Name: _____ **Address:** _____

City: _____ **State:** _____ **Zip:** _____ **E-mail:** _____

Law school attended: _____ **Graduation year:** _____

Please rate this product on a scale of 1 to 5:

General readability (style, format, etc.) .... *Poor* ① ② ③ ④ ⑤ *Excellent*

Length of outline (number of pages) .... *Too short* ① ② ③ ④ ⑤ *Too long*

Capsule Summary: Length .... *Too short* ① ② ③ ④ ⑤ *Too long*

Usefulness .... *Not useful* ① ② ③ ④ ⑤ *Useful*

End-of-book aids (tables) .... *Not useful* ① ② ③ ④ ⑤ *Useful*

Essay questions and answers .... *Not useful* ① ② ③ ④ ⑤ *Useful*

Outline's coverage of material presented in class .... *Incomplete* ① ② ③ ④ ⑤ *Complete*

OVERALL RATING ....*Poor* ① ② ③ ④ ⑤ ***Excellent***

Suggestions for improvement: _____
_____
_____

☛ **What other study aids did you use in this course?** _____
_____

☛ **If you liked any features of these other study aids, describe them:** _____
_____
_____

☛ **What casebook(s) did you use in this course?** _____

☛ **For other subjects, what study aids other than Emanuel do you use, and what features do you like about them?** ____
_____
_____

☛ **Plase list the items you would like us to add to our product line:**

Outline subjects: _____

Flashcard subjects: _____

Other products (e.g., software, multimedia, etc.): _____

☛ **If you win our drawing, what one study aid would you like?** _____

Send to: *Emanuel Law* **Survey**   OR   Fax to: *(914) 834-5186*
1865 Palmer Avenue, Suite 202
Larchmont, NY 10538

Cut here

**Please
complete & return
the Survey Form
on the other side**